PROJECT DELIVERY SYSTEMS
FOR CONSTRUCTION

3rd Edition

AGC of America
THE ASSOCIATED GENERAL CONTRACTORS OF AMERICA
Quality People. Quality Projects.

by Michael E. Kenig

All rights reserved. No part of this publication may be reproduced or transmitted in any form or by any means, electronic or mechanical, including photocopy, recording or any information storage and retrieval system, without permission in writing from the publisher (AGC of America).

Limit of Liability/Disclaimer of Warranty: While the publisher and the author have used their best efforts in preparing this book, they make no presentations or warranties with respect to the accuracy or completeness of the contents of this book and specifically disclaim any implied warranties of the merchantability or fitness for a particular purpose. No warranty may be created or extended by sales representatives or written sales materials. The advice and strategies contained herein may not be suitable for your situation. You should consult with a professional where appropriate. Neither the publisher nor the author shall be liable for any loss of profit or any other commercial damages, including, but not limited to, special, incidental, consequential, or other damages.

For general information about other AGC of America products and services, please call (800) 242-1767 or visit www.agc.org.

ISBN: 978-1-936006-28-1

Copyright © 2011 by

AGC of America
THE ASSOCIATED GENERAL CONTRACTORS OF AMERICA
Quality People. Quality Projects.

The Associated General Contractors of America
2300 Wilson Blvd., Suite 400
Arlington, VA 22201
Phone: (800) 242-1767
Fax: (703) 837-5405
Item No.: 2916

TABLE OF CONTENTS

ACKNOWLEDGEMENTS vii

PREFACE ix

A FOUNDATION FOR THE DISCUSSION

CHAPTER ONE
AN INTRODUCTION
Establishing a Context for a Discussion 2
How the Book Is Organized 12
Thoughts for the Reader to Consider 13
Self-Test 19

PROCUREMENT OPTIONS & BASIS OF REIMBURSEMENT

CHAPTER TWO
PROCUREMENT OPTIONS
Introduction 23
Defining Procurement Options 26
Procurement Processes 29
Selecting Procurement Options 40
Other Thoughts Regarding Procurement 41
Self-Test 45

CHAPTER THREE
BASIS OF REIMBURSEMENT
Introduction 48
Defining Basis of Reimbursement 51
Typical Basis of Reimbursement for Each Project Delivery Method 62
Self-Test 64

MANAGEMENT METHODS

CHAPTER FOUR
PROGRAM MANAGEMENT
Introduction 68
Defining Program Management 68
Clarifying the Term "PM" 71

TABLE OF CONTENTS

Developer as Program Manager 74
Future Trends 75
Self-Test 76
Case Study. 77

CHAPTER FIVE
AGENCY CONSTRUCTION MANAGEMENT

Introduction. 81
Agency CM Defined—Why Do Owners Use an Agency CM?. 82
Management System Overview and Roles of the Project Team Members 84
Types of Agency CM Organizations 90
Selection Criteria and Establishing the Fee 91
Risk Management 93
Future Trends. 94
Self-Test 95
Case Study. 97

DELIVERY METHODS

CHAPTER SIX
PROJECT DELIVERY CONSIDERATIONS/RELATED AREAS

Project Delivery Related Areas. 101
Basic Concepts 101
Project Delivery Considerations 102
Summary. 122
Self-Test 123

CHAPTER SEVEN
DESIGN-BID-BUILD

Introduction. 127
Definitions in this Project Delivery System 128
Delivery Method Overview/Structure. 132
Defining Characteristics and Typical Characteristics 135
Procurement and Establishing the Contract Amount. 137
Basis of Reimbursement Options 139
Roles and Responsibilities 140
Project Delivery Considerations 143
Lessons Learned. 151
Future Trends. 152
Self-Test 153
Case Study. 154

CHAPTER EIGHT
CONSTRUCTION MANAGEMENT AT-RISK

Introduction 159
Definitions in this Project Delivery System 160
Delivery Method Overview/Structure 163
Defining Characteristics and Typical Characteristics 169
Procurement and Establishing Contract Amount 171
Basis of Reimbursement Options 173
Roles and Responsibilities 176
Project Delivery Considerations 178
Lessons Learned 186
Future Trends 186
Self-Test 188
Case Study 190

CHAPTER NINE
DESIGN-BUILD

Introduction 195
Concept of Single Point Responsibility 196
Definitions in this Project Delivery System 197
Delivery Method Overview/Structure 200
Defining Characteristics and Typical Characteristics 202
Procurement and Establishing Contract Amount 203
Basis of Reimbursement Options 205
Roles and Responsibilities 207
Project Delivery Considerations 209
Lessons Learned 217
Future Trends 218
Self-Test 219
Case Study 221

CHAPTER TEN
INTEGRATED PROJECT DELIVERY

Introduction 225
Definitions in this Project Delivery System 227
Delivery Method Overview/Structure 233
Defining Characteristics and Typical Characteristics 237
Procurement and Establishing the Contract Amount 237
Basis of Reimbursement Options 238
Roles and Responsibilities 238
Project Delivery Considerations 240
Lessons Learned 248

TABLE OF CONTENTS

Future Trends...248
Self-Test..250

CHAPTER ELEVEN
DELIVERY METHODS INVOLVING FINANCING OR OPERATIONS AND MAINTENANCE

When Financing or Operations Become Part of the Project...............253
Financing Public Construction Projects..............................258
Financing Commercial Construction Projects..........................261
New Roles for the Original Parties..................................264
Public/Private Partnerships...265
Strategies for Offering Financing Services..........................267
Agreements Involving Financing.....................................267
Operations and Maintenance...268
Summary..271

GLOSSARY...275

SELF-TEST ANSWERS..287

RELATED CONTRACTS..291

INDEX..295

ACKNOWLEDGMENTS

The Associated General Contractors of America wishes to express its sincere appreciation to the principal author of this publication, Michael E. Kenig.

Mike is Vice Chairman of Holder Construction Group LLC in Atlanta, GA. He is also an adjunct professor at the Georgia Institute of Technology where he teaches a graduate study course on "Integrated Project Delivery Systems." He is a graduate of Purdue University with a B.S. in Construction Engineering and Management.

Mike is a recognized leader in the area of construction project delivery and is an active participant in numerous industry organizations. He has led or participated in numerous industry initiatives and is a frequent speaker at construction industry seminars and events across the nation.

Mike has served in various leadership roles within AGC of America. He is the past chair of the Building Division, past chair of the Project Delivery Committee, and a former three-year member of the AGC of America Executive Board. Mike currently chairs the Training, Education and Development Forum and is a member of the Project Delivery Forum, Industry Liaison Committee, Public/Private Industry Advisory Council, and the AIA-AGC Joint Committee.

AGC would also like to thank those who gave their time and expertise reviewing and commenting on the many drafts that were created during this process:

- Kevin A. Delorey — Quarles & Brady LLP
- Marcy D. Louza — Consultant
- Stanley A. Martin — Duane Morris LLP
- Tom Porter — Tom Porter Services LLC
- Michael F. Stark — AGC of America

As this book is an updated edition of the 2004 *Project Delivery Systems for Construction-2nd Edition*, AGC would like to thank the authors of that publication:

- Daniel Donohue
- Dirk Haire
- Damian Hill
- Michael Kenig
- Stan Martin
- Rick Poppe
- Stephen Shapiro

PREFACE

A FOUNDATION FOR THE DISCUSSION

The subject of project delivery continues to evolve. When the second edition of this book was published in 2004, the industry lacked a common vocabulary when it came to the subject of capital project delivery. In 2004, only a segment of the construction market was addressing this varied terminology—mostly participants from the public sector working in vertical construction. In 2011, the discussion on project delivery now includes more participants; the private sector as well as those from the horizontal markets including highways, tunnels, and bridges are also now engaged. Though there is closer consensus on some terminology, such as CM at-Risk, new terminology, such as IPD, has emerged that continues to add to the confusion within the industry.

Going into a topic that confuses even the "experts" within an industry, what can the reader hope to gain from this book? One studying the subject of project delivery will do well to come away with enough understanding for a meaningful discussion on the subject. Upon completion of this book, the reader should expect to have gained a basic understanding of the most common project delivery methods.

The construction industry, like numerous other industries, has evolved in so many different directions simultaneously that the meanings of industry terms have become quite diverse. Without the benefit of established, widely accepted definitions of terms, individuals and groups continue to independently decide on their own meanings.

Over a period spanning several decades, each group or individual has independently selected the characteristics they feel best define each delivery method. Because many were starting with the same basic "raw materials," they often chose similar words. What has resulted? We now have an industry vocabulary full of similar words with different meanings and different words with similar meanings. Sometimes the meanings vary only slightly, but other times, as with the term "IPD," for example, the meanings vary considerably.

PREFACE

This book does not try to convince everyone to use one vocabulary but rather to promote the next best thing—understanding one another's vocabulary. Specifically, this book hopes to give readers the ability to listen to others' definitions of delivery methods, management approaches, procurement options, and basis of reimbursement and then relate these to their own definitions. Without trying to label any terminology as right or wrong, this textbook offers a framework of definitions and templates with which to understand the subject of project delivery. We don't expect everyone to agree with the definitions put forth here, but they provide us with a starting point as we begin to understand one another's vocabulary.

Just what terms are put forth here? This textbook limits the list of delivery methods to the four most common: Design-Bid-Build (DBB), Construction Management at-Risk (CMAR), Design-Build (DB), and Integrated Project Delivery (IPD). Our challenge has been to make every hybrid fall into one of these four categories. We, therefore, needed to establish definitions that were as broad as possible; otherwise we would end up with hybrids that do not fit into any of the four delivery methods. We tried our best to avoid giving these hybrids new names, as that would have forced us to expand the list beyond these four methods.

The biggest vocabulary challenge with respect to delivery methods continues to be how to distinguish between Design-Bid-Build and CM at-Risk. The most common and current definitions leave gaps between these two delivery methods. The result has been more confusion and the creation of yet more delivery method names. Our goal in meeting this challenge has been to choose definitions that close the gap between Design-Bid-Build and CM at-Risk in the absence of industry definitions that work.

The definitions proposed in this book are not any one individual's, but rather they are definitions that appear to be the most consistent with those currently being used by most in the industry. The definitions in this 2011 third edition are updated from the 2004 edition to reflect the evolution of the terminology and the slight shifts in industry consensus.

Recognizing the continued lack of an industry standard, it is understood that no matter which definitions we select, there will be those who disagree. But if we don't select definitions (or even worse, if we create new terms), then we are no further along in eliminating the confusion. In fact, we would be adding to it!

Has the industry existed for so long without consistent definitions—a situation that has compelled everyone to develop their own definitions—that any effort to straighten out all this mixed up vocabulary is now futile? There are two schools of thought on this. The first is, "Yes, any effort to create a common vocabulary is an exercise in futility." The second view, and the one offered by this textbook, is that it is never too late to establish a framework for discussion.

PREFACE

This is the essence of this textbook—to establish a context for the discussion on project delivery. Perhaps one day, if everyone is able to reconcile to the same templates, the industry can debate the names we use in the template itself. If this can occur, we will have standard industry terminology. For now, being more realistic, we are not expecting to have a common vocabulary in which everyone uses the same words, but instead to reach the point at which we all understand one another's vocabulary.

WHAT'S NEW IN THE 3RD EDITION?

There are a number of additions and updates to this third edition. The updates reflect the continuous evolution that the subject of project delivery continues to go through. Highlights of the updates to the third edition include:

- **The addition of Integrated Project Delivery**—In recognition of the growing use of Integrated Project Delivery (IPD) with a multi-party contract, IPD has been added as the "fourth" delivery method. Along with this new delivery method, a new basis of reimbursement, Target Price, has been added as well.
- **Updated definitions**—Project delivery and procurement definitions have been updated to be closer to where the industry consensus has evolved. One key update is the expansion of Best Value procurement into two procurement types: 1) Total Cost and 2) Fees. Closely related, the previous edition of this textbook referred to Best Value competitions where price was based on the total cost (now referred to as Best Value: Total Cost) as a type of CM at-Risk; in this edition, the definition of Design-Bid-Build has been broadened to include the Best Value: Total Cost procurement option.
- **The addition of BIM, lean construction, and sustainability**—These terms have been added and are discussed relative to each delivery method.
- **Expanded discussion on procurement**—In addition to separating Best Value into two types of procurement, the discussion on procurement options that previously spanned across separate chapters has now been consolidated into one chapter (Chapter 2) and expanded.
- **The addition of basis of reimbursement**—We have also consolidated and expanded the discussion on this subject into a new chapter (Chapter 3) due to the growing importance of the basis of reimbursement on successful implementation. This chapter includes expanded discussion on Guaranteed Maximum Price (GMP) and an introduction to the Target Price basis of reimbursement.
- **Updated Appendix and Glossary**—The Appendix, which lists the contracts specifically related to the implementation of the different project delivery methods, and the Glossary of Terms have both been updated.

CHAPTER ONE

AN INTRODUCTION

Establishing a Context for Discussion
- What Is a Project Delivery Method?
- No "Perfect" Project Delivery Method
- Evolution of Project Delivery Methods
- The Four Stops on the Road to Implementing a Project Delivery Method
- Responding to the Industry's "Need for Speed"
- Fundamental Relationships Among the Parties
- "Defining" Characteristics
- "Typical" Characteristics and Hybrids
- Procurement Method and Its Importance
- Having a List—The Delivery Method Options Matrix
- Using the Delivery Method Options Matrix to Compare Different Lists
- Related Areas
- Management Methods vs. Delivery Methods

How the Book Is Organized
- Section 1: Introduction
- Section 2: Procurement Options & Basis of Reimbursement
- Section 3: Management Methods
- Section 4: Project Delivery Methods
- Section 5: Reference

Thoughts for the Reader to Consider
- Selecting an Appropriate Delivery Method
- Accelerated Procurement Approaches: IDIQ, On-Call Contracting, Term Contracting, and JOC
- Multiple Prime Contracting and Direct Subcontracting
- Agreements—Making Them Work for You
- Standard Forms of Agreement

Self Test

ESTABLISHING A CONTEXT FOR DISCUSSION

What Is a Project Delivery Method?

A project delivery method is the comprehensive process of assigning the contractual responsibilities for designing and constructing a project. A delivery method identifies the primary parties taking contractual responsibility for the performance of the work. The delivery method process includes:

- Definition of scope and requirements of a project
- Contractual requirements, obligations, and responsibilities of the parties
- Procedures, actions, and sequences of events
- Interrelationships among the participants
- Mechanisms for managing time, cost, safety, and quality
- Forms of agreement and documentation of activity

It is crucial to the success of a project that all participants understand the goals and objectives of the delivery method being used and how all parties are related to each other contractually. The essential elements of any project delivery method are cost, quality, time, and safety. Responsibilities for implementing these elements vary from method to method.

A project delivery method is fundamentally a people method because people remain the most valuable construction resource. The success or failure of any delivery method depends upon the performance, trust, and cooperation among the parties.

There are numerous hybrids and variations of the delivery methods discussed in this book. The result has been a confusing landscape of terms and definitions. To help establish a context for a project delivery discussion, this book introduces "defining" characteristics. Defining characteristics distinguish one delivery method from all other delivery methods. This book offers defining characteristics broad enough to cover almost any known hybrid.

Most common delivery methods, regardless of the name applied, should align with one of the delivery methods defined in this book. Using this simple set of definitions, readers should be able to align their list of methods with the methods used in this book.

Readers are encouraged to use this book to facilitate an intelligent discussion on the subject. The goal is to help everyone establish his or her own list and then compare them. Everyone can travel down the road of using various project delivery methods and develop the experience necessary to implement all the delivery methods successfully. The ability to compare lists increases the ability for best practices to be shared more easily across the industry even though individuals may still be using different terminology to describe their methods.

It is not the intention of this book to argue in favor of any one delivery method over another. Rather, this book strives to provide readers with a meaningful way to discuss project delivery methods.

No "Perfect" Project Delivery Method

Most groups agree that there is no perfect project delivery method. Every project is unique and has its own unique set of challenges. Therefore, industry consensus is that every project should be considered on a case-by-case basis to determine the most appropriate project delivery method.

Evolution of Project Delivery Methods

Delivery methods respond to changing circumstances. The Design-Bid-Build method is frequently described as "traditional." It involves competitively bid construction contracts that are based on complete and prescriptive contract documents prepared by architects and engineers. The documents include drawings, specifications, and supporting information.

For most of the 20th century, public work routinely has been built under the Design-Bid-Build delivery method. The basis of reimbursement for these projects is typically Fixed Price/Lump Sum, which uses competitive bidding among general contractors. Performance bonds, liquidated damages, and various other statutory requirements are employed to protect taxpayers' investments. These agreements are also called "Hard Money" contracts. All states and the federal government have detailed statutes on public advertisement of projects, bid submission procedures, and constructor selection.

Much private work also has been performed under the Design-Bid-Build method, in the belief that the marketplace ensures economic discipline and yields the best value. Particularly those private organizations with large constituencies, such as religious institutions and schools, use public-like project delivery methods, with sealed bids and formal procedures. In addition, many private corporations still employ the Design-Bid-Build method, but many now also use other delivery methods.

The Four Stops on the Road to Implementing a Project Delivery Method

As the adoption of multiple project delivery methods becomes more common for more owners, the process for deciding which project delivery method to implement has four stops:

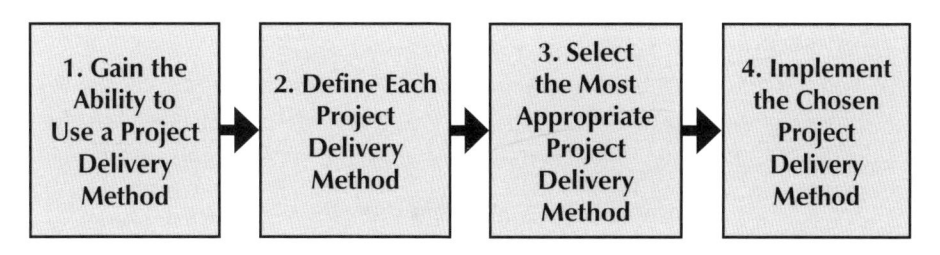

| 1. Gain the Ability to Use a Project Delivery Method | → | 2. Define Each Project Delivery Method | → | 3. Select the Most Appropriate Project Delivery Method | → | 4. Implement the Chosen Project Delivery Method |

These stops are based on the premise that someone has (or eventually will have) the ability to choose from a list of project delivery methods and that there is no perfect delivery method.

There are many products, papers, and guidelines to help us understand each of these four steps. For example, AGC offers guidelines, documents, and assistance with implementing all project delivery methods (Stop 4). This book's primary purpose is to provide a list of delivery methods and definitions for the reader to use as a framework for discussion (Stop 2).

Groups all over the country, if not the world, that get to the first stop and gain the ability to use multiple delivery methods often skip to the third stop and attempt to select the appropriate method. Eventually, most realize they need a set of definitions and return to the second stop.

This is where much of the confusion begins. As associations, individuals, and firms return to the second stop, they find that there are no industry standards, so they create their own set of definitions. This results in numerous differing lists and definitions.

Recognizing that there is not any one list of detailed definitions with which all would agree, this book puts forth broad definitions that the reader can use as a starting point. When everyone can establish his or her own list and compare those lists, the result will raise the bar for everyone and promote continuous improvement throughout the industry.

Responding to the Industry's "Need for Speed"

Why did these various project delivery methods evolve, anyway? In large part they were an industry response to demand for faster completion of construction projects. The concept of "speed to market" is a result of intense global competition, which has made it more critical than ever to move new products and services to market ahead of competitors. To be late in the marketplace can be devastating to profitability.

Many organizations have dramatically compressed their product development time by improving technology and better integrating processes. A stumbling block, though, has been the comparatively slow pace of delivering the facilities needed to house production.

The construction industry has responded to this trend with new methods of project delivery. The construction industry accelerated the processes of design and construction while striving to maintain controls on cost, safety, and quality. Construction Management (CM) at-Risk, Design-Build and Integrated Project Delivery (IPD) are being used effectively to shorten project schedules.

Public and private owners, seeing the success of accelerated projects in other settings, are now looking for similar results on their building projects. Overall schedule compression is now expected of constructors. This is one of the main reasons many owners are looking at the various delivery methods.

Fundamental Relationships Among the Parties

The classic triangle of construction is made up of owner, designer, and constructor. These three parties are participants in all project delivery methods, but their relationships and alignments vary according to the method being used.

It is the owner's duty to decide on the delivery method, scope, program, budget, and funding source for a project prior to design. During design and construction, the owner monitors project progress and quality and makes periodic payments to design and construction practitioners. After construction, the owner—whether private or public—should protect and enhance the built investment by providing maintenance for the completed building.

It is the designer's duty to translate the owner's needs and requirements into plans and specifications to be used during construction. During that phase, the architect may assist the owner in monitoring the progress of the work by verifying that the specified level of quality is achieved and certifying payment applications. The architect should provide interpretations of the construction documents and give additional instructions as needed.

The constructor's duty is to build the project according to the designer's plans and specifications, within the time and budget specified in the contract. This should be done without sacrificing either the quality of the work or the safety of the workers. The constructor has complete responsibility for achieving the quality level required in the documents, and for doing so safely. The constructor also may be involved in training the owner's personnel in the operation of the building systems and may provide some maintenance after construction is complete.

"Defining" Characteristics

Because industry-wide accepted definitions of project delivery methods do not exist, it is of little surprise that many groups have chosen different characteristics to define their lists of delivery methods. There is no right or wrong set of definitions, but there is a need for consistency among definitions to facilitate communication. The following definitions of delivery methods are as broad as possible, using terms that are generally accepted in the industry. This allows the definitions to work with as many hybrids as possible. The definitions are based on what we shall refer to as "defining" characteristics.

Defining characteristics distinguish one delivery method from the others. The following are the *defining* characteristics of project delivery methods used in this textbook:

1. What is the contractual agreement between the core team of the owner, designer, and contractor? Are the design and construction:
   a. Under separate contracts directly with the owner?
   b. Combined under one contract?
   c. Separate but contractually bound by a single multi-party contract with the owner?
2. Is total construction cost part of the criteria in the final selection of the constructor?

Using these two simple defining characteristics creates the following uniquely defined delivery methods:

- **Design-Bid-Build**
  1. Design and construction are separate contracts (versus Design-Build, where the contracts are combined).
  2. Total construction cost is a factor in the final selection of the constructor (versus CM at-Risk).
- **CM at-Risk**
  1. Design and construction are separate contracts (versus Design-Build, where the contracts are combined).
  2. Total construction cost is not a factor in final selection of the constructor (versus Design-Bid-Build).

  Note: The eventual establishment of a Guaranteed Maximum Price is typical with CM at-Risk.
- **Design-Build**
  1. Design and construction responsibilities are contractually combined into a single contract with the owner (versus both Design-Bid-Build and CM at-Risk, where contracts are separate).
- **Integrated Project Delivery (IPD)**
  1. The designer, the contractor, and the owner (and possibly other key members of the project team) sign one multi-party contract (versus Design-Bid-Build, CM at-Risk, and Design-Build).

"Typical" Characteristics and Hybrids

There are many characteristics typical of each type of method, but these characteristics are not required to define the delivery method. The following scenario highlights an example of a "typical" characteristic—in this case, preconstruction services.

What would you call a constructor based on the following scenario?

If the constructor is...
- Under a contract directly to the owner (separate from the design firm),
- Selected on the basis of qualifications and other non-price criteria,
- Contracting directly with the trade contractors, and
- Brought on board after the design is complete.

What would you call this? Construction Management? General Construction? Do you refer to this as CM at-Risk? Or some other term? Are you without a name for it?

Applying the *defining* characteristics, the constructor described here is contracting with the owner directly (separate from the designer) and is holding the trade contracts (warranting the performance of the work). As the constructor was selected for something other than the lowest bid on the total construction cost, this method would still be defined as CM at-Risk. This is true even though the constructor was not providing preconstruction services during the design phase.

Being brought on board during the design process is an example of a "typical" characteristic. It is *typical* for the CM at-Risk to join the team during the design phase and provide preconstruction services before design completion. However, based on this definition, a provider of preconstruction services during the design is not a defined *requirement* of CM at-Risk; it is a *typical* characteristic of CM at-Risk.

The same logic applies to the schedule guarantee. Though it is *typical* to have the CM at-Risk provide one, it is not required by definition. Therefore, a schedule guarantee is a typical characteristic, not a defining characteristic, of CM at-Risk.

There is much debate in the industry over the meaning of "at-risk" in the phrase "CM at-Risk" if there is no cost guarantee. The answer assumes that "risk" refers to a cost guarantee versus the performance risk (i.e., holding the trade contracts). If the phrase "at-risk" refers to the performance risk (vs. agency CM), then the term "CM at-Risk" works even if there is no cost guarantee. It works because the word "risk" refers to the performance risk that the CM takes by holding the trade contracts. Many choose to avoid this debate over the phrase "at-risk" and instead use the terms "CM/GC" or "CMc" (CM as constructor) instead of CM at-Risk.

When someone labels a "typical" characteristic as a "defining" characteristic, a hybrid is created. People may (and often do) give their hybrid a new name. There's nothing inherently wrong with this, but the key is to recognize that with all hybrids, these "typical" characteristics can be stripped away. Using the above two defining characteristic questions, the reader can align any method with one of the four delivery methods defined in this book.

Procurement Method and Its Importance

Many people look at how projects are delivered separately from how the services are procured. This separation is fine, but there is a general belief that how a project is procured has such an impact on the delivery method that you should consider both aspects together. In other words, how a project is procured has such an impact on the delivery method, the process, and the ultimate outcome of the project that when one is considering the delivery method, one must also look at the procurement option.

The procurement method is also referred to as the "selection" method. Just as with project delivery methods, numerous terms exist for the different procurement methods. The following (described in detail in Chapter 2: Procurement Options) are the four procurement methods defined in this book:

- **Low Bid**—Total construction cost is the sole criterion for final selection (total construction cost = 100% of final selection criteria).
- **Best Value: Total Cost**—Both total construction cost and other factors are criteria for the final selection (total construction cost = between 0–100% of the final selection criteria).
- **Best Value: Fees**—Both fees and qualifications are factors in the final selection (total construction cost = 0% of the final selection criteria; fees are a criteria in the final selection).
- **Qualifications Based Selection**—Cost is *not* a criterion for the final selection; qualifications are the only factor used in the final selection (cost = 0% of final selection criteria).

When using the term "price" or "cost" when discussing how a project is going to be procured, it is critical to define what is meant by the term "price." When using some version of the often used phase, "price has to be part of the competition," parties should be certain to clarify which aspect of the price is being referenced. This topic is discussed in more detail in Chapter 2.

As previously discussed, to determine the most appropriate delivery approach, it is highly recommended to consider both the procurement method and the delivery method. When considering the procurement and delivery methods together, the following matrix is created:

Delivery Methods by Procurement Option

DELIVERY METHOD Common Nicknames	Low Bid	Best Value: Total Cost	Best Value: Fees	Qualifications Based Selection (QBS)
Design-Bid-Build Competitive Sealed Bid; Low Bid; Inv. to Bid (IFB)	☐	☐	N/A	N/A
CM at-Risk CM/GC; GC/CM; CMc; ECI	N/A	N/A	☐	☐
Design-Build Engineer-Procure-Construct (EPC)	☐	☐	☐	☐
IPD Multi-party; Alliancing	Not Typical	Not Typical	☐	☐

Note: There is no agreed upon definition of Best Value: Total Cost when used with separate contracts for design and construction. The previous edition of this textbook referred to Best Value: Total Cost as a type of CM at-Risk, but in this edition, the definition of Design-Bid-Build has been broadened to include this selection type.

If the CM at-risk is procured by Low Bid (total construction cost being the sole criterion) or Best Value: Total Cost, you have, by definition, Design-Bid-Build Low Bid or Design-Bid-Build Best Value.

Taking the approaches created by combining the delivery methods and procurement options, owners can use this matrix to determine the delivery methods and selection types they use in their own organizations.

Having a List—The Delivery Method Options Matrix

When the definitions used here for the delivery methods are combined with the definitions used for the selection types, the result by selection type is the "Delivery Method/Selection Approaches" options matrix, shown with commonly used industry terms:

Delivery Method / Selection Approaches

SELECTION TYPES	"Price" Definition	Designer & Contractor 2 separate contracts	Design-Builder 1 combined contract	Designer-Contractor-Owner 1 Multi-Party contract
1. Low Bid — "Price" only criteria for final selection	Total Construction Cost (TCC)	Design-Bid-Build Low Bid	Design-Build Low Bid	Not Typical
2A. Best Value: Total Cost — "Price" and other criteria in the final selection; Price = TCC	Total Construction Cost (TCC)	Design-Bid-Build Best Value: Total Cost	Design-Build Best Value: Total Cost	Not Typical
2B. Best Value: Fees — "Price" and other criteria in the final selection; "Price" = Fees	Fees, General Conditions, Etc.	CM at-Risk Best Value: Fees	Design-Build Best Value: Fees	IPD Best Value: Fees
3. Qualifications Based Selection (QBS) — "Price" is _not_ a factor in the final selection criteria	None	CM at-Risk QBS	Design-Build QBS	IPD QBS

This matrix is particularly useful for organizations that do not currently have a list of options. Using this along with the blank matrix in the next section, organizations can fill in a name for the approaches they use with the name provided if the organization does not already have a name.

Using the Delivery Method Options Matrix to Compare Different Lists

Because the industry has gone for so long without standard definitions, some readers may not entirely agree with these definitions. This is not unusual and highlights the purpose of this textbook: to provide a framework for these discussions. Because the "Delivery Method/Selection Approaches" matrix works with nearly every known method of delivering design and construction, readers are encouraged to insert into the following blank matrix the names YOU use to describe each approach:

Delivery Method / Selection Approaches

SELECTION TYPES	"Price" Definition	Designer & Contractor 2 separate contracts	Design-Builder 1 combined contract	Designer-Contractor-Owner 1 Multi-Party contract
1. Low Bid — "Price" only criteria for final selection	Total Construction Cost (TCC)			
2A. Best Value: Total Cost — "Price" and other criteria in the final selection Price=TCC	Total Construction Cost (TCC)			
2B. Best Value: Fees — "Price" = Fees / General Conditions, etc. (no TCC)	Fees, General Conditions, Etc.			
3. Qualifications Based Selection (QBS) — "Price" is not a factor in the final selection criteria	None			

If any of the approaches are not used within your organization, just write "N/A" to indicate that either the organization does not have that option available or does not consider that option one of its available options.

There are no right or wrong names. Organizations can use whatever names they would like, but they should try to avoid adding to the list within this matrix (try, rather, to ensure that all options are just hybrids of one of the ten listed). Even if an organization does not normally use all ten options, or does not agree with the use of all them, members should at least be aware that all ten options exist and that one or more options may not be included on the organization's list of "available" options.

Many institutions have already found this matrix to be an excellent tool for establishing its own list. In addition, if separate groups have used this matrix to articulate their list of delivery options and names, everyone can easily compare those different names.

Related Areas

In Chapter 6, you will be introduced to the concept of "related areas." These are topics closely related to the subject of project delivery. In fact, they are so closely related that they are often used by others as defining characteristics of delivery methods.

"Related areas" are defined as characteristics not unique to any one delivery method. Any topic characterized as a "related area" is one that can actually be applied to more than one project delivery method. Prequalification is one example of a related area. One could prequalify with *any* project delivery method.

Other examples include fast-tracking, bridging, and program management methods. These related areas are typical characteristics—common but not required to define a particular delivery method.

Management Methods vs. Delivery Methods

Is agency construction management a project delivery method? Based on our delivery method definition in the beginning of this chapter, for the delivery of design and construction services, the answer is, "No, agency CM is not a delivery method." Instead, agency CM is a project management method, a method of managing design and construction services.

Therefore, agency CM could be used in conjunction with any project delivery method, including Design-Bid-Build, Design-Build, or even CM at-Risk. For the purpose of this textbook, we offer the following definitions:

A construction manager is either:
1. A construction manager agent [an "agent CM" or "CMa" (CM as advisor)], or
2. A construction manager (CM) at-risk.

The CM is either holding the trade contracts and at risk for the delivery of the project (the performance of the work) or not. (All other variations of CM are just slight modifications of the responsibilities and expectations of the CM and do not change this fundamental separation into these two categories. For example, a CM/GC is essentially the same as a CM at-risk.)

Management methods include:
1. Owner's in-house options (within the user's group or operations unit or by the real estate/facilities or procurement groups), or
2. Third party options (including development managers, agent CMs, and program managers).

These methods are discussed further in Chapter 4: Program Management and Chapter 5: Agency Construction Management.

HOW THE BOOK IS ORGANIZED

This book is divided into five sections: Section 1: Introduction, Section 2: Procurement Options & Basis of Reimbursement, Section 3: Management Methods, Section 4: Project Delivery Methods (including a chapter on considerations when the constructor is involved in the financing or operation of the project), and Section 5: Reference.

Section 1: Introduction

This section includes the Preface and Chapter 1. It discusses the basic principles to be covered in the text and "sets the stage" for the rest of the discussion.

Section 2: Procurement Options & Basis of Reimbursement

Chapter 2: Procurement Options and Chapter 3: Basis of Reimbursement highlights two areas that are often separated from the discussion of project delivery. Since both have such an important impact on the discussion of project delivery, it is recommended that they be reviewed in conjunction with project delivery methods.

Section 3: Management Methods

Chapter 4: Program Management and Chapter 5: Agency Construction Management discuss the most common project management methods. The goal is to help the reader appreciate that any project delivery method can be used with any project management method.

Section 4: Project Delivery Methods

Chapter 6 expands on the concept of "Related Areas" and provides a brief explanation of each. Related areas are topics that are closely related to the subject of project delivery. Each of the delivery method chapters (Chapters 7–10) includes a section addressing each of the related area topics and how each may be affected when used with that chapter's delivery method. Chapter 7: Design-Bid-Build, Chapter 8: Construction Management At-Risk, Chapter 9: Design-Build and Chapter 10: Integrated Project Delivery are discussed as the project delivery methods. Chapter 11 discusses variations of the typical delivery methods that incorporate aspects of financing and real estate as well as operations and maintenance.

Section 5: Reference

Following the main chapters of the book are the Glossary, the answers to the Self-Tests found at the end of each chapter, a listing of related industry contracts sorted by project delivery method, and the Index.

THOUGHTS FOR THE READER TO CONSIDER

Selecting an Appropriate Delivery Method

Many factors might be considered when trying to determine which delivery method is most appropriate for a particular project. However, many find that only a handful of "major" factors need to be evaluated before it is reasonably apparent which method is most appropriate.

The major factors are typically derived from the owner's project-specific requirements. The most common major factors affecting the delivery method decision are:
- **Schedule**—Is there a need to overlap phases of the project?
- **Project complexity**—Is constructor input necessary during design?
- **Level of desired collaboration**—What level of collaboration is desired?
- **Changes**—Is there any potential for changes during construction?
- **Owner's in-house capability**—Are the appropriate skills available?
- **Quality definition and verification**—Will the designer handle this?
- **Experience with the desired method**—Has the owner used this delivery method before?
- **Timing/availability of funding**—Are design and construction funded?

The overall schedule constraints frequently become the key criteria for selecting a project delivery method. Traditionally, the design/construction process has been linear—that is, each party performs its duties and then passes relevant information and responsibilities on to the next participant. This deliberate process has certain advantages in regard to boundaries of responsibility—including careful design decisions, material selection, and project administration—and typically utilizes Lump Sum contracts.

But while this linear process may be valid for many projects, it takes a lot of time and reduces the integration of expert knowledge from the various parties. In a complex project, the design process alone may take more than a year, and construction may take two or three years more. Integrated or clustered decision making and fast-tracking can shorten the process, but they require project delivery methods different from the traditional Low Bid Design-Bid-Build/Lump Sum process.

Accelerated Procurement Approaches

Many owners find it appropriate for some projects to use a process that allows accelerated procurements. These include smaller projects, time-sensitive projects, projects with difficult-to-define scopes, or projects with indefinite timeframes. Owners are also implementing alternate delivery approaches to address the myriad of repair, renovation, and remodeling projects that occur on an ongoing basis.

These approaches allow industry participants to deliver projects more efficiently than they might through a traditional advertisement/procurement/contracting process.
- Indefinite Duration, Indefinite Quantity (IDIQ)
- On-Call Contracting
- Term Contracting
- Job Order Contracting (JOC)

The first three approaches (IDIQ, On-Call, and Term) are generally used to describe open-ended contractual relationships that are not tied to specific scope. They are often used by owners who want to have contracts in place quickly to accommodate certain project types such as small or emergency projects. These types of projects benefit from having contracts that have already met the required procurement rules and can move quickly into the execution stage. Job Order Contracting is a type of IDIQ contract that, similar to the other three, has an open-ended contractual relationship that is not tied to a specific project, but is typically tied to a specific scope.

An IDIQ contract is a long-term contract in which the precise scope and timing of construction delivery is not defined at contract procurement. The contract term is typically well-defined, and is often broken down into a base contract term (typically a year or two) with option years which must be accepted by both the owner and the contractor. IDIQ contracts will often have a guaranteed minimum value and/or a contractual maximum per term. Individual projects are delivered through the use of delivery orders, and can have dollar limitations at this level, as well.

IDIQ contracts have the advantage of providing owners with an on-call contractor who is familiar with the complexities of working in their specific facilities environment. By establishing an IDIQ contract to facilitate use of the same contractor for multiple projects, owners avoid the delays associated with the project team's learning curve, making project delivery faster. When multiple projects are being executed simultaneously, there is also an efficiency and economy of scale for owner and contractor alike in project supervision, facility security requirements, and ongoing communication.

In selecting an IDIQ contract structure, owners must consider laws governing procurement or procedures, typical project size and total volume, and preferred degree of collaboration. Selection of an IDIQ contractor can be based on Low Bid, Best Value: Total Cost, Best Value: Fees or Qualifications Based Selection. Since the contracts result in a multi-year relationship, some consideration of qualifications is often desired.

A Job Order Contract (JOC), a type of IDIQ contract, traditionally relies on unit prices, though some JOCs are appearing in the market with alternative pricing structures. A JOC is typically based on a Unit Price Book (UPB) which establishes pricing for tens of thousands of construction tasks. The unit prices are all-inclusive, capturing not only labor and materials but general conditions, overhead and profit as well as incidental costs such as bonds and permits. At the outset of a contract the contractor will propose or compete based on a coefficient which modifies this pricing. This coefficient, also sometimes called a multiplier or a factor, is applied to all unit prices in the UPB across the board. Construction inflation is addressed by updating either the UPB or the coefficient periodically (usually annually) over the life of the contract. For example, a coefficient of 1.12 would represent a 12%

markup on all line items, and a coefficient of .88 would represent a 12% discount on all line items.

JOC projects are priced according to the contractual unit prices, prior to proceeding with work. The delivery order scoping process typically takes 1-3 weeks and results in a detailed scope of work that is tied to a proposal comprised of line items from the UPB with appropriate quantities applied. The unit pricing is typically prepared by the contractor and validated by the owner. This hybrid pricing approach typically resulting in a lump sum ensures that the owner knows the total project cost before proceeding and can incentivize contractor efficiency.

The JOC scoping process is often a collaborative one which explores various options for accomplishing the desired project result. The JOC contractor can manage the design process with a design professional as a subcontractor, as in a Design-Build, or they can be engaged to advise a design professional under contract to the owner, as in CMAR. There is seldom a separate fee for preconstruction services—they are included in the coefficient as are scoping and proposal services and there is no cost recovery for delivery orders that do not proceed to construction. The generation of line item proposals can commence before design is 100% complete, resulting in faster project delivery. Flexible contractual terms such as use of typical rates and unit costs for common scope items are negotiated only once. Terms of special or unique situations are also established in the contract. Once selected, the chosen team is then under contract and available when needed.

All of the accelerated procurement options allow owners to satisfy their procurement requirements and deliver projects more effectively. They can also be used by owners to retain design firms, program or construction managers, CM at-risks or design-builders. They all entail a distinct project development process and include relationship, responsibility, selection and pricing approaches similar to the project delivery systems for larger projects. Some of these accelerated procurement approaches are often characterized by some as separate project delivery methods. This is especially true for Job Order Contracting that is procured using a Unit Price Book with price competition through a coefficient. IDIQ qualifies under the Federal Acquisition Requirements for the use of Federal Funds and under most State procurement codes.

These accelerated procurement approaches are better characterized more as a procurement methodology than as a separate definable project delivery method. These approaches can be used in conjunction with any of the typical project delivery methods. What makes them different from delivery methods is not how the design and construction services are delivered, but rather how and when they are contracted.

Multiple Prime Contracting and Direct Subcontracting

Multiple Prime Contracting and Direct Subcontracting are contracting approaches that can be used with any of the delivery methods described in this book. As the names imply, instead of an owner contracting with a single general contractor, construction manager, or design-builder, the owner (or its representative) contracts directly with multiple trade contractors for the completion of the work and assumes the responsibility for its coordination.

Multiple Prime Contracting is generally applied when the project is awarded in a limited number of packages (typically fewer than ten). Packages are a combination of several trade contracts. Typical packages include sitework, structure, general construction, mechanical, and electrical. Each package is referred to as a "prime contract" and is contracted directly to the owner.

Direct Subcontracting applies when each trade contract and supplier is awarded individually and contracted directly to the owner. The number of direct contracts is typically greater than 10 and is often 50 or more.

Several states and local governments have laws requiring construction to be performed using Multiple Prime Contracts. Proponents of this contracting method point out that the owner gets the benefit of the lowest cost for each of the trades. The method also prevents bid shopping by the general contractor or construction manager. In addition, this contracting method can be used to fast-track a project without involving one of the other delivery methods in those jurisdictions where the other approaches are not available.

An owner using these approaches essentially becomes the general contractor. The owner holds the multiple contracts and assumes responsibility for coordinating them. Because there is a risk of poor coordination among the various trades, many owners do not wish to be burdened with this task. They might solve the problem by hiring an agent CM or by assigning one of the multiple prime contractors this responsibility. Even so, the ultimate responsibility for coordination remains with the owner.

Agreements—Making Them Work for You

What is the role of contracts? Simply stated, a contract is a written document describing the terms and conditions of an agreement, which in turn determine the legal rights and obligations of the parties to the contract.

Contracts are agreements that specify who does what when it comes to implementing the chosen delivery method. The terms and conditions of an agreement are set forth in legal documents. Ideally, the documents define many considerations beyond the fundamentals of cost, time, quality, and safety. It is important in modern management of construction to avoid having contracts become barriers to cooperation among the parties.

The industry-recognized best practice is to first select the management approach, project delivery method, procurement method, and desired relationship, and then use a contract to further specify the details of the relationship.

Standard Forms of Agreement

Contracts are either standard or specially prepared agreements. In the United States, standard forms of agreement, such as ConsensusDOCS, are promulgated by and are available from several construction industry associations, the federal government, and most state and local governments. The section at the end of this book, Related Contracts, provides a side-by-side comparison of the ConsensusDOCS to the American Institute of Architects (AIA) Contract Documents.

Self Test

1. Which of these is not a typical step on the Road to Implementing a Project Delivery Method?
   a. Obtaining the funding for the project
   b. Gaining the ability to use a project delivery method
   c. Developing definitions and a list of delivery methods
   d. Selecting the appropriate delivery method
   e. Implementing the chosen delivery method

2. Fast-tracking is a defining characteristic of which of the following delivery methods?
   a. Design-Bid-Build
   b. Construction Management at-Risk
   c. Design-Build
   d. All of the above
   e. None of the above

3. Which of the following are considered "defining" characteristics?
   a. Are the design and the construction under separate contracts directly to the owner, or are they combined under one contract?
   b. Is final selection of the constructor based on criteria other than just the lowest total construction costs?
   c. The construction can be fast-tracked
   d. Both a and b
   e. All of the above

4. Which of the following are considered "typical" characteristics?
   a. A Guaranteed Maximum Price (GMP) contract
   b. A contractual schedule guarantee
   c. Preconstruction services
   d. The construction can be fast-tracked
   e. All of the above

5. If an owner selects a contractor using a competition based on the total construction cost based on less than complete design and a final selection based on both the price and other non-price criteria, which procurement method is this?
   a. Low Bid
   b. Best Value: Total Cost
   c. Best Value: Fees
   d. Qualifications Based Selection
   e. None of the above

6. Based on the definitions used in this chapter, in which procurement method are fees and the contractor's general conditions part of the final selection criteria but not the total construction cost?
   a. Low Bid
   b. Best Value: Total Cost
   c. Best Value: Fees
   d. Qualifications Based Selection

7. Third party options for program management include:
   a. Development manager
   b. Agent CMs
   c. Program managers
   d. All of the above

8. Based on the definitions used in this chapter, the difference between Multiple Prime Contracting and Direct Subcontracting is:
   a. The type of contract being contracted
   b. Whether the owner directly holds the contracts
   c. The number of contracts
   d. None of the above

CHAPTER TWO

PROCUREMENT OPTIONS

Introduction
- Defining "Price"
- Prequalification

Defining Procurement Options
- Low Bid
- Best Value: Total Cost
- Best Value: Fees
- Qualifications Based Selection

Procurement Processes
- Determining the Type of Procurement Process
  - Understanding Procurement Rules
  - Design Services
  - Construction Services
- Invitation to Bid
  - Pre-Bid Conferences
  - Bid Strategy
  - Bid Day
- Request for Qualifications/Request for Proposals
- Request for Qualifications
- Request for Proposals
- Request for Proposals Including Price
  - Price Is Fees
  - Price Is Total Cost
- Interviews
  - Final Evaluation and Selection

Selecting Procurement Options
- Design-Bid-Build
- Construction Management at-Risk
- Design-Build
- Integrated Project Delivery

PROCUREMENT OPTIONS

Other Thoughts Regarding Procurement
- Sole Source
- Negotiated
- Subcontractor Procurement Options

Self Test

INTRODUCTION

The manner in which the owner makes the final selection of the primary members of the project team is considered the procurement process. Depending on the project delivery model, the selection may extend to the design professionals, the prime constructor, the design-build team, or, in the case of Integrated Project Delivery (IPD), all the signatories to the multi-party contract. The procurement process is also referred to as the "selection" method. The solicitation, advertisement, bid, Request for Qualifications (RFQ), Request for Proposals (RFP), timing and basis of the firm selection, type of contract, administration processes, and procedures are all elements of procurement affecting the project delivery process.

Many in the industry separate the discussion of project delivery methods from the discussion of procurement. This approach is acceptable; however, the subjects of project delivery and procurement are so tightly intertwined that they should be considered together.

The best example of this interrelationship is with the Design-Build project delivery method. Design-Build can be procured with any one of the procurement approaches described in this chapter. However, to procure a Design-Build project with a Low Bid or Best Value: Total Cost procurement, the owner might choose to require more highly developed design criteria or even create bridging documents to provide to the design-builders competing for the project. Developing these design criteria takes time and may call for bringing in an outside consultant. This can be very different from procuring a Design-Build project using Qualifications Based Selection, which requires little or no design information during the selection process.

Even though both examples are referred to as Design-Build projects, the strategies and business dynamics are very different. This illustrates that the procurement process used to select the design and construction teams does have a major impact on the delivery method and the resulting relationship. Consequently, the definitions of the project delivery methods used throughout this book are often discussed in conjunction with the procurement options.

This chapter discusses the four typical procurement options:
- Low Bid
- Best Value: Total Cost
- Best Value: Fees
- Qualifications Based Selection

There are numerous terms for the four typical procurement options. For example, Low Bid is sometimes referred to as a "Sealed Bid." These synonymous terms are discussed later in the chapter.

PROCUREMENT OPTIONS

Each of these four procurement options is typically executed with one of two processes, either an Invitation to Bid process or a Proposal process. The Request for Qualifications (RFQ)/Request for Proposals (RFP) process discussed here is a common example of the Proposal process. There are many variations of these processes and many different names that are used to describe these two basic approaches to implementing a procurement process. Sometimes this is referred to as a One-Step or Two-Step (or Two Stage) process, Negotiated, or a Competitive Negotiation.

This chapter also explores the impact the four typical procurement options have on the project delivery methods and their implementation. The procurement process can affect the timing of the selection of the design and construction teams, the amount of information required at the time of selection (e.g., whether bridging documents were required), and the likely basis of reimbursement most appropriate for each delivery/procurement combination. (Basis of reimbursement is explored further in Chapter 3.)

Because of the impact the procurement process has on the project delivery method, it is highly recommended that when looking at either, both be considered. To determine the most appropriate delivery approach, consider both the procurement option and the delivery method. When combining the procurement and delivery methods, the following matrix is created:

Delivery Methods by Procurement Option

DELIVERY METHOD Common Nicknames	Low Bid	Best Value: Total Cost	Best Value: Fees	Qualifications Based Selection (QBS)
Design-Bid-Build Competitive Sealed Bid; Low Bid; Inv. to Bid (IFB)	☐	☐	N/A	N/A
CM at-Risk CM/GC; GC/CM; CMc; ECI	N/A	N/A	☐	☐
Design-Build Engineer-Procure-Construct (EPC)	☐	☐	☐	☐
IPD Multi-party; Alliancing	Not Typical	Not Typical	☐	☐

Taking the approaches created by the combination of the delivery methods and procurement approaches, owners can use this matrix to determine the delivery method and selection types they use in their own organizations.

By definition, procurement of the Design-Bid-Build delivery method is only by Low Bid or Best Value: Total Cost. Procurement of CM at-Risk can result from either Qualifications Based Selection or Best Value: Fee selection. (If a CM at-risk is procured with Low Bid, this, by definition, is Design-Bid-Build.) Design-Build can be procured with any of the four procurement options.

Because the procurement type can have significant impact on the process, it is critical when referring to a delivery method to be sure to identify the method of procurement at the same time. Formally or informally, the first thing experienced industry people do is classify the delivery method, whether using these terms or their own. Contractors and designers evaluating an RFQ/RFP will quickly determine whether they need to team up with someone and will evaluate which criteria the owner intends to use as the basis for the final selection.

Defining "Price"

One cannot have a meaningful discussion of project delivery and procurement without understanding the elements of the term "price." Exercise caution anytime the word "price" is used during a discussion on project delivery. It is very important to clarify which element(s) of the total cost is being referred to when the word "price" is mentioned.

Discussions about project delivery methods require an understanding of how total construction costs (TCC) are categorized. The three components of TCC are:
1. Construction cost of the work
2. Constructor's general conditions
3. Constructor's fee

Depending on the delivery method and procurement option chosen, one or more of these may be part of the price portion of the competition.

Prequalification

As discussed in more detail in Chapter 6, prequalification is the process by which the qualifications of prospective designers or constructors are examined prior to those persons/companies being solicited to compete for the project. The purpose of prequalification is to ensure that those designers or constructors competing for and bidding on the work are capable of performing the necessary services.

Prequalification is a process that occurs prior to the final selection and can be used with any project delivery method. One process used for procurement, RFQ/RFP, essentially has prequalification built into the process. Assuming the owner creates a shortlist of firms after evaluating the RFQ, the RFQ and subsequent shortlisting is essentially a prequalification step.

It is critical to understand that the distinction among the four procurement methods turns on the criteria used as the basis for the final selection. Some confusion continues to appear over the term "qualifications." As a procurement option, Qualifications Based Selection, or QBS, refers to making a final selection from among various proposers based on qualifications. Prequalification is an evaluation occurring early in the procurement process and can be used with any procurement option. One can prequalify with Low Bid, either type of Best Value, or Qualifications Based Selection.

DEFINING PROCUREMENT OPTIONS

Classifying the procurement options depends on the answer to these three questions. Is price part of the final selection criteria? If yes, is the price the total construction cost? If yes again, is price 100% the final and sole selection criterion? These three questions create these possible results:

Is price part of the final selection criteria?	If yes, is the price the total construction cost?	If yes again, is price 100% the final and sole selection criterion?	Then the procurement type is:
Yes	Yes	Yes	Low Bid
Yes	Yes	No	Best Value: Total Cost
Yes	No	N/A	Best Value: Fees
No	N/A	N/A	Qualifications Based Selection

Low Bid

The Low Bid procurement process is defined as a competition where price is a factor in the final selection criteria, the price is the TCC (or design and construction costs if it is Design-Build), and the TCC is the sole criterion for final selection.

> **Low Bid**
> - Total construction cost is the sole criterion for final selection
> - Price = Total construction cost
> - Final selection criterion = 100% total construction cost
> - Other names: Competitive Sealed Bid, Sealed Bid, Hard Bid

Most owners require the contractor's bids to be both responsible and responsive and must meet these criteria to be considered for final selection. (See Chapter 7 for explanation of these terms.) Once determined to be both responsible and responsive, the sole criterion for final selection is the TCC.

Best Value: Total Cost

The Best Value: Total Cost procurement process is defined as a competition where price is a factor in the final selection criteria, the price is the total construction cost (or design and construction costs if it is Design-Build), and the total construction cost is not the only criterion for final selection.

> **Best Value: Total Cost**
> - Total construction cost and other factors are criteria in final selection
> - Price = Total construction cost
> - Final selection criteria = between 0–100% total construction cost and other factors
> - Other names: Competitive Sealed Proposal, Best Value Source Selection, Competitive Proposal Selection (CPS)

Best Value: Total Cost, with separate contracts for design and construction, is probably furthest from having an industry consensus on a standardized name. The previous edition of this book referred to Best Value: Total Cost as a type of CM at-Risk, but in this edition, the definition of Design-Bid-Build has been broadened to include this selection type and no longer considers this approach a variation of CM at-Risk.

For guidance on best practices when using Best Value selections including total construction costs, see the most recent version of *Best Practices for Use of Best Value Selections*, jointly produced and published by National Association of State Facilities Administrators (NASFA) and AGC of America.

Best Value: Fees

The Best Value: Fees procurement process is defined as a competition where price is a factor in the final selection criteria, the price is the fees, and the fees are not the only criterion for final selection.

> **Best Value: Fees**
> - Both fees and qualifications are factors in the final selection
> - Price = Fees (which might include general conditions, preconstruction fees, etc.)
> - Final selection criterion = between 0–100% fees and other factors
> - Other names: Best Value Source Selection (fees), Competitive Sealed Proposal (fees)

Typical Best Value: Fees selections might include a weighting of fees for preconstruction, construction, and/or general conditions. For example, the following elements could be considered:
- Fee
  - Preconstruction services
  - Construction services
  - Post-construction services
- General conditions
  - Estimate of anticipated expenses based upon the project definition
- Project budget estimate
  - Divided into the major categories of work, based on the project definition documents
- Recommended contingency
  - Design contingency (preconstruction)
  - Construction contingency

In states that require the selection of a contractor through competitive pricing, the owner has the opportunity to select the most qualified contractor at a competitive price. It is up to the owner to determine the weight given to the fee criteria. The weight of each factor should reflect the relative importance of the fee, but it should never be the sole determining factor. In the "Request for Proposals" section below, further guidance is offered on handling of Fee and Pricing Proposals if the Best Value: Fees procurement process is used. For more information, see the most current edition of the AGC and NASFA publication, *CM/GC Guidelines for Public Owners*, which includes discussion on Best Value: Fees procurement of CM at-Risk.

Qualifications Based Selection (QBS)

The Qualifications Based Selection procurement process is defined as a competition where price is a not a factor in the final selection criteria.

> **Qualifications Based Selection**
> - Price is not a criterion for the final selection; qualifications are the only factor used in the final selection
> - Price = 0% of any component of price
> - Final selection criteria = 100% non-price criteria
> - Other names: Negotiated, Competitive Negotiation, or Single Source

Several states, including Arizona for example, statutorily or by policy prohibit any element of price to be part of the selection process for contractors on public work using CM at-Risk. Thus, these states strictly use a QBS procurement process similar to the one they use to select other professional services including designers. For more information, see the most recent edition of AGC of America's publication, *Qualifications Based Selection of Contractors*.

PROCUREMENT PROCESSES

Determining the Type of Procurement Process

Selecting the optimal procurement process can be critical to the success of the project. Once the owner has defined the project and the project goals, the best way to deliver and procure the project can be determined. All procurement processes come with risks and rewards. Each process should be weighed against the project requirements to determine the best method by which to deliver the project.

Understanding Procurement Rules

Most jurisdictions have specific laws and regulations concerning the solicitation and engagement of design- and construction-related services for public work. While there are variations among jurisdictions, the general process is similar. Public notice must be given in which the service being procured must be described and the factors or process for selection and contract award included. These selection factors may be based on qualifications, price, or a combination of the two, depending on the type of service or work being procured.

Design Services

The architect/engineer (A/E) is generally selected with a Qualifications Based Selection process when contracting directly with the owner. In most instances, there are advertisements or Requests for Qualifications/Proposals, responses from interested A/E firms, the development of a shortlist of fully qualified and suitable firms, interviews of shortlisted firms, the selection of the A/E, a negotiation of fees based on the scope of the services to be provided, and the award of the contract.

In selecting an A/E, the public owner should be aware of the different circumstances a designer may encounter when working under each of the different delivery methods. For example, with CM at-Risk the A/E will be working closely with a constructor during the design phase. The A/E needs to be aware that it will be working in a CM at-Risk process that includes the budget and schedule control functions that require its cooperation. The A/E will be challenged to coordinate the user's wants and preferences with the constructor's preferred systems, methodologies, and cost considerations. The CM at-risk's preferences for sequencing the work and trade/subcontract bid packages will also impact the A/E's development of the construction documents. This may be a reason to consider the selection of the CM at-risk first. However, where the architect is selected prior to the CM at-risk, the A/E should become familiar with the proposers responding to the RFQ or RFP for the CM at-risk, as the A/E can provide valuable input into the selection of the CM at-risk.

PROCUREMENT OPTIONS

The A/E's contract should encourage collaboration with the other members of the project team. Clauses such as the basis of reimbursement should be aligned with the specific requirements of the project. There are some who believe that an hourly fee with a not-to-exceed total fee allows for a more collaborative process, especially in situations where the scope may not be clear or the budget and program may not be aligned. A fixed price, negotiated lump sum approach to the fee may unintentionally inhibit some of the needed collaboration. Generally speaking, a fixed price for an A/E's fees is fine for scopes of service that can be defined. For projects without defined scopes, an hourly with a not-to-exceed fee may better support the needed collaboration. In other words, if the contractor's contract is an open-book, collaborative, team-approach type of contract, on projects requiring a high level of collaboration and integration during the design, the A/E's contract should be as well.

Construction Services

The figure below shows the typical procurement options for the contractor for each delivery method and selection type. The figure also shows the basis of reimbursement (Lump Sum, GMP, or Target Price) for each approach and the typical process (Invitation to Bid or RFQ/RFP). AGC of America has developed RFQ/RFP training that includes recommended practices and is available to assist in the training of managers responsible for implementing selections using RFQ/RFP.

Typical Delivery Method / Procurement Options with Typical Basis of Reimbursement

DELIVERY METHOD Common Nicknames	Low Bid	Best Value: Total Cost	Best Value: Fees	Qualifications Based Selection (QBS)
Design-Bid-Build Competitive Sealed Bid; Low Bid; Invitation to Bid	Inv. To Bid Lump Sum	RFQ/RFP Lump Sum	N/A	N/A
CM at-Risk CM/GC; GC/CM; CMc; ECI	N/A	N/A	RFQ/RFP GMP	RFQ/RFP GMP
Design-Build Engineer-Procure-Construct (EPC)	Inv. To Bid Lump Sum	RFQ/RFP Lump Sum	RFQ/RFP GMP	RFQ/RFP GMP
IPD Multi-Party; Lean Project Delivery; Alliancing	Not Typical	Not Typical	RFQ/RFP Target Price	RFQ/RFP Target Price

Invitation to Bid

On projects procured with the Low Bid procurement option, the procurement process used is the Invitation to Bid process, often referred to as the "traditional" process. Most owners, particularly public owners, have well established processes and procedures, many of which are regulated, for how they procure with Low Bid. Whether or not it is specifically referred to as an Invitation to Bid process, the process is probably very similar to the Low Bid process described here.

Pre-Bid Conferences

Owners or designers may call pre-bid conferences to explain unusual aspects of jobs and answer constructors' questions about the documents or the design. Such meetings are recommended for complex projects, such as major remodeling or buildings with sophisticated components, and participation at the pre-bid conference is often mandatory. Conferences should be scheduled at about the midpoint of the bid period and should include all constructors that have taken out documents, been prequalified, or been invited to submit bids. Conferences may be held at or near the construction site to review such things as traffic, construction limits, and unusual conditions. Typically, the owner documents the details of pre-bid conferences and distributes the information to all bidders.

Bid Strategy

Some constructors obtain all their work by bidding on Low Bid contracts. Others seek a balance between Low Bid and selections based on some amount of subjective criteria. In either case, constructors develop strategies to determine which projects to bid and which ones to bypass. The variables they use in devising their strategies include:

- Number of jobs available for bidding
- Attractiveness of a particular job compared to others
- Success in bidding on various types of projects
- Current and projected work load (backlog)
- Bonding limits now and in the future
- Perceived profit potential of particular jobs
- How prospective jobs fit the capabilities of the constructor
- Desire to keep key personnel employed during down markets (which may lead to bidding on less attractive projects)
- Characteristics of probable other bidders on a particular job
- Availability of key management personnel for a particular type of project

The number of competing bidders on a particular project depends not only on the condition of the marketplace but also on the level of specialization required. Projects with relatively little specialty work attract many bidders. Specialty projects, such as historical restorations and fire rehabilitation, attract fewer bidders. Specialty projects present a higher profit potential, but they represent a narrow portion of the construction market.

Success patterns develop over time, and constructors become adept at recognizing in advance which projects they should bid. Nonetheless, investigation is warranted before deciding to respond to any Invitation to Bid.

Bid Day

Prior to bid day, the general contractor prepares a recap covering all divisions of the work and a checklist of all items to accompany the bid, including the bid bond (if required) and various legal requirements. Also, the mark-up, defined as the difference between all the constructor's expected costs (buying the job) and the price to be submitted on the bid form (selling the job), is discussed among company executives. Sometimes called the fee and considered to be the profit after accounting for all, the mark-up is an important decision based on current market conditions, desirability of the project, and any other factors deemed important.

The bid forms are filled out as far ahead of time as possible. Then, often in the final hours before the deadline, bids come in from subcontractors and suppliers by phone, fax, hand delivery, and email. Participants are concerned that early submissions may hurt the confidentiality of their bids. Usually the general contractor's final price is determined within less than an hour of submission time, and a frantic period ensues. There is a final tally, check and recheck, application of the mark-up, completion of bid forms, and then the actual submission to beat the deadline.

Factors influencing the general contractor's bid include:
- Location of the job
- Marketplace conditions
- The number of bidders (not necessarily known in private work, but in public work, the parties obtaining documents is public information)
- Historic bidding patterns in this type of work
- Desirability of the project compared to other work being considered at the same time
- Prospects that the project will help to develop good relations with an owner
- Degree of uncertainty, including weather, labor supply, and the owner's and designer's reputations for reliability

Bid day is hurried, competitive, and deadline-oriented. Constructors focus aggressively on the challenge at hand when bidding and tolerate few distractions. In public work, the deadline is fixed. If the advertisement says noon, a public official will usually declare the bid period over precisely at noon. Bids submitted after the deadline will not be accepted. Private work may have more latitude, but it is good practice to adhere to a schedule. The frantic activities of bid day have long been considered among the worst aspects of bidding on Lump Sum projects. Not only is it hectic, it also can be expensive.

Request for Qualifications/Request for Proposals

On projects procured with Qualifications Based Selections, Best Value: Fees, or Best Value: Total Cost, the most commonly used process is a two-phase selection process; the first phase is a Request for Qualifications (RFQ) and the second a Request for Proposals (RFP). During the Request for Qualifications phase, consideration is given to the qualifications and expertise of the proposed firm. During the Request for Proposals phase, the firm submits its general qualifications of the proposed team relative to the requirements of the specific project, the cost of any preconstruction services, the proposed fee, the proposed general conditions cost, and the commitment of the firm to the owner's construction budget and schedule. With a QBS and Best Value: Fees selection, the cost and schedule commitment is defined after the selection, often near the end of the design process.

While the two-phase selection method is preferred by many, several hybrid selection processes have been developed as a result of owner's requirements.

The owner should develop a timeline for the overall procurement process. This can be done during the project definition development by the owner, or it can be done in parallel or as soon after the selection of the A/E as possible. For those using a Qualifications Based Selection process, industry studies show that the project benefits from selecting a contractor early in the process in order to have the construction expertise to draw upon at the right time.

The owner needs to know its internal team's management approach to the project. Once this is understood, it can assist in generating the schedule and aligning the in-house commitments and resources. Preparation of an RFQ/RFP, schedule, and the evaluation forms should occur before the selection process begins. The following figure shows a typical timeline for the selection process:

PROCUREMENT OPTIONS

Task \ Weeks	1	2	3	4	5	6	7	8	9	10	11	12	13	14	15
Advertise/Solicit Interest and Issue RFQ	▇														
Contractor Responds to RFQ		▇	▇	▇											
Review RFQ and Develop Shortlist of Proposers				▇	▇										
Issue RFPs						▇									
Contractor Responds to RFP							▇	▇	▇						
Review RFPs									▇	▇					
Contractor Interview Preparation											▇	▇	▇	▇	
Interviews/Evaluation and Selection															▇

■ Public Owner Tasks
■ Contractor Tasks

Note: Local statutory or policy- and project-specific requirements may require that the activities and time periods shown in this sample be adjusted accordingly.

Sometimes, particularly in the private sector, the owner elects to accelerate the procurement process and use a hybrid approach by combining the RFQ into the RFP. Essentially, this eliminates the time to prepare and distribute RFQs, wait for and evaluate responses, and create an initial a shortlist. Instead, much of the information requested in the RFQ is combined into the Request for Proposals. Then, upon receipt of and evaluation of responses, a shortlist can be created of the firms to be invited to the interview, or a selection can be made directly from the RFP responses.

Request for Qualifications

The RFQ is used to identify which firms are interested in the project and to pinpoint their relative qualifications. The qualifications under consideration at this stage normally are limited to non-monetary issues. The owner should provide information about the project to the firms interested in applying for it. This material should provide some definition of the project under consideration.

The following outline represents typical information required in an RFQ. (For a more detailed outline, see the most current edition of the AGC and NASFA publication, *CM/GC Guidelines for Public Owners*.)

- Basic company information
- Form of ownership
- Office submitting qualifications
- Authorization/license to do business in state
- Personnel capability
- Consultants
- Financial and fiscal responsibility information
- Bonding capacity
- Safety information
- Experience in project delivery system and project type
- Statement of why the proposing firm should be selected

Once the RFQs have been received, the owner reviews them to identify firms that have the best and most relevant experience, references, and financial capability. The owner may use weighted criteria in reviewing the RFQs to focus on firms that have background in areas most important to the owner. Selected firms are then typically shortlisted.

Assuming the owner received a significant number of RFQs, the shortlist would be limited to the best three to five firms that have demonstrated they are capable of providing the services and skills required by the project. By limiting the list to these firms, the owner produces a more motivated group of firms, as their individual odds of success have increased. Because these firms are competing against high quality companies, they will tend to be more competitive and thorough. The shortlist also allows those firms that are not selected to move on to more viable opportunities quickly and with limited expense.

Request for Proposals

The second phase is the RFP. The RFP is more detailed than the phase one RFQ process and involves more time, effort, and expense for all parties. The number of firms invited to propose should be limited to a number that allows for an efficient competition among the most suitable respondents to the RFQ, usually between three and five competitors. The proposals are reviewed and ranked following procedures specified in the solicitation. Finally, the firm determined best suited is selected, and the final negotiations for the award of the contract (if any) take place.

Very specific, objective evaluation criteria should be described in the RFP. All criteria should be listed in the order of importance to selection. Only evaluation

PROCUREMENT OPTIONS

criteria listed in the solicitation should be considered in ranking proposals. In determining the criteria, the owner should define project priorities and should indicate its intentions to achieve maximum value for the owner.

The shortlisted firms are given the Request for Proposals, which is a more in-depth request for information. At this time, they should also receive all the material that was developed by the owner to define the project, including the contract, budget, and schedule expectations. The more information the owner can provide to the firms about the proposed project, the more specific information the firms can provide about their approach to delivering the completed project.

The following outline represents typical information required in an RFP. (For a more detailed outline, see the most current edition of the AGC and NASFA publication, CM/GC Guidelines for Public Owners.)

- Experience
  - Resumes and references of proposed project staff members
  - Organizational chart describing how the project will be organized during preconstruction and construction
  - Specific firm experience on similar projects, including costs, schedule, and quality
  - Experience with Building Information Modeling (BIM), including 4D scheduling and 5D estimating (if applicable)
- Detailed project approach (Management Plan), including preconstruction services
  - Conceptual estimating
  - Detailed estimating
  - Value analysis
  - Systems analysis
  - Scheduling services for all team members and public authorities
  - Constructability reviews
  - Long-lead item strategies and purchasing
  - Bid package development
  - Cultivation of specialty contractor and supplier interest
  - Design support
- Construction services
  - CPM scheduling
  - Short interval scheduling
  - Cost control and cost forecasting
  - Change order management
  - Self-performed work
  - Specialty contractor and supplier procurement
  - Punchlist and warranty programs
- Budget
  - Budget for project (if enough information is available)

- Outlined specifications that define budget
- Qualifications and clarifications of the budget
- Weighting
  - Criteria and weighting factors
- (If Best Value: Total Cost or Best Value: Fees)
  - Business relationship (in a separate sealed package)
  - Proposed contract form or qualifications to the owner's proposed contract
  - Proposed fee (usually expressed as a percentage at this stage)
  - Proposed general conditions or reimbursable costs

Once the RFPs have been received, the owner evaluates them using either a formulaic approach or a trade-off analysis approach to determine which firms best satisfy the criteria established in the RFP. Then the owner generally moves to the next step in the procurement process, an interview.

A suggested best practice if fees are not part of the selection process is to require the owner to negotiate at first only with the highest ranked firm. If those negotiations are not successful, the owner must go to the next firm in rank, continuing with each firm in ranked order until a successful negotiation has been achieved. In addition, it is best not to allow an owner to return to a higher ranked firm with which it previously rejected. Instead, the owner must proceed to the next ranked firm. If it reaches the end of the list of qualified firms without a successful negotiation with any of them, the owner must start the whole selection process over again.

Request for Proposals Involving Price

If the procurement is Best Value: Total Cost or Best Value: Fees, regardless of whether it is Design-Bid-Build, CM at-Risk, or Design-Build, the RFP process will include price. The RFP must define how much the price will be weighted relative to the non-price criteria. Regardless of whether the price is the total cost or some combination of the fees, general conditions, and reimbursables, industry best practice is to have the price proposal be submitted in a separate envelope from the rest of the proposal response. Who gets to review the price proposals, and when, varies considerably. As a general rule, though, it is a best practice to keep those reviewing the technical or non-price criteria from having access to the price proposals until as late in the process as possible. For more information on Best Value: Total Cost, see the most recent edition of AGC and NASFA publication, *Best Practices for Use of Best Value Selections*.

Price Is Fees

When the price is only fees, the evaluation process is very similar to a Qualifications Based Selection, but in this case, there has to be an analysis of the proposed fees and possibly general conditions. If the selection team is using a formulaic approach, the fees usually just get entered into a formula which then, based on the formula, provides the score to be factored into the overall selection.

Regarding general conditions, the industry has developed three typical ways of compensating contractors for their general conditions costs: 1) The owner and the contractor can agree on a lump sum amount for all general conditions costs, 2) an amount not to exceed a stipulated maximum, or 3) a percentage of the construction costs. Often there is uncertainty about what items are included in "general conditions" and how to calculate the appropriate costs. There is no substitute for making clear—in the RFP—what is included in each part of the price proposal, especially the general conditions.

Fees based on a percentage of the work should be considered with the overall scope of the project in mind. A lower fee percentage combined with a high-cost producer may not be as good a value to the owner as a higher fee percentage with a low-cost producer. For this reason, it is recommended that the fee percentage not be the sole determining factor in the selection process.

Owners should understand fully the importance of fees in the overall selection process and should clearly state this importance in the instructions accompanying the RFP. More owners are recognizing that the real ability to impact overall project cost lies in controlling direct project costs, which can represent over 85–90% of the total project costs. Owners are encouraged to focus on selecting the contractor likely to have the most positive impact on the direct project costs and recognize that this firm may not offer the lowest proposed fee.

Preconstruction fees should be separated from the construction fees, and any correlation between them should be made clear. Also, it is recommended that the fees and costs for construction services be separated to show the fixed management fee, the costs for the general conditions work (Lump Sum, fixed percentage of construction cost, or an agreed upon not-to-exceed maximum cost), the contractor's construction contingency (Lump Sum or percentage of estimated construction cost), and the proposed proportioning of cost savings.

While price is always important because of tight budgets and fiduciary responsibility, the owner should carefully balance the complexity of the project with the quality and technical capabilities of the competitors to determine which proposer is most likely to provide the maximum value.

Price Is Total Cost

When the price is the total construction cost, the analysis of the price proposals is very similar to a Low Bid, and the proposals must be analyzed like a bid in the Invitation to Bid. If the bids are received with no clarifications and there is only a price to evaluate, this can be a relatively quick process. However, if the prices are submitted with detailed information and clarifications, which is often the case in the private sector, the analysis could take time. If the project is Design-Build, then the analysis can be even more time consuming because the designs and scopes of each price proposal could be different. Likewise, if the amount of design criteria provided to the proposers was minimal, the scope that each price proposal is based on could be very different.

Interviews

From the shortlisted firms who have submitted RFPs, the owner will normally select two to three firms to participate in organized interviews or presentations to the owner and other members of its team. The number of firms selected for interview should be based on the initial scoring of the proposals and should be limited to those firms that may reasonably be expected to receive an award. In almost all cases, the owner's selection team will determine weighted criteria for all elements of the interview. In some jurisdictions, these criteria may be set by regulation.

There are a number of best practices for the interview portion of the selection process. Some of these best practices for owners include:

- One member of the selection committee should check the references provided and distribute the results.
- The selection committee should consist of people who are stakeholders in the project. This group includes representatives of the owner and of the end user of the facility. In the case of a public owner, it is highly recommended to include a representative of the public owner who is there solely to guarantee fairness of the process. Often this person has a procurement background but is not a member of the end user organization.
- A second shortlisting, after the RFP responses but prior to the interviews, is generally a good practice. If the selection committee determines that a firm, based upon the proposal or other good evidence, has no chance of success, the firm should be spared the expense of interviewing.
- A set timeframe and agenda should be established in advance of the interview.
- The selection committee should meet prior to the first interview to review the plan for the day and receive any last-minute instructions. Scheduling short breaks between interviews will also allow time to fill out evaluations and discuss each interview.
- Recommendation for final selection should be made immediately following interviews.

It is important to review with the selection committee the criteria established by the RFQ/RFP. It is critical that once a set of selection criteria is established and published to the shortlisted teams, it is followed. Many times during the interviews and the final selection meetings, the selection committee will want to change or modify the selection criteria. This is almost never, with rare exception, a good practice. The teams are competing in good faith and are spending several thousand dollars apiece. To change the criteria at the last minute to favor one over the other is unfair. Selection committees that decide, even with good intentions, to change or deviate from the original selection criteria are exposing themselves to possible accusations of impropriety, or even to litigation.

Another practice growing in popularity is to include on the selection committee an industry representative who is not competing for the project. This person usually represents a peer firm of the competing firms. Though this committee member may not have a vote, the industry representative does participate as a member of the committee throughout all steps of the process and provides objectivity.

To maintain the integrity and credibility of the process, it is important that the selection committee have full and independent authority to make a final selection. The committee's decision should not be overridden by a board, commission, or other public official.

Final Evaluation and Selection

After all the firm's proposals have been evaluated against the original criteria and the most qualified firms have been interviewed, best practice strongly suggests that the selection committee come to a final group ranking before leaving the interview room. The selection committee should deliberate, reviewing as a group all evidence to the extent deemed necessary, including the responses to the RFQ, the proposals, and any references. Each selection committee member should submit to the chair a final personal ranking of the firms. Upon conclusion of selection committee work, each member should endorse his or her official documentation of the group's decision. The successful and unsuccessful firms should all be notified within a reasonable period of time.

SELECTING PROCUREMENT OPTIONS

The selection of design and construction practitioners significantly affects the types of relationships created and the ultimate outcome of a project. There are a whole myriad of elements of the project delivery process that are directly affected by the procurement process chosen by the owner.

First, and perhaps most important, because of the impact the procurement method has on the delivery method and the tie to the definition of the delivery method, the choice of the procurement option will often define the delivery method. For example, if an owner hires an architect and proceeds with developing the design, then decides to procure the contractor based on a Qualifications Based Selection, the owner is using CM at-Risk, whether or not the owner uses the term.

Examples of other areas that are affected by the chosen procurement option include:
- The likely choice of the basis of reimbursement
- Whether the contract is open-book
- The amount of information required at the time of the selection
- The duration of the overall team selection
- The ability of the contractor to include contingencies for work that is not clear
- The manner in which changes are addressed, especially during construction
- How much information is shared and when
- The owner's access and participation in the subcontracting process

Design-Bid-Build

By definition, Design-Bid-Build can be procured with either Low Bid or Best Value: Total Cost.

Construction Management at-Risk

By definition, CM at-Risk can be procured with either Qualifications Based Selection (QBS) procurement or a Best Value: Fees.

Design-Build

Because Design-Build can be procured with any of the four procurement approaches, it is particularly important when referring to Design-Build to clarify whether it is a Design-Build Low Bid, Design-Build Best Value: Total Cost, Design-Build Best Value: Fees, or Design-Build Qualifications Based Selection. The impact of the procurement is probably best illustrated with Design-Build.

Integrated Project Delivery

Though Integrated Project Delivery (IPD) can theoretically be procured with any of the four procurement approaches, given that the primary motivator to use IPD is higher collaboration, it is hard to conceive of procuring it with Low Bid or Best Value: Total Cost. Most IPD projects to-date have been procured with Qualifications Based Selection, if not outright Negotiated Single Source.

OTHER THOUGHTS REGARDING PROCUREMENT

Sole Source

A situation where the owner either elects to or has no choice but to negotiate directly with a single firm is often referred to as a "Sole Source" or Direct

Negotiation procurement. In some cases, an owner may have reasons for believing that negotiating an award with a single contractor is in its best interest.

An example of when an owner may be forced to use Sole Source includes emergency situations such as a road collapse, where there is no time to go through a formal procurement process. Another example is when there is only one contractor that can provide the required services, such as a fabric roof manufacturer that owns the patent on the system to be used on a new domed roof stadium. In both of these examples, the owner is forced into or has no choice but to directly negotiate with a single contractor.

Some in the industry refer to this as another separate type of procurement. Here, Sole Source is referred to as a type of Qualifications Based Selection because there is no price considered in the final selection. It does not matter that there was not a procurement process with an RFQ, RFP, or interview prior to the selection; those are just the typical processes used to procure with a Qualifications Based Selection. The fact that there is no price element is what defines Sole Source as a type of QBS.

Negotiated

The term "negotiated" is used to describe procurements and, in most cases, it is probably referring to any procurement in which the price is finalized after a single firm has been chosen but prior to their award being finalized. This distinction, where the selection is final but the award is not, is important, but it is not necessary to define the procurement process.

The procurement is defined and linked to the final selection. If the subsequent negotiation results in a contract award, that is assumed to be the outcome. If the subsequent negotiation does not result in an award, the owner makes another selection, but that selection would still be based on one of the procurement options outlined in this chapter.

The term "negotiated" can also refer to any procurement based on a proposal rather than a bid. Essentially all procurements other than those procured with an Invitation to Bid are negotiated. Given such a wide ranging application of the term, it is generally avoided here.

There is another reason that the term "negotiated" has been avoided here. In many circles within the industry, the term has picked up a negative connotation and sometimes implies that there has not been any competition. All of the procurement options here are competitive and, if managed properly, can be held up to any level of scrutiny. Since some of the procurement options described here often refer to some type of negotiated selection, rather than subject the discussion to this debate, the term is generally just not used here.

Subcontractor Procurement Options

With many contracts, particularly those procured with Qualifications Based Selection or Best Value: Fees and contracted with an open-book GMP, Cost-Plus, or Target Price basis of reimbursement, the owner is able to actively participate in the subcontractor procurement process. This includes reviewing the scopes, pricing, and clarifications of each subcontractor as well as evaluating, recommending, and awarding approval of each subcontract award.

Some owners' procurement rules require that the contractor procures under the same rules as the owner when it subcontracts the work. Some rules require that all subcontracts be procured through Low Bid. It is critical that the owner understands this aspect of the buyout process and clearly explains the rules in the selection documents. This will allow the contractor to procure the project with the greatest possibility for savings for the owner since the open-book GMP passes most, if not all, of this savings back to the owner.

A growing number of owners are able to encourage selection options for the contractor to use in the selection of subcontractors. Every project has unique elements the contractor must consider as it selects or procures its subcontractors. In theory, the same processes available to the owner are available to the contractor when selecting subcontractors. These can include:

- **Design-Build subcontractor**—Another option is to use the Design-Build method at the trade contractor level. The selection of the trade contractor could be based on any of the procurement options. It is crucial that if this approach is desired, it should be fully discussed with the entire team before proceeding. This can be done on projects procured with any project delivery method at the prime contractor level. For example, on Design-Bid-Build projects, if only performance specifications are provided as is typical with fire sprinkler systems, the selected subcontractor takes the responsibility to complete the design, fabricate and install the work as a design-build subcontractor.
- **Design-Assist contracting (for subcontractors)**—Typically used with a QBS or Best Value: Fees procurement, this is similar to the process described above, in which a Request for Proposals is developed and the subcontractor responds with qualifications and sometimes a price.

Whereas the terminology works when you push the Design-Build methodology down the line to the subcontractor, the industry trips when the CM at-Risk methodology is pushed down the line. For the most part, the industry applies the term "Design-Assist" to describe the application at the subcontractor level of a methodology similar to CM at-Risk.

This is not to say that this is the only way Design-Assist is done. Although the term primarily refers to a Qualifications Based Selection with the expectation to work open-book providing preconstruction services collaboratively until a mutually agreed upon GMP for the scope of work can be provided, the term "Design-Assist" also is used to describe the early involvement of the subcontractor even when procured with a Best Value: Total Cost process, or essentially a competitive pricing of the subcontractor's entire scope as part of its selection.

This is a process that allows the subcontractor to bring the best information to the design team through consultation. In the Request for Proposals, it is clearly spelled out that the subcontractor will work in the first phase as a design assistant to the design team. The subcontractor will collaborate and provide full cooperation and information to the design team on details, installation, fabrication, budget, and all aspects of the project. For this effort the subcontractor will be compensated the same as the contractor being reimbursed for preconstruction.

If at the end of the first phase (the Design-Assist phase) the subcontractor is willing to sign a contract for the agreed upon budgeted amount based upon its work, it will be awarded the subcontract. If, on the other hand, the subcontractor is not able to arrive at the agreed upon budget, then the contractor has the right to use all the information developed by the subcontractor and the designer to bid the project competitively. This process has produced excellent results on projects, as it limits risk to the owner and provides knowledge and skill to the design professional in the design and construction phase.

To use the Design-Assist method of contracting, the owner should indeed expect to pay more upfront for consulting fees and coordination. The owner should expect savings later thanks to fewer change orders, delay claims, and chances of litigation.

Self Test

1. Which of these is not a procurement option?
   a. Low Bid
   b. Invitation to Bid
   c. Best Value: Fees
   d. Best Value: Total Cost
   e. Qualifications Based Selection

2. Which of these selection types does not typically employ a RFQ/RFP process?
   a. Low Bid
   b. Best Value: Total Cost
   c. Best Value: Fees
   d. Qualifications Based Selection

3. Which of the following can be used as a prequalification process?
   a. Low Bid
   b. Best Value: Fees
   c. Best Value: Total Cost
   d. Qualifications Based Selection
   e. All of the above

4. Which of these processes is typically used with Best Value: Total Cost procurements?
   a. Low Bid
   b. Invitation to Bid
   c. Request for Qualifications/Request for Proposals
   d. Direct Negotiations

5. True or False: A Request for Qualifications typically focuses on the experience of the proposed personnel and the detailed Management Plan.

6. If an RFP includes a request for a price proposal and the price is only fees and general conditions, which of the following is this?
   a. Low Bid
   b. Best Value: Total Cost
   c. Best Value: Fees
   d. Qualifications Based Selection

CHAPTER THREE

BASIS OF REIMBURSEMENT

Introduction
- Contract Types
- Open-Book Contracting
- Risk Shifting
- Changes

Defining Basis of Reimbursement
- Lump Sum
- GMP—Cost-Plus with a Not-to-Exceed Guaranteed Maximum Price
  - Cost of the Work: General Conditions and the Contractor's Fee
  - Fixed Fee Approach
  - GMP—A Challenge and an Opportunity
- Cost-Plus—Without a Not-to-Exceed Guaranteed Maximum Price
- Target Price
  - Target Price vs. Cost-Plus
  - Target Price vs. GMP
  - The "No GMP" Misnomer
  - Pooled Contingencies
- Unit Price

Typical Basis of Reimbursement for Each Project Delivery Method
- Design-Bid-Build
- Construction Management at-Risk
- Design-Build
- Integrated Project Delivery

Self Test

BASIS OF REIMBURSEMENT

INTRODUCTION

Often brought into the discussion of project delivery is the "basis of reimbursement," or how the contractor is reimbursed by the owner (also referred to as the compensation approach). Chapter 2 discussed the typical procurement options and their direct impact on the project delivery method chosen and the implementation of that chosen method. Examples from Chapter 2 of how the procurement process affects implementation of the delivery methods included: the timing of the selection of the design and construction teams, the amount of information required at the time of selection (e.g., whether bridging documents were required), and the likely basis of reimbursement most appropriate for each delivery/procurement type combination. This last example, the basis of reimbursement and how it impacts the delivery method, is explored further in this chapter.

The basis of reimbursement defines how the contract amount is going to be determined and reimbursed. Is the contract amount going to be reimbursed as one overall price (Lump Sum)? Is the contract amount going to be capped by a Guaranteed Maximum Price (GMP)? If there is no pre-established contract amount, will costs be reimbursed as they are incurred (Cost-Plus)? Is the contract amount going to be treated as a target with incentives tied to hitting that target and consequences tied to missing it (Target Price)? Is the contract amount going to be based on specific units of work with payment rate tied to each unit (Unit Price)?

The basis of reimbursement also is often directly related to how information is shared and how much access the owner has to information possessed and controlled by the contractor (i.e., whether the contract is "open-book"—more transparent—or "closed-book"—less transparent). This is another one of the issues that directly impacts the process typically resulting from the chosen project delivery method.

One of the most significant impacts of open-book contracts that use a Cost-Plus approach to cost reimbursement is how changes to the originally agreed upon scope are addressed after the original contract amount has been established or during construction.

It is very important to note that the basis of reimbursement is not exclusively tied to any project delivery method. If they were, they would be considered "defining characteristics" and incorporated into the definition of each delivery method. In theory, any delivery method could be contracted with any of the basis of reimbursements. In practice, the industry has learned that each delivery model works best if it is paired with a suitable basis of reimbursement.

Experience has also shown a strong correlation between the choice of the basis of reimbursement and the procurement type chosen. Low Bid and Best Value: Total Cost procurements are typically Lump Sum. Best Value: Fees and Qualifications Based Selections are typically Guaranteed Maximum Price (GMP) or sometimes, though much less frequently, Cost-Plus. The emerging trend with Qualifications

Based Selections on Integrated Project Delivery projects is Target Price. While these trends are not universal, they are fairly representative across the industry as a whole.

Many owners have a responsibility to provide some limit to the financial exposure that they accept on behalf of their organizations or institutions. This requirement usually limits the use of uncapped Cost-Plus contracts and is currently a subject of close scrutiny with the emergence of Target Price, multi-party contracts. The misuse of one of the basis of reimbursements can be very costly to the project owner. For example, procurement best practices generally caution against the use of Lump Sum, closed-book type contracts on procurements that are not based on competitive pricing, such as QBS or Best Value: Fee procurements. These negotiated-type procurements generally are recommended to be open-book contracts that allow the owner to participate in the review of all pricing.

Similarly, projects with a high likelihood of having minor changes during construction (e.g., renovation of a historic building) would not typically lend themselves to the use of the closed-book, Lump Sum contract. The administration of minor changes likely to arise on such a project would typically be more easily managed with the transparency offered by an open-book GMP contract because of the typical approach of openly identifying a contingency within the GMP. Depending on the contract terms established (i.e., if the contractor's fees are fixed and not a percentage of the construction cost), the contractor's incentive to increase profit on changes is eliminated. This common practice with GMP contracts directly contributes to the team's ability to effectively manage these minor changes. This does create a new challenge on GMP contracts—good contingency management. Without experienced personnel using well established practices for good contingency management, there can be a tendency to overuse the contingency and allocate it for costs that should have been included in the original project scope.

It is also worth noting that on the same project, just as a variety of delivery approaches can be used, different basis of reimbursements can be used as well. At the trade contractor level, different subcontracts can be different basis of reimbursements. For example, on a CM at-Risk project, the major trade contractors, such as the mechanical and electrical trades, may be contracted early with a Qualifications Based Selection and contracted under a Guaranteed Maximum Price, while the majority of the other trade contracts may be Lump Sum contracts.

Not only can the same project have multiple contracts with multiple basis of reimbursements, but a single contract can also have some or all of the pricing methods included. As an example, on a project with a GMP contract there is an overall GMP, but one component of the work may be priced at a unit cost (sitework), while another is a time and material allowance (deep foundations), and still another component (concrete) is a lump sum.

BASIS OF REIMBURSEMENT

As the industry and delivery methods used by the industry have evolved, the corresponding basis of reimbursement has evolved as well. Like other industry vocabulary, the terminology used to describe contract and payment approaches has evolved into a variety of terms. Once again, the terms used here are chosen to provide a baseline for the industry to use for aligning terminology.

Contract Types

The term "contract type" is another term used by many industry participants to mean several different things. Some use contract type to refer to the basis of reimbursement (e.g., Lump Sum or GMP contract type). Others use contract type to refer to the delivery method (e.g., Design-Bid-Build or Design-Build contract type). Based on the many uses of the term "contract type," this textbook does not use the term to describe any one of these topics specifically, but may generally be used to refer to any one of these topics.

Open-Book Contracting

Open-book refers to a contractual requirement to share information related to the project, particularly project cost information. This includes estimates, bids from subcontractors and suppliers, invoices, and any information directly related to the cost of executing the project. Cost-Plus refers to the manner in which actual costs associated with the project are marked up for overhead and profit by the contractor and then billed to the owner—the "plus" in Cost-Plus, referring to the contractor's fee. For example, a contract might specify a specific cost plus a fee of 10%. In this instance, the contractor would add up all of the actual costs that are required by the contract to be reimbursed by the owner and add 10% to this total for overhead and profit.

The Cost-Plus contract approach is commonly used in cases such as emergencies (e.g., a road collapses and needs to be replaced immediately) or on unique projects where it is difficult to define a scope and corresponding contract amount. The obvious downside of the Cost-Plus contract to the owner is that, without a GMP feature attached, there is no upper limit to how much a project might cost. As an alternative to a GMP, the owner and contractor might be using an estimated budget to give the owner some order of magnitude of the estimated total cost.

Risk Shifting

These basis of reimbursements are one of the most important mechanisms used by owners to address how much risk they are able and willing to take on for a specific project. With most of these different approaches, risk is shifted from the owner to its contractor. As a general rule, there is cost associated with the risk when it is shifted, and the more risk the owner shifts to the constructor, the greater that cost should be. The contract type and the basis of reimbursement play a significant role in how much risk an owner chooses to either assign or retain, but as is almost always the case, they are not the only factors. Using one basis of reimbursement versus another may have a major impact on the ultimate outcome of the chosen delivery approach, but the use of one over another by itself is never a guarantee of success.

Changes

Changes to the project scope or to other aspects of a project affecting budget and/or schedule that occur during the project continue to present one of the largest challenges to project teams. Determining what is and is not a change, who caused the change, when the change occurred, and who is responsible for the cost and schedule impacts resulting from the change are all aspects that need to be resolved. Addressing all of these issues is one of the more daunting challenges almost every project team faces at some point.

There is no perfect solution to the endless variation of scenarios. That said, the transparency offered by the open-book approach that is typical with GMP, Cost-Plus, and Target Price basis of reimbursements does have a direct correlation to how changes will be addressed, particularly those that occur either after the GMP amount has been agreed upon or after construction has begun. This open-book practice can work against a contractor's ability to enhance profit during the project while significantly increasing the ability to keep the team focused on the project's best interest.

DEFINING BASIS OF REIMBURSEMENT

Lump Sum

The most common basis of reimbursement is Lump Sum. Lump Sum contracts are a basis of reimbursement defined by having a set price in exchange for providing a prescribed scope. The set price is typically fixed at the time of the contract and is intended to be inclusive of all services including labor, materials, equipment, and other related costs.

There are many terms used interchangeably with Lump Sum including: 1) "Stipulated Sum," a synonym for Lump Sum that is frequently used in contract language, 2) "Fixed Price," a term favored by some owners meaning essentially the same thing as Lump Sum or Stipulated Sum but tending to be more broadly applied to other types of contracts such as "Negotiated Fixed Price," 3) "Firm Fixed Price," a term used in the federal sector, and 4) "Hard Bid" or "Hard Money," colloquial terms for any agreement where the constructor is under contract with a Lump Sum basis of reimbursement.

BASIS OF REIMBURSEMENT

A Lump Sum or a Firm Fixed Price contract is generally not open-book, and access to the contractor or design-builder's information is limited. The contract terms usually describe a scenario where the general contractor assumes the risk of increases in cost to complete the work required. Increased costs beyond that lump sum are allowed only through formal amendments (change orders) agreed upon by the owner and general contractor. While the owner has no right to disclosure of the contractor's cost for the base contract work, there may be a right to see cost information pertinent to the pricing of change orders.

The Lump Sum basis of reimbursement can be used with any delivery method procured with any procurement type. (It should be noted, however, that though theoretically possible, it is difficult to conceive how a Lump Sum basis of reimbursement can be used on an IPD contract and still maintain the desired level of collaboration.)

There are some typical applications when the Lump Sum basis of reimbursement is used:
- The Lump Sum type of reimbursement is most common with projects procured with a Low Bid or Best Value: Total Cost selection. Since, by definition, Design-Bid-Build uses either Low Bid or Best Value: Total Cost selections, Lump Sum contracts are most common with Design-Bid-Build.
- Lump Sum contracts are not limited to Design-Bid-Build, however; Design-Build, particularly those procured with Low Bid or Best Value: Total Cost selections are often Lump Sum contracts as well.

Much less common is the use of Lump Sum when procured with Best Value: Fees or Qualifications Based Selection. Since, by definition, Construction Management at-Risk is procured with either Best Value: Fees or Qualifications Based Selections, the use of Lump Sum contracts with CM at-Risk is not common. (Instead, CM at-Risk is most often contracted with a GMP basis of reimbursement.) Similarly, Design-Build or Integrated Project Delivery arrangements procured with Best Value: Fees or Qualifications Based Selection are rarely contracted with Lump Sum.

Lump Sum is frequently the basis of reimbursement in subcontracts and supply agreements in all project delivery systems. In all these situations, when contracted with Lump Sum as the basis of reimbursement, subcontractors or suppliers accept the risk that if they are required to complete the required work at a cost greater than the contract sum, they will have to cover the cost overrun (except for those costs due to change orders or other permissible grounds under the contract for adjusting the lump sum price).

GMP—Cost-Plus with a Not-To-Exceed Guaranteed Maximum Price

A Guaranteed Maximum Price, sometimes referred to as a "GMP" or "G-Max," is a basis of reimbursement where the owner agrees to reimburse the cost of the work up to a prescribed ceiling amount—the Guaranteed Maximum Price. In return, the contractor agrees to provide the agreed upon scope of work and is at risk for cost overruns due to any fault of its own that causes the total contract amount to go above the GMP. Again, the contractor would not be responsible for those costs due to change orders or other permissible grounds under the contract; the GMP amount is subject to adjustment for change orders in a manner similar to adjustment of the contract amount under a Lump Sum basis of reimbursement.

Overruns caused by the owner or the designer would be considered changes and not part of the original GMP. Note that this is an area where CM at-Risk and Design-Build contracts differ. In a GMP Design-Build contract, the category of overruns due to errors in design, after the establishment of the GMP, shifts from the owner to the design-builder and would not be considered a change to the original GMP.

Conversely, in CM at-Risk, design errors would generally be the owner's responsibility (reference the Spearin Doctrine as discussed in Chapter 7) and would be considered a justification for changes to the original GMP. There are some who question how much the owner's responsibility for the design may be eroded due to the early (preconstruction) involvement of the CM at-risk. The involvement of the contractor during design has created an issue relative to how much, if any, responsibility the CM at-risk assumes for the design.

GMP contracts are almost always open-book. The transparency an open-book GMP contract offers can play a major role in enhancing collaboration, particularly when compared to closed-book Lump Sum contracts. One example is the ability to manage changes; many owners use open-book GMP contracts to better manage changes mainly when changes are expected after the establishing of the GMP. On the other hand, GMP contracts can be difficult to manage, especially for owners not experienced with doing so. Since the owner has access to the contractor's cost information (with detailed itemized billings), this can present owners and contractors with a whole new set of challenges.

The use of Fixed Price and Cost-Plus contracts is not unique to the construction industry. In an industry often maligned for its lack of innovation, the construction industry does deserve credit for having evolved a basis of reimbursement approach that provides both the benefit of an upper limit to the owner's cost exposure *and* facilitates a much higher level of collaboration than a traditional Lump Sum contract (GMP). The GMP is a feature added to a Cost-Plus contract whereby the cost reimbursement is limited by a GMP amount. When added to a traditional Cost-Plus contract, the not-to-exceed cost limitation that is tied to a fairly well, but not completely, defined scope of work creates a contract with maximum price that has some guarantees associated with it. The GMP basis of reimbursement has been around and improved by the industry for decades. It is not a foolproof approach and, especially for owners or contractors with little or no experience using it, the GMP basis of reimbursement can present an entirely new set of challenges.

BASIS OF REIMBURSEMENT

Cost of the Work: General Conditions and the Contractor's Fee

Costs associated with GMP contracts are typically categorized into three buckets for reimbursement purposes: cost of the work (COW) (the actual labor and materials going into the final construction product); contractor's general conditions (the contractor's project-specific overhead, such as the supervision salaries, and the support items, such as trailers and temporary utilities) and the contractor's fee (corporate overhead and gross profit). GMP contracts usually define in specific detail which costs are reimbursable as cost of the work versus costs that are attributable to the other buckets.

Many owners view the contractor's general conditions as a component of the cost of the work and thus end up with two buckets, the cost of the work and the contractor's fee. This is logical when the contractor is hired early in the design process and the scope of the work is not really well defined in order to provide a precise estimate of the general condition line items such as size and duration required of staffing, typically one of the largest components of the general conditions.

A GMP contract also may contain a savings split provision regarding any savings between the GMP and the project's actual cost. It might provide that the owner shares a percentage of the savings, or it may state that the owner retains all such savings. A savings split provision is an incentive to the contractor to help minimize costs. However, such provisions sometimes are criticized because they may provide an incentive for the contractor to inflate the estimate to create savings later. This is an example of a new challenge that is involved in managing GMP contracts.

Fixed Fee Approach

One of the practices used on GMP contracts by many owners is fixing the contractor's fee as a lump sum amount. This is usually done after using a percentage fee for estimating purposes, but then at the time of establishing the not-to-exceed Guaranteed Maximum Price, the fee is fixed. Typically, there is a clause that limits increases to the GMP to no more than a mutually agreed upon percentage (typically around 10%). This practice of fixing the contractor's fee can dramatically change the contractor's behavior and virtually eliminate the contractor's personnel from being subject to the scrutiny that they are benefitting from changes to the scope of the project. In fact, the contractor is now incentivized to efficiently manage and incorporate changes. On the other hand, if the GMP were to increase by more than the 10% through owner-initiated change orders, the contractor's fee would increase as well.

BASIS OF REIMBURSEMENT

GMP—A Challenge and an Opportunity

Other examples of the differences with GMP contracts include:
- The ability to have access to the contractor or design-builder's information via contractually established audit rights throughout the project
- The ability to have access to the trade contractor's and supplier's bids
- The ability to participate in the review and buyout process
- The ability to convert the GMP to Firm Fixed Price later in the project
- The volume of supporting information often received with progress billings
- How to assure that the costs being proposed are reasonable for the work being performed
- Defining and enforcing what elements of cost are and are not included in the contract definitions of cost of the work, and how those costs are determined
- Determining what kind of audit, if any, to perform

These are just a few of the differences between an open-book GMP contract and a closed-book Lump Sum contract. These differences can be advantages or disadvantages depending on how they are managed and also depending on whether you are looking at them from the perspective of the owner or the contractor.

The timing for establishing the Guaranteed Maximum Price varies. Typically it is established before the design is complete, but it can be deferred until after the design is complete or the trade packages are bid. Often the GMP is set near the completion of design development documents (sometimes referred to as 60–65% completed drawings). It can be set earlier, at the end of the schematic design phase (perhaps 20–25%), but it must be understood that the contractor's contingency will be much higher to address the contractor's increased risk due to the lack of definition and the number of unknowns at that time.

The art of managing a GMP contract is closely tied to the ability to successfully manage contingencies. Different contingencies take on different meanings and significance depending on who is holding the contingency and the basis of reimbursement being used. With GMP contracts, it is typical for the contractors to include a design phase contingency to accommodate unknowns within the as yet incomplete design and corresponding estimate. The less complete the contract documents at the time the GMP is established, the larger the design phase contingency.

BASIS OF REIMBURSEMENT

Contingency

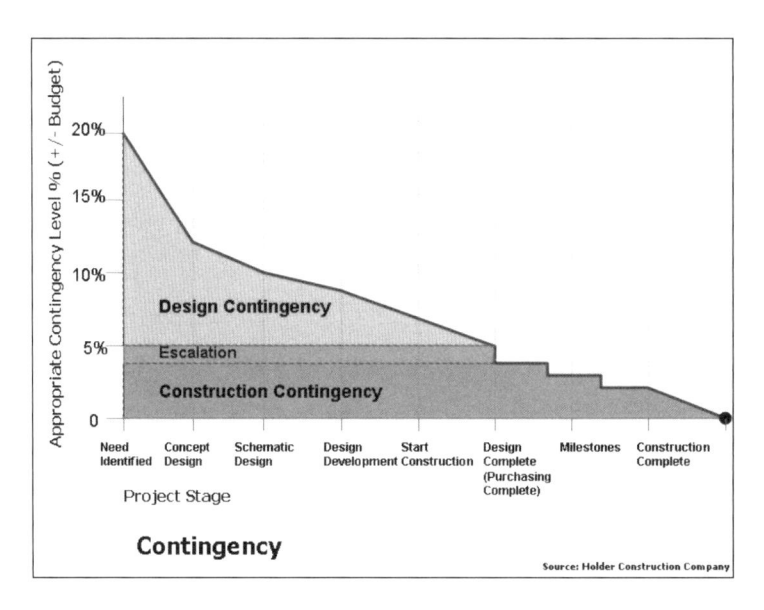

Source: Holder Construction Company

The three fundamental approaches to implementing GMPs prior to the completion of the design include:
1. Establishing a "preliminary GMP" for the entire project early in the design process and continuously tracking the design and corresponding pricing against this baseline.
2. Establishing a "progressive GMP" or component change order approach where components are contracted individually building to a GMP. The progressive GMP approach starts at zero and "builds" a GMP by adding cumulative change orders as each bid package is completed, bid, and awarded.
3. Establishing the GMP early in the design and accepting that the GMP will include the risk of design completion, typically in the form of a higher contingency.

The progressive GMP or component change order approach presents a higher chance of a surprise when the last component is added to the total and, only then, the project is found to be substantially over budget. Conversely, the preliminary GMP approach establishes an early GMP, sometimes as early as the concept design. More typically, the GMP is set at a point in the design development when the entire team feels confident that the scope is adequately defined to narrow the margin of error contained in the preliminary GMP to an acceptable level. The amount of design contingency that will have to be included, along with the unknowns that typically exist this early in the design process, makes this approach an exercise in design and contingency management, a process that is well established and manageable for experienced owners.

All of these approaches can be successful, but owners should be cautious with the progressive, component change order approach because this approach is riskier to the owner. Since the component change order approach is less risky from the contactor's viewpoint, pricing should be reflective of this lower risk. In instances where establishing a reasonable estimate is difficult or impossible, such as a unique project, using the component change order rolling up to a GMP may be the only option if a GMP basis of reimbursement is the method of choice.

While there is also the risk with the preliminary GMP approach that there will be a "surprise" at the end (this is the owner's main risk of using GMP contracts), experience has shown that the rigor created by having a preliminary GMP reduces the likelihood of having a project substantially over budget at the end of the design. Well managed GMP contracts identify this potential early on and address this issue continuously throughout the design process by working collaboratively to find ways to balance the owner's program with the budget.

Also worth noting is confusion on the use of the term "target." Since the preliminary GMP approach goes by many names including "early GMP" and "target GMP," many are quick to compare these uses of the word "target" and think they are referring to essentially the same thing (as noted in the later discussion on the Target Price basis of reimbursement, this is not the case).

The use of the term "target" in the context of the GMP basis of reimbursement is the early estimate of the amount that will become the Guaranteed Maximum Price once it can be tied to a defined scope of work. In a multi-party contract, which, in its purest form, assumes there is no "guarantee" on the reimbursement of the cost, the term "Target Price" is referring to a process in which IPD participants are incentivized to work collaboratively to maximize the value that an owner will receive for a specified amount of money. Project participants collaboratively establish the Target Price at some point in the project design (or conceptualization) phase and are incentivized to hit that target rather than guaranteeing that they will. This is discussed in greater detail below in the Target Price basis of reimbursement and in Chapter 10: Integrated Project Delivery.

Cost-Plus—Without a Not-to-Exceed Guaranteed Maximum Price

A Cost-Plus contract without a not-to-exceed Guaranteed Maximum Price is essentially the same as a GMP contract as far as the treatment of cost reimbursement, but it differs dramatically from the standpoint of not having any cap or maximum amount. These contracts are generally used only where owners can afford the risk of incurring unlimited financial exposure on a specific capital project and by owners for whom other factors outweigh the comfort of having a GMP in place.

Although riskier, owners often use Cost-Plus contracts on projects that have to be done quickly where there is not adequate time to define the scope of work to be used as a basis for a meaningful contract amount. In practice, owners often use Cost-Plus contracts. Examples include emergency projects such as replacing a road that collapsed into a sinkhole or situations where the public safety or other public benefit outweighs the risk of having a cost guarantee.

BASIS OF REIMBURSEMENT

A growing sentiment exists in the highly collaborative project arena, where owners place a high value on the benefit of collaboration, that GMP contracts can actually deter project teams from working in the project's best interest. There is some merit to this idea; removing the disincentive created by having one party at a significantly greater financial risk is at the heart of the risk/reward sharing of the relational multi-party contract used in Integrated Project Delivery.

Target Price

In conjunction with Integrated Project Delivery, a new basis of reimbursement is emerging. This new basis of reimbursement is most commonly being referred to as "Target Price" although the term "Estimated Maximum Price" (EMP) is also coming into use. Under the Target Price basis of reimbursement, the project participants (at a minimum, those who are signers to the multi-party contract) collaboratively establish a target price for the project and then work together to maximize the value that the owner receives for that amount—that is, to see to it that the value proposition proposed by the owner at the outset of the project is achieved for a cost no greater than the target price. At the heart of the Target Price basis of reimbursement is a multi-party agreement with terms requiring that the parties share in the costs that exceed the target price. The contract terms describing this "pain/gain sharing" of risk and reward are the main thrust of the multi-party contract and are generally attributed to being a catalyst driving changed behaviors and a resulting higher level of collaboration on IPD projects.

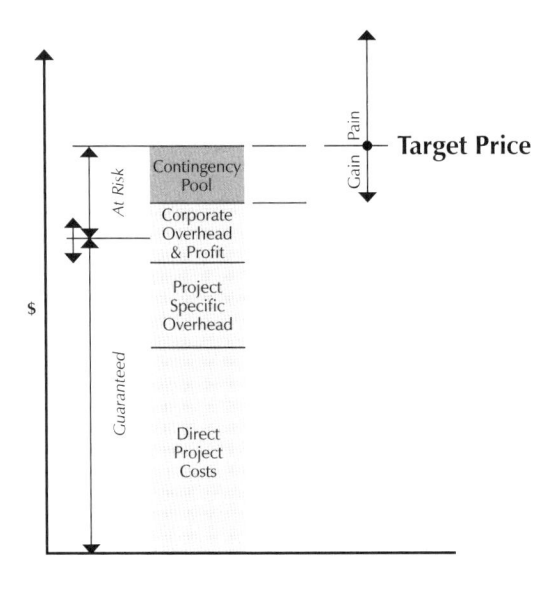

Target Price vs. Cost-Plus

With typical Target Price contracts, unlike with any other basis of reimbursement, the design team participates along with the owner and the constructor in the risk/

reward sharing and typically has a financial incentive for the project to hit or come in under the target price. This risk sharing often includes placing at least a portion of both the design team's and the construction team's compensation at risk. So now when the "team" is being referenced pertaining to risk, instead of referring to only the contractor, it refers to all primary parties signing the multi-party contract including the designer.

On projects using the Target Price basis of reimbursement, the owner agrees to reimburse the contractor all of the actual direct project costs (cost of the work) and the project-specific overhead (general conditions). In that respect, Target Price is similar to Cost-Plus, but how the team members' profit, including corporate overhead, is addressed varies on Target Price projects. On some projects, the team's entire profit is placed at risk and is tied to the project team's success with hitting the target price. On other projects, the team's profit is guaranteed and is not tied to the success of hitting the target price. A third approach is to put only a portion of the team's profit at risk.

Conversely, Cost-Plus contracts usually do not put the team's profit at risk. It is common to provide an incentive to the team to increase profits by completing the project within budget through performance-based incentives. In the Target Price context, as indicated above, the owner funds the actual costs of the project up to the target price (which usually includes the contractor's and designer's fees). Once the target price is exceeded, the contractor and designer bear the additional costs up to a set amount (that is, the agreed upon portion of their fees). Once that "shared pain" is reached, any additional excess costs are paid by the owner.

One significant difference between the Target Price basis of reimbursement and Cost-Plus basis occurs when there is serious overrun and the actual project costs surpass the target price. That is, with Target Price, the owner again incurs all the upside cost risk but with one important change. From the time the target priced is surpassed, neither the designer nor the contractor receives any further fees (i.e., the owner guarantees only the actual cost of the work to complete the project). Some speculate that insurance companies are evaluating this risk, and an insurance product that will mitigate this risk may soon become available. However, until such products are commercially available and affordable, this upside risk will continue to provide pause to owners and lenders considering multi-part IPD contracts that include this risk.

On the more positive side of these shared pain/shared reward contracts, if the project is completed for less than the target price, the contract provides a sharing of that savings in percentages agreed upon at the time the contract is signed. In addition, multi-party IPD contracts typically also include incentives for things such as safety, schedule, collaborative behavior, achievement of sustainability goals, and so on, all aimed at creating a collaborative, trust-based project culture that is believed will enable the project team to act in the best interest of the project and, accordingly, in their collective best interest.

Target Price basis of reimbursement is unique in that it aligns the parties' economic interests, the idea of risk acceptance, and the resulting collaborative management of risk. While the traditional practice of shifting and avoiding project risk is believed by some to be the catalyst for an actual reduction in project risk, others perceive the practice creates an increase in project risk. Over time, as more IPD projects are completed, this theory will be validated one way or the other.

Target Price vs. GMP

As mentioned previously during the discussion of Guaranteed Maximum Price, the term "target" is often confused with a preliminary or target amount used in GMP contracts. This confusion exists primarily among many of those approaching Integrated Project Delivery for the first time as a delivery method and this relatively new Target Price as a basis of reimbursement in the multi-party contract. The use of the term "target" in the context of the GMP basis of reimbursement is the early estimate of the amount to later become the Guaranteed Maximum Price and is tied to a defined scope of work. Again, in the Target Price basis of reimbursement, participants are incentivized to hit the target rather than guaranteeing that they will.

Another difference between a typical GMP contract and a Target Price contract is the design team's interest in the financial outcome of the project. Under most GMP contracts (or for that matter, Cost-Plus or Lump Sum contracts), there is no direct relationship between the design team's reimbursement and the contractor's reimbursement. Even with Design-Build, the designer is often a subcontractor to the design-builder, and its compensation is either a percentage of project cost or an hourly rate—in either case often with a not-to-exceed, but it is not tied to the GMP. Traditionally, the designer does not have a financial incentive tied to the overall project's financial outcome. With Target Price basis of reimbursement, the design team does have a vested interest in the financial outcome of the project. Though the designer's interest is much smaller and subject to contract negotiation, there is a perceived project benefit to the design team's having a shared interest in not only its own success but the rest of team's success as well.

The "No GMP" Misnomer

The Target Price approach is often mistakenly referred to as a "no GMP" basis of reimbursement. This reference is deceiving because it implies that it is fully Cost-Plus or cost-reimbursable with the owner taking the full risk for the actual project costs. Referring to Target Price as "no GMP" is not an accurate representation of the Target Price basis of reimbursement.

Pooled Contingencies

Project teams need the latitude to work in an environment where errors and changes that are not easily assigned to a single party do occur and are tolerated. To provide a buffer to the risk of having some or all of their profit at risk, teams are often allowed to carry a pool of contingency within the target price. With Target Price basis of reimbursement contracts, it is typical for the parties to pool their separate (and often redundant) contingencies. This shared pool of contingencies is then included in the target price and tied to the shared risk/reward portion of the contract.

With typical GMP contracts, the sharing of cost risk is tied to the direct cost of the project, with contingencies often specifically excluded from the savings split clause. At the end of a typical GMP contract, unused contingencies are often held separate and returned 100% to the owner; thus, any savings achieved within the direct cost are shared in accordance with the savings split. This is one of the biggest differences between the Target Price basis of reimbursement and the typical GMP contract.

The opposite essentially is true with Target Price contracts. Because there is no risk tied to the direct costs (all of these costs are 100% reimbursed by the owner), there is no sharing of savings on the direct costs. Instead, the savings is tied to a benchmark (the target price) that includes the direct costs, the project-specific overhead, the contractor's and designer's profit, and if the owner chooses, the team's pooled contingencies. Any savings comes from the proper management of the project costs and the team's success in working together to not spend the pool of contingencies. This savings is what is then shared among the parties signatory to the multi-party contract in accordance with agreed upon percentages stated in the multi-party contract.

This difference of how cost risks are shared is a major factor affecting the behavior of project teams and is believed to have a significant impact on driving these projects to a higher level of collaboration, even beyond the level of collaboration typically achieved with GMP contracts. This higher level of collaboration does come at a price to owners and lenders who must accept some of the risks that are, at least theoretically, otherwise assigned to others when using a GMP or Lump Sum basis of reimbursement.

Some owners who have been willing to accept this perceived risk and have used multi-party contracts with the Target Price basis of reimbursement have indicated anecdotally that they believe they have received a better value both through time savings and completed projects that do a superior job in meeting their user's needs. A multi-party contract with a Target Price basis of reimbursement may not be suitable for every project, but for those owners who place a value on this higher level of collaboration, it provides another option.

BASIS OF REIMBURSEMENT

Unit Price

Occasionally some contracts are reimbursed based on specific defined "units" of work and prices associated with each unit, referred to as unit prices. Unit Price basis of reimbursement is used on projects where the substantial amount of the project costs can be defined by these specific items of work. Examples include highway projects that are usually defined by specific scope items such as lineal footage of piping or square yards of base or pavement, or interior renovations that are easily defined by the amount of wall types, square footages of floor area, and so on.

Unit Price basis of reimbursement contracts vary considerably. Some are "converted" to Lump Sum contracts once the quantities are agreed upon and extended into dollar amounts with applicable unit prices. Others are more similar to Cost-Plus, where the owner accepts the risk associated with establishing the quantities. In these cases, contractors compete based solely on unit prices, and unit prices must be clear in terms of what they include and what they do not. Hence, the contract must state whether the contractor's labor, materials, equipment, general conditions, and fees are included in the unit prices.

Job Order Contracting and On-Call Contracting are both commonly executed with the use of Unit Price contracts. It is also common to use unit prices within other contracts such as Lump Sum, GMP, or Cost-Plus to do work that is not defined at the time of establishing the original contract amount or that is likely to change. Allowances are often established as an example and then reconciled with the use of unit prices.

TYPICAL BASIS OF REIMBURSEMENT FOR EACH PROJECT DELIVERY METHOD

The figure below shows the typical basis of reimbursement (Lump Sum, GMP, or Target Price) for each delivery approach. The typical process (Invitation to Bid or RFQ/RFP) is also shown for each approach. (*Note:* AGC of America has developed RFQ/RFP training that includes recommended practices and is available to assist in the training of managers responsible for implementing selections using Requests for Qualifications and Requests for Proposals.)

BASIS OF REIMBURSEMENT

Typical Delivery Method / Procurement Options with Typical Basis of Reimbursement

DELIVERY METHOD Common Nicknames	Low Bid	Best Value: Total Cost	Best Value: Fees	Qualifications Based Selection (QBS)
Design-Bid-Build Competitive Sealed Bid; Low Bid; Invitation to Bid	Inv. To Bid Lump Sum	RFQ/RFP Lump Sum	N/A	N/A
CM at-Risk CM/GC; GC/CM; CMc; ECI	N/A	N/A	RFQ/RFP GMP	RFQ/RFP GMP
Design-Build Engineer-Procure-Construct (EPC)	Inv. To Bid Lump Sum	RFQ/RFP Lump Sum	RFQ/RFP GMP	RFQ/RFP GMP
IPD Multi-Party; Lean Project Delivery; Alliancing	Not Typical	Not Typical	RFQ/RFP Target Price	RFQ/RFP Target Price

Design-Bid-Build

The typical basis of reimbursement used with Design-Bid-Build project delivery is Lump Sum.

Construction Management at-Risk

The typical basis of reimbursement used with Construction Management at-Risk is GMP.

Design-Build

The typical basis of reimbursement used with Design-Build is usually directly correlated to the procurement process that is used to select the contractor or design-builder:
- Design-Build procured with Low Bid—The typical basis of reimbursement is Lump Sum.
- Design-Build procured with Best Value: Total Cost—The typical basis of reimbursement is Lump Sum.
- Design-Build procured with Best Value: Fees—The typical basis of reimbursement is GMP.
- Design-Build procured with Qualifications Based Selection—The typical basis of reimbursement is GMP.

Integrated Project Delivery

The typical basis of reimbursement for Integrated Project Delivery is Target Price.

BASIS OF REIMBURSEMENT

Self Test

1. Which of the following is not a basis of reimbursement?
   a. Lump Sum
   b. Guaranteed Maximum Price (GMP)
   c. Cost-Plus
   d. Target Price
   e. Low Bid

2. Which delivery method(s) typically use Lump Sum basis of reimbursement (choose any that apply)?
   a. Design-Bid-Build
   b. CM at-Risk
   c. Design Build procured with Low Bid or Best Value: Total Cost
   d. Design-Build procured with Best Value: Fees or QBS
   e. Integrated Project Delivery

3. Typical GMP contracts differ from typical Lump Sum contracts in which of the following respects?
   a. Owner access to contractor price information
   b. Owner access to trade contractor's bid information
   c. Owner ability to participate in the buyout process
   d. The amount of information typically submitted with monthly billings
   e. All of the above

4. Which of these describes the impact on the design contingency if the design is less complete?
   a. It will be greater
   b. It will be less
   c. It will not be affected

5. Which one is potentially more risky to the owner?
   a. Preliminary GMPs
   b. Progressive GMPs
   c. Neither, they are both equally risky

6. With regard to Target Price basis of reimbursement, which of these statements is incorrect?
   a. The designer's financial success is tied to the project's financial success
   b. The owner is taking more risk in exchange for higher collaboration
   c. Referring to Target Price as "no GMP" is an accurate representation
   d. It is common to pool the participants' separate contingencies

7. Once the actual costs on a Target Price project exceed the target price and the team's at-risk profit, the project essentially turns into which of these?
   a. A Lump Sum contract
   b. A Guaranteed Maximum Price contract
   c. A Cost-Plus contract
   d. None of the above

CHAPTER FOUR

PROGRAM MANAGEMENT

Introduction

Defining Program Management
- Five Phases of Every Project—The Construction Phase Model
- Leadership vs. Administration
- Delivery Method or Management Method?

Clarifying the Term "PM"
- Common Elements of Program Management and Project Management
- Distinguishing Between Program Management and Project Management
  - Distinguishing Characteristics of a Program Manager
  - Distinguishing Characteristics of a Project Manager

Developer as Program Manager

Future Trends

Self Test

Case Study

PROGRAM MANAGEMENT

INTRODUCTION

Program management may be the least consistently used term in the project delivery lexicon. Program management is sometimes referred to as a delivery method; in other instances, the term is used to describe a method for managing the construction phase of the building process. This paradox has created confusion that makes it difficult to consistently identify what a program manager is or does. Adding to the confusion is the overlap between the description of services within some definitions of program management and the description of services provided by construction managers, fee developers, project managers, architects, and engineers. This textbook attempts to resolve these ambiguities by defining program management as a management method that is typically used on multi-structure or multi-site building programs.

The use of program management as a management method is broadening. The evolution of alternate forms of project delivery (such as Construction Management at-Risk and Design-Build) has led to more expansive use of what had previously been considered unconventional forms of project delivery and management. This change in thinking has led to the use of program management for much smaller projects.

Many owners and developers, particularly in the public sector, now favor program management in situations where they lack sufficient internal expertise or resources to manage various elements of construction. Program management has emerged as a useful tool when outside resources are required. It also helps public bodies that receive large infusions of new capital through bond offerings, or that require the expeditious and efficient development of public works projects to manage those funds.

Program managers are typically involved in most of the five phases of the construction process (real estate, financing, design, construction, and occupancy). Often they provide services on multiple projects or on multi-building undertakings. This multifaceted scope of work is what most distinguishes program management from other project management methods. The broad scope of responsibility also makes program management unique in the construction industry, because program managers assume many responsibilities traditionally undertaken by owners using in-house resources.

DEFINING PROGRAM MANAGEMENT

A fundamental challenge in defining program management is determining whether it is a delivery method or a management method. The term "project delivery method" has been used by many to describe both a delivery method and a management method, contributing to the ambiguity of the definitions. Let's briefly analyze the distinctions between a delivery method and a management method:

Five Phases of Every Project—The Construction Phase Model

Every construction undertaking comprises five basic components or phases. While the terminology used to define a phase may differ, each construction project can be outlined using the definitions provided below. Keep in mind that the scope of work within one phase can overlap with that in another. The more the scope of work within each phase overlaps, the greater the opportunity for duplicated effort. Watch out for this potential redundancy when selecting an appropriate management method and delivery system.

The five phases of the construction process are as follows:
1. **Real estate**—Consists of locating and purchasing real property; identifying its appropriate use; arranging for zoning, permitting, and environmental compliance; and handling other front-end development issues.
2. **Financing**—The process of obtaining funds to pay for and develop real property.
3. **Design**—Includes all architecture and engineering work associated with building improvements on real property. It includes programming and predesign activities.
4. **Construction**—The process of making improvements to real property.
5. **Occupancy**—During this phase, the finished construction product is leased or sold, and basic property management services such as operations and maintenance are set up. This phase also includes decommissioning at the end of the project's useful life.

Note: The "bidding phase" referred to in other sections of this book may be part of either the design or the construction phase.

Whether formally assigned or not, someone must take responsibility for each phase in the construction phase model. Someone must also manage each of these phases and be responsible for the overall outcome. This textbook refers to the process of managing at least the design and construction phases as a "management method." The responsibility for implementing a desired management method is either retained by the owner or outsourced. Program management is one of several outsourcing options.

Construction owners often select a management method based on their comfort level with respect to the various phases of project development and available in-house resources to manage those phases effectively. For example, most commercial developers and public owners are confident in their ability to manage the real estate, financing, and occupancy phases, so they accept direct responsibility for those efforts. They often perform the work in these phases on their own, or they retain specialists to assist with locating suitable building locations, obtaining loans, or maintaining the property.

While many owners have some degree of expertise in all five phases, they may have less experience (or fewer internal resources) to manage the design and construction processes. It is a fundamental principle that someone needs to take overall responsibility for each phase of the construction process. This responsibility can either be delegated to an in-house resource or outsourced. Many owners retain independent sources to manage design and construction phase work.

Program managers are typically used in situations where: 1) the owner lacks resources to properly manage the work, 2) a program manager is desired to provide leadership during the overall construction process, 3) the owner believes program management is the most effective way to contain program costs, or 4) program management is the owner's traditional management method.

Leadership vs. Administration

Using a program manager as an extension of the owner's project staff contemplates an administrative relationship between the owner and constructor that does not include a delegation of authority to the program manager to bind the owner. Outsourcing to a program manager for project leadership contemplates an agency relationship between the owner and program manager through which the program manager is delegated authority to bind the owner. Whether responsibility for making binding decisions is retained in-house or outsourced, a decision regarding the nature of the relationship between the owner and program manager should be made promptly and then clearly defined in all contractual relationships associated with a project.

Delivery Method or Management Method?

In broad terms, a management method is the set of techniques by which construction is administered and supervised. A delivery method assigns responsibility and risk for the delivery of design and construction services. A management method has broader implications with respect to the life of a construction project because it involves a defined level of responsibility for some or all of the five basic phases described above. In contrast, a delivery method is typically focused only on the design and construction phases and does not address the other three phases of the construction phase model.

Based on the dichotomy between a management method and a delivery method, Construction Management at-Risk, Design-Build, and Design-Bid-Build are readily characterized as delivery methods. By definition, these delivery methods relate to the provision of the design and construction phases. In contrast, these distinctions indicate that agency construction management is a management method because it relates to the set of techniques by which construction work is supervised and administered. Program management is appropriately defined as a management method as well, because program management relates more to the means by which the project is managed and a program manager's scope of work may include the management of all five phases on a single project or multiple projects.

Theoretically, any management method may be used with any delivery method. Program management is one of several options. It is important to choose a management method that best allocates responsibility and accountability for all five phases with minimum duplication of effort. It also is important to assign responsibility to the party that is in the best position to manage potential risks.

It is advisable to select a management method before locking into a delivery method. Each construction project has a stated objective, and each construction phase requires an organizational structure and implementation plan to achieve this desired result. Typically, it is more efficient and logical to decide how the overall project will be organized and run before making a final decision on which delivery method best suits that organizational model and the owner's objectives.

For example, the primary objectives of most construction projects involve quality, price, and time. An owner with limited available in-house resources may have a project where the goal is to achieve the highest quality project regardless of cost or duration. In this situation, the owner desires a management method that provides significant peer review, inspection, and oversight. The owner also will desire a delivery method that allows sufficient time for this management method to be effectively implemented. Therefore, program management overseeing a Design-Bid-Build design and construction process may be preferred. In situations where speed is the overall goal, it may be better to use a program manager supervising a Design-Build constructor or separate designers and trade contractors working on a fast-track basis. Where cost is the primary concern, the owner may choose to rely on its own resources to manage the project and use the Construction Management at-Risk delivery method or a general contractor.

CLARIFYING THE TERM "PM"

Common Elements of Program Management and Project Management

Another gray area in the definition of program management may be attributable to the overlap between functions provided by program managers and project managers. The common use of the acronym "PM" to describe both a program manager and a project manager also contributes to this confusion. It often is difficult to distinguish a program manager from a project manager because they perform many of the same functions and offer many of the same services. As a result, program managers and project managers often have similar skills and frequently compete for the same types of work. Specifically, program managers and project managers are similar because they oversee the full range of preconstruction and construction services.

On a fundamental level, project managers and program managers are similar because they are both owner representatives. Both entities have a direct contractual relationship with the owner of real property through legal documentation that contemplates that the program manager or project manager will oversee specified design and construction work. More significantly, each is expected to be a representative of the owner. As such, the program manager and project manager protect the owner's interests and guide the project in a direction that serves the owner's objectives. Furthermore, program managers and project managers frequently have delegated authority to act on behalf of the owner in areas where the owner lacks the inclination, expertise, or resources to do so on its own.

On a practical level, project managers and program managers are similar to the extent that each assumes a broad spectrum of responsibility during the design and construction phases of a project. During the design phase, it is not unusual for program managers and project managers to be required to provide feasibility studies and conceptual and logistical planning, establish design criteria, and oversee the design process. To perform these services, program managers and project managers are required to have similar skills. Both should be well versed in government regulations; building codes; and the use, selection, and availability of construction materials. They also should possess the skills necessary to assist in constructability reviews, drawing coordination, estimating, scheduling, and bidding.

There also is overlap in the services provided by program managers and project managers during the construction phase of most projects. Program managers and project managers are frequently involved in negotiating contracts for labor, material, and professional services. They also are asked to establish and monitor project control systems and oversee insurance, safety, quality control, and compliance programs. Both entities are involved in overseeing the actual construction process—from establishing construction building controls and schedules through inspection, testing, commissioning, training, and certain operations and maintenance levels for the finished project. It is common for program managers and project managers to be involved in administrative functions such as processing requisitions, evaluating and negotiating change orders, and assisting in claims management.

Distinguishing Between Program Management and Project Management

Despite the overlap between program management and project management, there are distinctions. A program manager is responsible for a larger scope of the construction process than a project manager. This scope of responsibility for the building effort is the key line of demarcation between the two entities.

Distinguishing Characteristics of a Program Manager

Program managers typically oversee the construction of multiple structures on the same site or handle coordinated building efforts at multiple locations or under multiple contracts. For example, program managers are frequently asked to manage the construction of several buildings on sites such as corporate or academic campuses, office parks, or military bases. Program managers also oversee the construction of various structures for a single owner in multiple locations, such as retail centers, commercial office buildings, and certain types of public works projects. The term "program management" is used by some to define a situation in which a single entity has responsibility for all five phases of project development. Using this definition, an entity that manages one or more project phases beyond the design and construction phases can be considered a program manager.

Due to the broad nature of the work, the program manager is frequently the single point of contact for most participants in the construction processes. As such, the program manager often controls the design and construction and reports to the owner on the project's financial controls. A program manager also may be responsible for locating suitable project sites, obtaining financing, and arranging for the end-use of the finished building. Program managers may negotiate contracts held by the owner with construction professionals such as architects, engineers, construction managers, and project managers.

Distinguishing Characteristics of a Project Manager

A project manager's scope of responsibility is more limited than a program manager's. Typically, a project manager oversees a single-phase project or is responsible for overseeing the construction phase of a multi-building project. In some situations, a project manager is given specifically defined responsibilities for other phases; for example, the scope of work provided by a project manager may overlap with finance or design. Nevertheless, as a general rule, when a project manager's level of responsibility moves beyond construction on a single project, the manager becomes a program manager.

A project manager's responsibility for the overall financial success of a project is generally more limited than a program manager's. Typically, project managers are required to control construction costs and participate in value engineering. They also may be asked to develop an overall budget for design and construction. Project managers are less likely than program managers to become involved in identifying advantageous building locations or suitable financing. It also is unusual for a project manager to be involved in leasing, sales, or operations and maintenance.

DEVELOPER AS PROGRAM MANAGER

As described above, the definition of a program manager depends largely on the scope of responsibility that a manager has within the five phases in the development of a construction project, as well as upon the nature of the project itself. Based on these criteria, a project manager who assumes responsibility for more than the construction phase of a single project can become a program manager. There are situations in which others in the construction process, such as certain categories of commercial developers, could be considered program managers.

Three entities that fall under the generic label "developer" are:
- **Developer**—An entity that develops real property and maintains an ownership interest in a project or multiple projects.
- **Fee developer/development manager**—An entity that develops real property in which it has no ownership or equity interest.
- **Fee developer at-risk**—An entity that develops real property in which it has no ownership or equity interest but holds contracts with, and is financially responsible to, architect/engineers, general contractors, and/or trade construction contracts. On a practical level, there is little to distinguish a fee developer at-risk from a design-build contractor with financing responsibilities.

Theoretically, any of the three categories of developer could be considered a program manager using the criteria previously described. The key distinguishing characteristic would be whether the developer assumes responsibility for all five phases of project development. Therefore, a developer holding an equity interest in real property could be considered a program manager if it expanded its traditional level of responsibility from the real estate, financing, and occupancy phases to include design and construction. In this situation, the developer would become its own program manager. That raises the question of whether such an entity requires an additional label.

A fee developer/development manager or fee developer at-risk also may be considered a program manager if it assumes responsibility for overseeing the design and construction phases. The traditional core competencies of a program manager, particularly on a single project, relate to work performed during the design and construction phases. Therefore, a fee developer/development manager assuming the role of a program manager would be required to accept those responsibilities.

A fee developer at-risk requires less of a shift in focus to become a program manager because it already holds the major contracts for design and construction and is experienced with those phases of a project. A design-build contractor with financing responsibilities must have core competencies much closer to those associated with a program manager. Either entity, upon assuming the role of program manager, would need to accept additional duties and obligations.

FUTURE TRENDS

The program management model for overseeing construction should continue to expand during the next several years. Program management has gained favor in the public sector because it eases the burden on government agencies, which require major public works programs but lack the expertise or resources to effectively manage a large construction effort. Many private sector entities are choosing program management to develop relationships with a single entity that understands its interests and can gain efficiencies through familiarity. While this model is not appropriate in every situation, proper program management is an effective tool in the management of the construction process.

Self Test

1. Program management is a:
   a. Construction project delivery method
   b. Project management system
   c. Course of study leading to a degree in Management

2. Program management is differentiated from project management by:
   a. The roles played by the parties involved in the construction process
   b. The degree and complexity of the project
   c. The expanded scope of work performed by the program manager

3. Program managers are:
   a. Used exclusively in the public sector
   b. Not necessary when CM at-Risk is used
   c. Typically involved in all or most of the five phases of the construction of a multiple structure or building site

4. The basic difference between a *management* method and a *delivery* method is:
   a. Who approves the pay requests
   b. Whether a developer is involved in the project
   c. Whether responsibility for actual delivery of design and construction services is assumed

5. A *management* method can be:
   a. Used with any *delivery* method
   b. Extremely difficult to identify
   c. Compared with a course of study in college called Industrial Management

6. The key difference between a developer and fee developer/development manager is:
   a. Whether the developer holds an ownership or equity participation position
   b. Whether the developer is in the United States or abroad
   c. The degree to which the developer is involved in the day-to-day operations of the project

Case Study

The following is an example of a typical project. Evaluate the circumstances described and recommend how to proceed. Questions are offered for group discussion. Be prepared to explain and defend your recommendations.

Acme Development LLC ("Acme") is planning to build a mixed-use commercial development in a large metropolitan area. The project will include seven high-rise buildings, preferably on a waterfront location, which will house retail, office, and residential units. Although Acme has identified several potential sites for the project, it is just beginning the five phases of the construction process. Acme's senior management has asked its Senior Vice President for Construction, Jane Doe, to provide recommendations regarding which delivery and management methods will best suit Acme's objectives.

To recommend a management method, Ms. Doe considered the number and variety of the buildings that would be constructed and the possibility that design and construction for the various buildings might be performed as separate undertakings with staggered start and finish dates. She also considered the possibility that separate designers and constructors might be used for some or all of the buildings. Ms. Doe then considered Acme's internal resources. Acme had significant experience in developing large construction projects and had internally managed each of the construction phases in the past. Nevertheless, Acme had a higher comfort level with the real estate, financing, and occupancy phases of the construction process than it had with design and construction. Acme also was involved in several other large construction efforts, which were utilizing most of its available in-house resources.

Based on this understanding of the nature of the project, Acme's comfort level with the design and construction phases, and Acme's available resources, Ms. Doe determined that program management would best suit Acme's needs to manage the project. She felt that a program manager would provide resources that could supplement Acme's in-house staff. Ms. Doe also felt that the program manager would take a leadership role in the project to provide a single source of responsibility for oversight and coordination of the multiple design and construction efforts required and would be in the best position to effectively monitor costs. Therefore, Ms. Doe concluded that the program manager should be given a clearly defined delegation of authority to act on Acme's behalf and bind Acme to the program manager's decisions in appropriately delineated areas.

Ms. Doe also determined that CM at-Risk was the best delivery method for the project. Their outsourced program manager would provide the resources and expertise necessary to manage the design. Acme desired to construct the project as quickly as possible, limit its debt obligations, and maximize revenues. They planned to do this by staggering the completion of certain buildings to accelerate the commencement of profitable commercial and residential leases and condominium sales. The CM at-Risk delivery method suited these objectives by allowing a single entity to take responsibility for the construction of each of the buildings. Separate construction managers at-risk could be retained to construct individual buildings if necessary. Ms. Doe also felt that a CM at-risk would help Acme to track, manage, and contain costs. Finally, the CM at-Risk delivery method shifted certain risks to the constructor and provided the level of comfort that Ms. Doe knew Acme was accustomed to.

Based on this analysis, Ms. Doe recommended that Acme retain an outsourced program manager with leadership responsibilities to oversee construction using the CM at-Risk delivery method.

DISCUSSION ISSUES:

1. Why did Acme choose a program manager as its management method? Can you think of other reasons?

2. Did the waterfront location affect the choice to use a project manager?

3. By choosing program management, did Acme have greater or fewer project delivery options?

4. How did the fact that the project was actually "several" projects affect Acme's decision (or yours)?

CHAPTER FIVE

AGENCY CONSTRUCTION MANAGEMENT

Introduction
- Program Management (PM) vs. Construction Management (CM)

Agency CM Defined—Why Do Owners Use Agency CM?
- Leadership vs. Administration
- A Fundamental Characteristic of Agency CM

Management System Overview and Roles of the Project Team Members
- Programming—Predesign Phase
- Design and Preconstruction Phase
  - Consultation
  - Project Schedule
  - Budgets
  - Construction Document ("Constructability") Review
  - Additional Agency CM Preconstruction Services
- Construction Phase
  - Administration
  - Project Schedule
  - Budgets
  - Review of Safety and Work Programs
  - Provision of General Conditions Items
  - Project Closeout
  - Commissioning
- Occupancy Phase

Types of Agency CM Organizations

Selection Criteria and Establishing the Fee
- Selection Criteria
- Fee

Risk Management
- Warranties
- Fee
- Insurance and Related Issues

Future Trends

Self Test

Case Study

INTRODUCTION

In introducing agency construction management (agency CM), it is important to note that the construction manager acting as the agent (agent CM) plays an important consultative and advisory role for the owner and the owner's team. This consultative and advisory role is somewhat in contrast to a principal focus of a construction manager at-risk, which is to assume and control risk in a manner that is most beneficial to both the owner and the constructor. Both agency CM and CM at-Risk have grown in use and popularity since the 1970s, and both have proven effective on numerous types of projects. This chapter will focus on how and when agency CM can be employed most effectively.

A common misconception is that agency CM is a *project delivery method*. An agent CM is not contractually responsible for delivering the bricks and sticks construction. Rather, the agent CM is responsible for furnishing the management services necessary to deliver construction. Thus, it is more accurate to describe agency CM as a *construction management system*, a way to manage the process of construction, not a way to physically deliver construction. Consequently, agency CM can be considered a type of project or program management, as described in the previous chapter.

Program Management (PM) vs. Construction Management (CM)

Another way to understand this distinction is to ask which delivery systems can be used on a project with agency construction management. The answer: All of them. For example, an owner may hire an agent CM to represent it throughout the process under a Design-Bid-Build system. In this example, the agent CM may interview and select the designer, prepare the bid package based on the completed design, and bid the project to a general contractor who then constructs the project.

A second example is that an owner may hire an agent CM to represent it throughout the process under a Design-Build system. In this example, the agent CM may interview the design-builder, review certain trade bid packages, and otherwise serve to protect the owner's interests and monitor the design-builder's performance. This monitoring may be particularly appropriate in Design-Build, where the traditional checks and balances between design and construction do not exist because design and construction are integrated into one contract.

A final example is that an owner may hire an agent CM to represent it throughout the process under a CM at-Risk system. In this example, the agent CM may interview and select the designer, interview and select the construction manager at-risk, coordinate activities among the parties, and otherwise serve to protect the owner's interests based on the scope of services in the agreement.

A key element of agency construction management is that a firm is paid a fee to provide a management service. Under this arrangement, the owner, not the construction manager, enters into the contract(s) for the performance of the trade construction work. As a result, the agent CM does not guarantee, and is not directly responsible for, construction performance risks such as schedule delays, cost overruns, or construction defects. Instead, the agent CM is responsible for providing management services that are consistent with industry norms. In this regard, to the extent the agent CM improperly delivers its services, the agent CM may be liable.

Agency construction management fills the role of owner representation. Many different types of firms have entered the agency CM market, including general contractors, architectural firms, engineering firms, consulting firms with an accounting background, consulting firms with an architectural/engineering/construction background, and construction professionals with public and private owner backgrounds. With such a range of experiences from which to choose, an owner must select an agency CM firm based on the owner's specific project objectives and the firm's specific capabilities.

Agency CM tends to work best where the owner vests sufficient authority in the agent CM to enable the agent CM to make timely decisions and hold other project team members accountable for those decisions. Many private owners have found that using an agent CM in this manner enables them to manage a building program with limited in-house resources. Agency CM is least effective where the owner vests decision-making authority for the same or similar decisions in multiple project parties, including an agent CM.

AGENCY CM DEFINED—WHY DO OWNERS USE AGENCY CM?

Agency construction management is a management system based on an owner's agreement with a qualified construction management firm to provide coordination, administration, and management within a defined scope of services. The agent CM works throughout the various phases of a project and cooperates with the project team in furthering the interests of the owner. A key feature of this management system is that the contracting entity operates as an agent to the owner, operating under traditional legal obligations pursuant to an agency relationship. While agency CM is not limited to projects of a certain size, agency CM is frequently used effectively on large, complex projects where the owner desires to supplement its in-house staff and expertise.

Leadership vs. Administration

Using an agent CM as an extension of the owner's project staff contemplates an administrative relationship between the owner and constructor that does not include a delegation of authority to the agent CM to bind the owner. Outsourcing to an agent CM for project leadership contemplates an agency relationship between the owner and the agent CM through which the agent CM is delegated authority to bind the owner.

The degree of authority varies, and the owner should assign the agent CM enough authority to be effective. Whether responsibility for making binding decisions is retained in-house or outsourced, a decision regarding the nature of the relationship between the owner and the agent CM should be made promptly and then clearly defined in all contractual relationships associated with a project.

All members of the construction team should understand the agent CM's agency obligation to the owner. An agent is someone authorized to act on behalf of another. In the agency CM context, this means that the agent CM is acting on behalf of the owner. For an agency CM in a leadership capacity to be successful, the owner must empower the agent CM to make key project decisions in a timely manner.

The owner must be clear about the role and responsibilities of the agent CM and avoid having another layer in the project structure, which can be counterproductive. If the agent CM has little decision-making authority during the design phase or in the field, the owner has essentially hired an organization that is little more than an intermediary. Often, this type of agency arrangement results in an administrative role rather than the intended leadership role. In contrast, if the agent CM has substantial decision-making authority during the design and construction phases, potential for delay is substantially diminished.

It is crucial that the owner understand, before the design phase, how it will administer the project. This decision will drive not only the scope of the agent CM relationship but also the types of design and construction entities that will be most effective in achieving the owner's project objectives.

A Fundamental Characteristic of Agency CM

There has been great confusion in the design and construction industries over the differences between "agent" and "at-Risk" CMs. In most standard industry contracts and educational materials, the distinction is between CMs who hold the trade contracts and are at risk for the performance of the work and CMs who do not hold the trade contracts and are not responsible for the performance of the work. As such, a fundamental characteristic of the agent CM, no matter how involved in project administration, is that it is not at risk for the cost or schedule of building the job—in other words, for the *performance* risk. This is a critical issue and one that is commonly misunderstood. It can create more misunderstandings and problems both during contract negotiations and on the job.

Often, agent CM arrangements will cap the liability of the agent CM for negligence in the furnishing of its services at its fee or professional insurance coverage for the project (the premiums of which are typically paid for by the owner). Yet, on all projects, and particularly on larger, more complicated projects, an agent CM's negligence related to its performance (e.g., with scheduling or inspections) can have actual cost consequences to the owner many times greater than the agent CM's fee or insurance. It is important for the owner to consider this fundamental characteristic of agency CM at a project's programming stage.

MANAGEMENT SYSTEM OVERVIEW AND ROLES OF THE PROJECT TEAM MEMBERS

Programming—Predesign Phase

Some owners select an agency CM firm to help them define the scope of their program or even a specific project. When an agency CM firm is selected for this role, it is important that the owner evaluate the firm's core competencies in critical predesign functions such as planning.

Based on this understanding, the importance of the predesign phase with respect to agency CM is the owner's role. Owners that utilize agency CM must commit to creating a project team and project objectives that are clear and understandable from the predesign phase onward. These objectives include:

- Creating clear project goals and objectives regarding cost, quality, and schedule.
- Obtaining substantial input from the end user of the project, particularly if the owner will not be the end user.
- Selecting a designer that is willing to embrace the agency CM process fully and enthusiastically.
- Selecting an agent CM that understands the program and the design intentions, and that is experienced in preconstruction services.
- Assigning owner's personnel to the project who understand the project objectives, who are willing to make decisions on behalf of the owner quickly and confidently, and who let the designer design and the agent CM manage.
- Aligning project incentives so that the owner, agent CM, designer, and other team members are working toward the same objective.

Design and Preconstruction Phase

Preconstruction phase services are delivered primarily during the design phase, although there can be considerable overlap on certain CM at-Risk or Design-Build projects where speed of delivery is critical. During the design phase, it is important that the owner, designer, agent CM, and other preconstruction team members (e.g., design-builder or CM at-risk) understand and agree with the design phase process typical of agency CM, including the functions of value engineering, constructability, and cost control. The owner must hire a designer that is willing to cooperate with the agent CM and that appreciates and is responsive to potential changes based on recommended schedule and cost savings. The designer must also design based on the owner's program. Likewise, the agent CM must actively cooperate in reviewing the design and be prepared to consider the value of architectural considerations and not simply cost considerations. In short, there is no substitute for good cooperation and communication among the parties.

The scope of an agent CM's preconstruction phase services can vary substantially depending on the type of delivery method being used to construct the project. Although the basic preconstruction activities are often similar to those of an at-risk CM—evaluating the design for constructability, cost, schedule, and other variables that will ultimately drive the success or failure of the project—an agent CM may or may not take an active role in developing the scheduling, developing estimates, etc.

The use of CMs before, or very early in, the design process has allowed owners to make changes in the design at little or no expense to final project cost. Also, involving a CM at this stage can dramatically reduce unexpected and potentially costly risks. It is most effective to hire an agent CM before hiring the designer. This is because the owner's best chances for project success involve establishing its management approach before hiring service providers to design and construct its project.

Several preconstruction services, discussed below, are typically offered by an agent CM.

Consultation

As part of the project team, the agent CM is expected to attend and participate in regular meetings with the owner and/or owner's representatives, constructor, and architect. The agent CM should provide advice and consultation regarding a range of issues, including:
- Site use and improvements
- Programming and establishing the scope of work
- Selection of materials, building systems, and equipment
- Construction feasibility
- Methods to minimize adverse effects of labor or materials shortages
- Time requirements for procurement, installation, and construction completion
- Factors related to construction cost, including estimates of alternative designs or materials

AGENCY CONSTRUCTION MANAGEMENT

Project Schedule

Once project requirements have been identified, the agent CM should review a preliminary project schedule and advise the owner regarding any suggested changes. This schedule should:

- Account for coordination and integration of the services and activities of the owner, agent CM, architect, constructor, relevant government entities, and any other parties that could impact the schedule's critical path
- Track the proposed activity sequences, durations, and/or milestone dates for the following: receipt and approval of pertinent information, issuance of construction documents, preparation and processing of shop drawings and samples, delivery of materials or equipment requiring long-lead time procurement, owner's occupancy requirements, and estimated dates of substantial and final completion
- Be updated if milestones in prior versions of the schedule will not be met, and show how to recover the schedule
- Reflect sequencing and issuance of construction documents for a phased project

Budgets

Typically, if an agent CM is involved in the project, either the agent CM or another party (such as a design-builder or CM at-risk) develops a budget early in the design process that reflects the experience of construction professionals. Although the initial budget is typically based on conceptual designs and objectives, the agent CM can help the owner evaluate the realistic construction cost range of the project. The initial project budget is typically prepared once the owner has sufficiently identified its program and requirements and the designer has prepared basic design criteria. Thereafter, the budget is updated throughout key points in the design process, until the owner is ready to prepare a construction budget for use in negotiating or bidding the actual construction work.

This type of review process has the advantage of generally eliminating major "sticker shock" when the bids or proposals are received. It also helps the owner refine the project early enough to get an idea of whether it is constructible within the owner's budget.

Construction Document ("Constructability") Review

Another service provided by most agent CMs is a constructability review. This service is similar in scope to the budget process described above, although its primary objective is to evaluate whether there are major coordination, schedule, or technical obstacles posed by the design. The constructability review can identify project constraints at a time when adjustments can be made most economically.

Additional Agency CM Preconstruction Services

The agent CM often has within its scope a number of additional advisory and administrative services, depending on the needs and experience of the owner's in-house construction staff and the type of delivery system being used. Among these other services are:

- Locating temporary facilities for project team members
- Identifying and facilitating orders of long-lead items
- Recommending how to divide the bid or proposal packages
- Coordinating, receiving, and awarding trade bids and proposals
- Helping the owner select consultants
- Helping the owner obtain permitting and government approvals

Construction Phase

Under the agency CM system, construction phase services typically begin once the preconstruction phase services are completed. However, as noted above, it is becoming more common to have some overlap between the preconstruction and construction phase services, particularly on larger, more complex projects that are on a tight schedule.

Administration

Agency CM has evolved as a response to increasing construction administration pressures placed on in-house owners' staffs. The pressures are brought to bear by owners seeking to increase profitability by focusing on core competencies (and outsourcing non-core competencies such as administration of capital construction programs). This reduction of owner in-house capabilities has coincided with increased owner demands to deliver projects more quickly, more cheaply, and with higher quality, and often in an environment of increasing project complexity. For reasons related to experience and risk tolerance, owners now recognize that certain aspects of project administration and management, traditionally within the architect's scope of work, might be more effectively implemented through an agent CM. A review of the agent CM's standard administrative responsibilities bears out this trend. Agent CMs typically:

- Advise the owner regarding terms and conditions of general and/or trade construction contracts. Depending on the type of project, this may include helping the owner prepare, negotiate, and enter into trade contracts.
- Act as the owner's onsite representative, which may include an active role in scheduling and project coordination meetings.
- Provide onsite administrative reporting to the owner, including daily reports on all project site activities.
- Assist the owner and designer, if relevant, in the review, evaluation, and documentation of claims.

- Coordinate the work of the trade contractors (if acting as the owner's agent for multiple prime contracts) and, if necessary, re-sequence the time, order, and priority in which the work is performed by trade contractors.

Project Schedule

If the agent CM is representing an owner that holds multiple prime trade contracts, typical agent CM arrangements call for it to evaluate work schedules provided by the trade contractors and coordinate and update the overall project schedule. If the owner does not provide the agent CM with sufficient authority to change trade contractors' schedules, significant delays and claims could occur. It is important that the agent CM have sufficient authority to implement the schedule, including key activities that can impact the schedule, such as Requests for Information (RFI) turnaround from the architect or engineer of record.

If the owner is using an agent CM and a design-builder, CM at-risk, or general contractor, the agent CM will typically not have control over the schedule and sequencing. In this case, the agent CM should actively participate in scheduling conferences, represent the owner's needs and concerns relative to scheduling, and regularly advise the owner of project progress relative to the schedule.

Scheduling can become confusing if the owner hires both an agent CM and a traditional general contractor but fails to delineate clear responsibility for schedule management. Thus, it is extremely important for the owner to delineate who controls the schedule and other project administration issues (such as safety programs).

Budgets

Once the construction phase begins, an important service provided by the agent CM is to provide financial oversight, including monitoring payment requests and the overall construction budget and, where relevant, each of the trade contractor budgets. The agent CM is typically required to provide regular updates on the budget to the owner throughout the construction phase. If the costs begin to trend above the budget, the agent CM should discuss the reasons for this trend with the owner and make recommendations regarding measures that may need to be implemented.

Review of Safety and Work Programs

Agent CMs typically are required to at least review and comment on trade contractors' safety and work programs but may have limited ability to control the implementation of a contractor's programs. Unless proper incentives are placed in the agent CM agreement, this lack of control can be a disadvantage to the owner seeking to implement a consistent, coordinated project safety plan. In some cases, the agent CM has responsibility to administer and enforce the project safety program.

Provision of General Conditions Items

If the agent CM is representing the owner on multiple prime contracts, the CM usually is responsible for providing general conditions items not likely to be within the scope of work for the various trade contractors or others providing services to the project. A standard list of these items may include:
- Incidental construction work
- Preparation for ceremonies
- Signs
- Security
- Photographs
- Field office and its related costs (such as equipment)
- Furnishings and office supplies
- Temporary toilets
- Communication equipment
- Computer equipment and software
- Temporary utility services
- Clean-up
- Refuse removal services
- Trash chutes
- Surveys
- Testing
- Temporary roads and parking

Project Closeout

When a project is substantially complete, the agent CM and/or designer advises the owner, and typically the agent CM collaborates with the designer to create a punchlist for project closeout. The CM also assists the designer and owner with final inspections. Among the other closeout services typically within the agent CM's scope are collecting the guarantees, affidavits, releases, bonds, waivers, keys, manuals, record drawings, and other relevant items from the trade contractors and delivering them to the owner.

Commissioning

Before it is occupied, the project's systems and equipment are tested and adjusted so that they perform as designed and will satisfy the project's requirements. The constructor's contract usually requires that this be done before the owner's final acceptance of the project. Frequently, the constructor has this responsibility; however, contract requirements for commissioning can vary widely. The actual commissioning work may be done by a commissioning consultant or a specialty contractor, and the designer may or may not have a dedicated professional on its staff working on behalf of the owner. The responsibility for the management of the commissioning is often assigned by the owner to the agent CM.

Occupancy Phase

Following project closeout, most agent CMs (at least under an agency CM agreement) will have completed their project responsibilities. Some agency CM firms offer expanded services related to move-in and post-occupancy operations and maintenance. This is discussed further in Chapter 11.

TYPES OF AGENCY CM ORGANIZATIONS

Three types of organizations that typically offer construction management services include:
- General construction firms
- Professional design firms
- Consulting firms

Sometimes viewed as a fourth option is an owner's in-house staff, if it has developed the experience and capabilities to offer service to other divisions within the firm (or even other clients outside of the firm). A good example is the U.S. Army Corps of Engineers, which actively seeks to provide services to other federal and non-federal government agencies. The capabilities of each organization influence the nature of services provided.

General construction firms offer:
- Experience in the actual construction of projects and firsthand knowledge of estimating, scheduling, site operations, and the factors that can drive price, time, and quality
- Knowledge of current construction technology
- Experience with dynamics of complex construction operations and managing the various members of the construction team
- Expertise with in-house estimating and scheduling resources
- Experience in dealing with public building departments, utility companies, inspection officials, and safety enforcement officers
- Skill in cash management and experience in payment processing
- Skill in bidding and awarding contracts and subcontracts
- Experience managing a construction budget in a risk-based compensation environment
- Ability to be bonded if required

Professional design firms offer:
- Experience in acting as the owner's agent

- Sensitivity to the quality and aesthetic factors that may be important to owners
- Familiarity with computer-based design and management systems

Consulting firms offer:
- Experience in the land development process, including project due diligence
- Experience in accessing various credit markets
- Broad-based design and construction experience, depending on the background of key principals in the firm (experience can vary widely among consulting firms in these areas)
- Familiarity with computer-based management systems
- Familiarity with modern management practices
- Access to market data for project financial due diligence

As in all construction activities, owners are advised to determine the exact personnel who will provide them service, regardless of the type of organization.

SELECTION CRITERIA AND ESTABLISHING THE FEE

Selection Criteria

Selection of an agency CM firm is nearly always decided on the basis of qualifications and sometimes includes the agency CM firm's proposed fee. The federal government has largely driven the standard for selection of licensed professionals on design procurements through the Federal Acquisition Regulation. These regulations typically limit the ability to factor fees into the initial selection.

Although in most jurisdictions agency CM firms are not required to be licensed as professional entities, the federal selection regulations, or portions thereof, are often used as the standard for selecting firms on both public and private projects. The federal standards largely require the following selection criteria:
- Professional qualifications commensurate with the type of services needed for the project
- Specialized experience and technical competency
- Project staffing and management approach to project administration
- Experience of key personnel
- Organizational capacity to complete the services on time
- Past performance related to managing project cost control, quality, and schedule
- Experience in and knowledge of the market where the project is located
- Other factors unique to the project

Fee

With a Qualifications Based Selection, it is common before finalizing the award to negotiate a fee for the required services. On occasion, where several firms are ranked closely on their technical capabilities, the fee may be the determining factor. It is extremely important that owners have an evaluation process that allows them to understand in significant detail how an agent CM will administer the project.

Owners must understand what is or is not included in the agent CM's fee. The reimbursable items of an agent CM typically including the salaries of the agent CM team are typically included in the agent CM's fee. This is in contrast to the contractor, CM at-risk, or design-builder in which the salaries of the team are considered a part of the general conditions or the cost of the work. Though the term "fee" is being used in both cases, the fees for an agent CM and the fees for a CM at-risk are typically not comparable in what they include and should be evaluated carefully.

While a number of options to calculate fees are used in the market (e.g., fixed fee, percentage fee, hourly fee with a not-to-exceed sum), it is essential that the owner understands exactly what it has purchased. One model for making this evaluation includes breaking down the fee by phases:

- **Preconstruction phase fee**—Compensation for preconstruction phase services is based on the scope of the services to be delivered and the projected overall value of the total project. This is often done on a Lump Sum basis, although many owners choose an hourly reimbursable costs basis.
- **Construction phase fee**—The critical element in comparing fee numbers in this phase is to determine what is included in the overhead and reimbursable costs. The composition of the overhead typically includes the following:
  - A proportionate amount of the salaries (and other mandatory or customary compensation) of the agent CM's employees at its principal and branch offices, except for employees at the project site or those otherwise designated as part of the reimbursable costs
  - A proportionate amount of the general and administrative expenses of the CM's principal and branch offices other than the field office, unless expressly included as part of the reimbursable costs
  - A proportionate amount of the agent CM's capital expenses, including interest on the agent CM's capital employed for the project

  The reimbursable costs can include the following:
  - Actual wages, salaries, and other compensation for employees directly associated with the project
  - Cost of payroll taxes, insurance, and all employee benefits and contributions

- Cost of temporary workers
- Reasonable transportation costs
- Purchase or rental costs, as relevant, of materials and supplies
- Total cost of all insurance required by the owner for the agent CMs
- All sales tax, use, gross receipt, or other taxes and duties related to the project for which the agent CM is responsible
- Permit fees, licenses, tests, royalties, damages for infringement of patents, and potential costs of defending such claims (depending on jurisdiction)
- Deposits lost for causes other than the agent CM's negligence
- Certain uninsured losses
- Minor administrative costs, such as long distance telephone calls, faxes, etc.
- Cost of clean-up and removal of waste to the extent relevant
- Emergency costs related to protection of persons or property
- Total cost of relevant data processing services
- Total cost of relevant legal, accounting, and other services
- Legal, mediation, and arbitration costs other than those arising from disputes between the owner and agent CM
- All costs and expenses related to general conditions items (only applicable under Design-Bid-Build/multiple prime scenario)
- Other relevant costs that can be demonstrated as directly incurred under the agent CM's scope of services

The agent CM's total reimbursable costs are sometimes included as a not-to-exceed or, in other cases, may be fixed as a lump sum.

Once the overhead and reimbursable costs have been calculated, profit will typically be represented as a lump sum or percent of the projected value of the total project. Thus, the fee under this scenario would equal overhead plus reimbursables plus profit.

Owners are cautioned when applying pressure to drive agency CM firm's fees downward. Although the market will drive the fee, owners should be aware that their fee awards will have a direct impact on the amount of resources, within the definition of the scope that an agency CM firm will be able to devote to a project. Out-of-market downward pressure on fees, driven by the owner industry, may unexpectedly result in some qualified firms being unable to remain in the agency CM market. As a result, owners may face substantial upward pressure on their fee.

RISK MANAGEMENT

Warranties

An agent CM typically warrants that it will perform its services in accordance with the standard of care normally practiced by other neighboring agency CM firms. If an agency CM firm violates its warranty, its damages usually take the form of having to provide additional services or costs to correct the deficiencies. Most agent CM warranties limit the agent CM's damages to its fee or its project insurance coverage. This can be a significant limitation if the agent CM's deficient project coordination results in actual construction damages that dwarf the agent CM's fee. Thus, it is imperative that the owner monitors project performance closely so that it can take informed, decisive action if an agency CM project is experiencing significant performance difficulties.

Fee

The fee/warranty limitation derives from the nature of the agent CM's performance guaranty. Unlike a traditional general contractor, at-risk CM, or design-builder—each of which guarantee to the owner that they will actually build a project—an agent CM guaranties only that it will manage the construction of a project in accordance with terms and conditions of its contract and prevailing professional standards.

Insurance and Related Issues

Typical agency CM agreements will require the agent CM to carry statutory workers' compensation, employers' liability, commercial general liability (CGL) (including contractual liability, broad form property damage, and products and completed operations), and business, automobile, and liability coverages. Requiring at least one million dollars of CGL coverage per occurrence and several million dollars of aggregate CGL coverage can, with proper contract language, provide the owner with some protection against some fee-based liability limitations. Umbrella policies can also be used to extend the limits of coverage beyond the primary layers.

FUTURE TRENDS

With many private and public sector entities operating with reduced staff during the most recent economic downturn and still facing corporate mandates to become more efficient and focus on core competencies, it is likely that agency CM will continue to be regularly used as a way for companies and governments to access experienced construction professionals without hiring that expertise in-house. This is particularly true for larger projects and multi-project programs.

In terms of client satisfaction, agency CM is in many respects a management system that is heavily dependent on how the owner structures its project relationships. Where the owner provides the agent CM with contractual authority to do its job, success or failure is determined by the agent CM's performance. If the lines of authority are unclear or duplicative, an agent CM, no matter how qualified, may prove unsuccessful in achieving the owner's project goals.

Self Test

1. Agency construction management is a:
   a. Construction project delivery method
   b. Project management system
   c. Company representing models for construction advertisements

2. With agency construction management:
   a. A project delivery system other than Design-Bid-Build is involved
   b. The designer reports directly to the agent CM
   c. The owner always holds multiple prime contracts
   d. The agent CM is not holding any of the trade contracts

3. A fundamental characteristic of agency CM is that the agent CM:
   a. Assumes full responsibility for the project
   b. Is not at risk for the cost or schedule of building the job (the performance risk)
   c. Is involved in all five phases of the construction process

4. Types of organizations that typically offer construction management services are:
   a. General construction firms
   b. Professional design firms
   c. Consulting firms
   d. All of the above

5. Selection of an agency CM firm is typically:
   a. On the basis of qualifications and sometimes its fee
   b. Based on the bid for total construction cost
   c. Based on a public advertisement and affecting selection of general contractors

6. An agent CM typically warrants:
   a. That it will not perform its services improperly
   b. The design in conjunction with the project designer
   c. The proper operation of all equipment selected for use on the project
   d. The quality of the construction

7. The fees of an agent CM usually include:
   a. The salaries of the agent CM team
   b. The cost of any insurance coverage required for the project
   c. The cost of the design of the project

8. If both the agent CM and the CM at-risk on the same project are being paid the same percentage "fee," which one is likely earning a greater profit?
    a. The agent CM
    b. The CM at-risk
    c. They are both likely making the same profit

Case Study

The following is an example of a typical project. Evaluate the circumstances described and recommend how to proceed. Questions are offered for group discussion. Be prepared to explain and defend your recommendations.

A public owner (Super County) is building a large civic center for public use. Super County has all the funding needed for design and construction and to operate the facility once it is built. The building is to be approximately twice the size of the largest project Super County has ever built. Its program elements for sports and entertainment go beyond what it has ever designed and constructed. Super County, though, does have an excellent staff that has overseen the management of all of its new capital improvement projects. They have built schools, courthouses, office buildings, and maintenance facilities, all delivered with a traditional Design-Bid-Build delivery approach.

The project is only in the conceptual stage but must be designed and built in time for a new minor league franchise opening its season in 18 months. The "normal" project duration under the best of circumstances is anticipated to be approximately 6–8 months to design and 16 months to construct. Everyone agrees that a fast-tracking approach, overlapping the design and construction, will be required. Knowing the cost of similar facilities, Super County is aware of its very tight budget and the need to manage the costs closely.

After evaluating the situation, Super County determines that, though it has good resources, it does not have the experience required to manage this huge project on a fast track. The county decides to hire an agent CM to oversee the entire design and construction process.

Super County conducts a pure Qualifications Based Selection process, soliciting proposals from all interested parties. From a dozen firms (design firms, contractors, program managers, developers, and others) responding to the initial Request for Qualifications, Super County shortlists the five that appear to be the most qualified. After a review of more detailed proposals and interviews with all five firms, the county selects a design firm with a construction management group to act as the agent CM.

With help from the agent CM, Super County decides that, although it has never before used it, Design-Build is the best approach for delivering the design and construction services. The county uses the Best Value bid approach; all competing design-build teams submit their proposed design solutions and bids for the total design and construction. The winning design-build team was awarded the project based on its price and technical proposals.

Once complete, the project was beautiful. It was finished on time, but only after a contentious design and construction process. There were seemingly endless controversies and numerous change orders. The project ended up costing over 20% more than the original bid. Claims from subcontractors and between the design-builder and Super County lingered for years after the construction was complete.

Throughout the project, Super County looked to its agent CM to represent it in the design and construction process. However, the agent CM never seemed to step up and take responsibility for the project. Instead, it seemed only to be documenting what was happening. The agent CM was always there; it was always able to explain the situation to Super County and show how it had represented Super County throughout the project. In the end, the agent CM had maintained excellent records of all the costs and was proud to have managed the project and completed it on time.

DISCUSSION ISSUES:

1. Why did Super County hire an agent CM? Did you agree with this choice?

2. Did Super County receive project leadership or project administration? Which one did Super County think it was getting?

3. Assuming the decision to hire an agent CM is already made, what did Super County do right? What could they have done differently?

4. Did using a pure Qualifications Based Selection of the agent CM make any difference?

5. What additional information would help you understand what role Super County played or did not play in the ultimate outcome of the project?

6. Did the decision to use agency CM limit the available project delivery choices? Could Super County also have hired a construction manager at-risk?

7. Did you agree with the county's choices to use Design-Build and a Best Value bid selection of the design-builder? Explain why you agree or why you would recommend a different delivery and selection approach. (To aid discussion of this particular question, refer to Chapters 7-10.)

CHAPTER SIX

PROJECT DELIVERY CONSIDERATIONS/ RELATED AREAS

Project Delivery Related Areas

Basic Concepts

Project Delivery Considerations
- Building Information Modeling
- Changes
- Claims and Disputes
    - Partnering/Collaboration
    - Dispute Resolution Alternatives
    - Dispute Avoidance/Management
- Design Phases
    - Sources of Design Information
    - Design Process
- Fast-Tracking
- Indemnification/Hold Harmless Clauses
- Insurance
    - General Liability Insurance
    - Builder's Risk Insurance
    - Professional Liability Insurance
    - Umbrella Liability Insurance
    - Automobile Coverage by Constructors
    - Workers' Compensation
    - Owner's Liability Insurance
- Other Insurance Coverage/Issues
    - Insurance by Subcontractors and Supply Contractors
    - Project Insurance
    - Self-Insurance
    - Wrap-Up Insurance
- Lean Construction

- Licensing
  - Architect/Engineer Licensing Requirements
  - Constructor Licensing Requirements
- Lien Waivers
- Prequalification
- Retainage
- Safety
- Standard Forms of Agreements
- Subcontracts
- Surety Bonds and Other Forms of Security for Performance
  - Bond Underwriting
  - Payment Bonds
  - Performance Bonds
  - Bonding of Subcontractors and Trade Contractors
  - Letters of Credit
- Sustainability

Summary

Self Test

PROJECT DELIVERY RELATED AREAS

Consideration and discussion of project delivery systems touches upon many different topics and issues. Participants in the design and construction industry use many terms to express, in shorthand fashion, complicated issues and conditions. There are many such basic concepts. For instance, what does the phrase "fast-track" mean, and how does a fast-track project methodology fit into a discussion on project delivery? What is "builder's risk" insurance, and who typically buys it? Sometimes terms in common use have a standard meaning throughout the industry, and sometimes their meanings differ for different constructors.

This chapter reviews many of these basic construction industry concepts so that the reader will have a baseline of information about, and understanding of, those concepts. Then, with a basic level of understanding as a foundation, the reader can more readily appreciate how a specific concept may vary in application from one delivery method to another. For example, a review of the typical design phases will lead one to ask how those phases may differ for a Design-Build project, as opposed to a Design-Bid-Build project.

BASIC CONCEPTS

Following are the basic concepts (listed in alphabetical order):
- A. Building Information Modeling
- B. Changes
- C. Claims and Disputes
    - a. Partnering/Collaboration
    - b. Dispute Resolution Alternatives
    - c. Dispute Avoidance/Management
- D. Design Phases
    - a. Sources of Design Information
    - b. Design Process
- E. Fast-Tracking
- F. Indemnification/Hold Harmless Clauses
- G. Insurance
    - a. General Liability Insurance
    - b. Builder's Risk Insurance
    - c. Professional Liability Insurance
    - d. Umbrella Liability Insurance
    - e. Automobile Coverage by Constructors
    - f. Workers' Compensation
    - g. Owner's Liability Insurance
    - h. Other Insurance Coverage/Issues
        - i. Insurance by Subcontractors and Supply Contractors

PROJECT DELIVERY CONSIDERATIONS/RELATED AREAS

        ii. Project Insurance
       iii. Self-Insurance
       iv. Wrap-Up Insurance
            1. Owner Controlled Insurance Programs (OCIP)
            2. Constructor Controlled Insurance Programs (CCIP)
- H. Lean Construction
- I. Licensing
  - a. Architect/Engineer Licensing Requirements
  - b. Constructor Licensing Requirements
- J. Lien Waivers
- K. Prequalification
- L. Procurement
  - a. Low Bid
  - b. Best Value: Total Cost
  - c. Best Value: Fees
  - d. Qualifications Based Selection
- M. Retainage
- N. Safety
- O. Standard Forms of Agreements
- P. Subcontracts
- Q. Surety Bonds and Other Forms of Security for Performance
  - a. Bond Underwriting
  - b. Payment Bonds
  - c. Performance Bonds
  - d. Bonding of Subcontractors and Trade Contractors
  - e. Letters of Credit
- R. Sustainability

PROJECT DELIVERY CONSIDERATIONS

Each of the chapters discussing a delivery system (Chapters 7–10) includes a section titled "Project Delivery Considerations" and includes a discussion of how that chapter's delivery method affects the basic concepts discussed here. The section aims to help the reader gain a better appreciation for the nuances of that delivery method. The rest of this chapter is devoted to general discussion about each basic concept (listed in alphabetical order).

Building Information Modeling

A Building Information Model (BIM) is an enhanced electronic representation of a facility for the purpose of design, analysis, construction operations, and facility management. BIM consists of geometric representations of the building elements plus additional information that needs to be captured and transferred in the project delivery process and in the facility operations. As the project moves through its lifecycle, different participants use BIM as a tool in different ways to enhance collaboration throughout. BIM is being used in many ways to improve the efficiency of project delivery. One of the major BIM benefits remains the ability to visualize information.

During its evolution, the concept of BIM was associated with different names, such as 4D (time), 5D (cost), XD, ND, and Virtual Design and Construction (VDC). While the different names all stressed certain model emphases and viewpoints, the name BIM has proven to be general enough to describe the landscape of applications of electronic building models. For project types other than buildings, other terminology, such as VDC, may be more applicable.

Other BIM benefits to the project delivery process can be attributed to these factors:

- Models exist in electronic, virtual form and can be easily shared and exchanged among project participants.
- Models represent geometrical information in three dimensions and enable more conscious design and coordination processes.
- Additional information can be associated with facility geometry. This means that information can be represented and stored in a single place and, therefore, data consistency can be enforced.
- Model characteristics allow practitioners to leverage BIM's benefits and represent information more accurately and consistently, exchange information more quickly, and analyze models in systematic and automated ways.

As a result of the higher fidelity coordination on BIM projects, subcontractors—particularly HVAC, mechanical, and electrical trades—are confident enough in what they can expect for actual site conditions to increase the level of prefabrication. This has positive effects on 1) the quality of work installed in the field, 2) the number of workers required on a job site, which can be lower, 3) site logistics due to reduced field work, and 4) the construction schedule. Prefabrication is one of the few quadruple wins that can be found in the industry. Prefabrication usually results in lower costs (win), higher quality (win), shorter schedules (win), and increased safety (win)!

BIM projects frequently report reduced numbers of field RFIs, shortened delivery schedules, less or no overtime for the workforce, fewer constructability-related change orders, and fewer unplanned, disruptive field conditions. For example, by associating quantity, quality, and unit cost information with building elements, BIM can be useful for estimating. Associating building elements, zones, and spaces with construction schedule activities allows BIM to be useful for 4D scheduling. The industry is just beginning to understand how models can be used in entirely new fields such as space management, crowd control analysis, daylighting studies, energy efficiency, emergency response support, and model-based code checking.

BIM's evolution in the industry has been rapid. Since the mid-2000s, BIM has been adopted by many major industry players. In the mature and competitive construction industry, new technologies survive only if they are practical and deliver tangible value. Experts estimate that in a few years BIM will be standard on most projects

BIM does not change the fundamental roles and responsibilities of project participants. Architects will continue developing great architecture, structural engineers will continue analyzing load characteristics and structural systems, and builders will continue evaluating means and methods to build efficiently. On the other hand, BIM does allow teams to automate tasks in design, coordination, fabrication, and construction. With BIM, designers can more easily create versions and derivatives of a given design and evaluate it with respect to building performance. Builders can extract quantities from models and efficiently develop cost estimates. Design changes can be efficiently analyzed and evaluated for cost and constructability. These changes lead to higher quality design and coordination on BIM projects than on projects that do not use BIM.

The ultimate BIM use for building owners is access to information from the Building Information Model after construction for more efficient facility operations, management, and planning. As delivery processes for capital projects evolve, handoffs from construction to operations are expected to evolve as well.

For more information, see AGC of America's *The Contractor's Guide to BIM*, 2nd Edition. This publication includes information on the process of incorporating BIM in organizations, as well as information about the currently available software tools.

Changes

The essence of a changes clause in a construction contract (changes clauses are typical in construction contracts, but not in design contracts) is that the owner has the right to direct changes in the work, and the constructor has the right to an equitable adjustment in the contract amount. The most common issues that arise under a changes clause are 1) under what circumstances does an owner's directive amount to a change in the scope of the work and 2) what amount of contract adjustment is called for as a result. Under a typical form of changes clause, the owner can direct that work be added. If the owner and constructor do not agree upon a cost adjustment as a result, the constructor is usually entitled to recover the incremental costs associated with the additional work. That may include the costs of running the job for a longer period of time, if that is the effect of the change. The changes clause does not vary as much with the project delivery method as with the basis of reimbursement.

Claims and Disputes

Partnering/Collaboration

In construction, partnering is an ongoing collaborative process. Partnering is typically set up on a particular project by a facilitated session at the outset of the project. At that session, attended by the major decision-makers of each principal participant, common goals and problems are discussed. The parties agree on a methodology for working out any issues that may arise and work together through the project's completion.

Collaboration is simply a form of partnering. In a collaborative setting, the parties communicate regularly in an effort to ensure that common goals are achieved. They try to work as a team to complete the project and to resolve issues and problems in a cooperative process.

Dispute Resolution Alternatives

The common dispute resolution alternatives include mediation, case evaluation, dispute review boards, mini-trials, arbitration, and litigation.

Mediation is a voluntary, facilitated settlement negotiation. In mediation, each party to the dispute (and there may be more than two) meets with a mediator or facilitator. That person is not empowered to make a decision on the dispute and, in fact, will typically not take any definitive position. The mediator listens to a discussion of the dispute by each side and then attempts to help the parties find a mutually acceptable framework for a resolution. If the parties reach a settlement, that agreement is documented and becomes enforceable. However, if the parties do not reach agreement, laws of all states provide that the discussions at the mediation are not admissible at any subsequent arbitration or litigation hearing.

Case evaluation is similar to mediation, involving a neutral third party or facilitator that is not empowered to make a decision on the dispute between the parties. However, in case evaluation, the neutral party examines each party's position and advises each party, confidentially, of the evaluator's independent analysis of that party's position on the underlying claims.

Dispute review boards (DRB) are boards of project representatives that are appointed in advance of the project and that meet periodically during the project. At each meeting, the DRB is given an update on the project as a whole. In the event of any disputes that are not resolved directly by the parties, the DRB hears each side's position on the issue and then renders a decision. Under most DRB structures, this decision is not admissible if the parties split ways and must resort to more formal arbitration or litigation. However, a party that is not happy with the DRB's decision should nevertheless seriously consider whether to challenge the decision of knowledgeable DRB board members who are familiar with the project.

Mini-trials are non-binding presentations of each side's case to a jury or panel of three persons. In this method of dispute resolution, each party is given a designated amount of time to present its position. The jury then evaluates the positions and issues a non-binding decision. Under some scenarios, the jury is not told until after the fact that its decision is not binding upon the parties. The parties receive a "reality check" from an independent group and should carefully consider whether they would challenge such a decision.

Arbitration is a more formal method of dispute resolution. The parties' claims are presented to a single arbitrator or a panel of three arbitrators for a decision. This form of dispute resolution exists either by written agreement—typically in the contract that is signed by the parties at the outset of the project—or by mutual agreement after the contract is signed. The arbitrators have authority similar to (but not as extensive as) that of a judge, and they take sworn testimony of witnesses and receive exhibits. Upon completion of the hearings, the arbitrator(s) will render a decision on the dispute, which in almost all instances is binding on the parties.

Litigation means filing a lawsuit in the court system and then proceeding under the court's rules to a trial—assuming no settlement is reached in advance of trial. Litigation in U.S. courts often involves extensive "discovery," during which each side learns about the other side's case; the extensive nature of litigation also increases the cost of the lawsuit.

Dispute Avoidance/Management

Disputes are common on construction projects. The design is usually unique, based upon the designers' application of judgment to the owner's program, and the construction is performed by a host of people and companies whose own financial interests may not be tied to the overall outcome of the project. In fact, given all the various interests represented on a construction project, it is sometimes a wonder there are not more disputes. Owners, designers, and constructors thus should learn dispute avoidance and management skills to have a successful project. This is one area that is not affected significantly by the project delivery method chosen.

Dispute avoidance involves good communication. Expectations must be clearly stated, and critical assumptions must be aired and not withheld from other players. When information is lacking or unclear, the party that recognizes this should raise the issue right away so that the appropriate parties can address the situation and correct it. It may sound trite, but treating other parties in an upfront and direct manner, and in a way that fosters dialogue, will help industry participants avoid disputes.

Dispute management involves finding ways to flag issues and resolve them promptly. Studies of construction claims have confirmed that claims rarely, if ever, go away on their own. Rather, unresolved claims fester and grow. Thus, effective dispute management techniques depend upon prompt handling of a dispute.

Some managers call for the construction foreman or superintendent and his/her counterpart on the owner's side to resolve issues in the field within three days. If they cannot, the dispute is sent up the chain to their respective bosses for resolution. If the bosses strike out, again within a very short span of time, the matter is referred up the chain to upper management on each side. The benefits of this process are two-fold. First, a dispute is not allowed to linger and is typically resolved while the matter is fresh in everyone's mind. The quicker the process, the more likely the dispute will be resolved. Second, this process creates both empowerment and added pressure to resolve issues at the lower levels of the management hierarchy.

This book is not about dispute avoidance and management. There are many sources of information on those subjects. Nevertheless, construction participants would be well advised to consider what steps can be taken on any project to encourage communication and solve problems.

Design Phases

Sources of Design Information

Normally the design for a construction project is performed by a licensed architect or engineer. The architect or engineer is a person who, by virtue of education, experience, or examination—or a combination of two or three—possesses the skill and knowledge to create a design that complies with applicable building codes, suits the needs of the project owner, and is buildable by the constructor.

Design Process

The design process comprises a series of steps through which the design evolves until the project is completed. The names or labels for those steps are universal, although there may be some variation in level of design represented by the label.

"Predesign" is the phase of an activity in which requirements are identified and when programming, site analysis, and other appropriate studies are conducted. These studies clarify essential information, including cost estimates, to support and advance the decision-making process before the design and implementation phases. Predesign lays the foundation for an effective response to an agency's documented requirements. It also allows more cost-effective document trade-off analyses related to scope, phasing, site options, and alternatives.

In the programming, or planning phase, the designer assesses the owner's present use of a facility and detailed requirements for the project. The designer then develops lists of relationships and analyzes options and alternative courses of action. During this phase, the client is trying to determine the amount of space needed for the building or facility, a general idea of what it should cost, and approximately how long it should take to build the facility. This is a very process-oriented step, often seen in accounting terms as much as in design concepts. It includes meetings with employees to determine the number of people to be accommodated, future expansion needs, equipment and meeting needs, adjacencies (who needs to work near someone else), work flow, etc. The time to develop a "wish list" for a project is early in this phase. Once all the most optimistic expectations have been established, the designer has the difficult task of helping the owner narrow down the expectations to a level that fits within the budget, time, and reality constraints of the project. In highway or bridge projects, the designer determines durability requirements, flow requirements, traffic maintenance, etc., and has the same "wish list" issues as in a building project.

Schematic design (SD) is the stage at which the design is developed on a conceptual basis. At this point in the design, basic relationships between functional spaces are established, preliminary decisions are made about the overall design parameters for the project, and the general scope and scale are determined. During the schematic design, the designer, now armed with the agreed upon space requirements and adjacencies, starts the actual design of the project. The size of the different floors is governed mainly by the adjacencies and square foot requirements. Through many considerations of what is reasonably possible, the designer also sets the sizes of the floors and how they will stack up (blocking and stacking diagrams). The designer starts putting an exterior enclosure design to the building. In a bridge or highway project, basic configurations, flows, intersections, signalizations, spans, etc., are shown in large scale. By the end of this stage, the design is generally considered to be ±15% complete. The designer has incorporated the results of detailed traffic analysis, drainage analysis, etc., into the design.

During the next stage, design development, relationships between various components of the design are finalized, and the design team starts to flesh out more details, materials, standards, and the like. The description of the design at this stage is clear, and the major building systems are defined, even though many details remain to be finalized. Design developments represent the next generation in the evolution of the project design. Design development documents are more typical of building projects than of heavy or highway projects. By the end of this phase, the design will be approximately 65% complete. By this point, the client and team have agreed on the size and scope of the project. The number of stories in the building, the location of elevators and loading docks, and the arrangement of offices or residences in the building have been determined. Critical design details are worked out in this stage: how the structure will be tied together, how interfaces between the structure and exterior enclosure will work, selection of materials and where they will be used in the project, details on what the exterior of the building will look like, etc. Also considered during this stage are traffic circulation, detailed site analysis by the civil engineer, and other elements that allow the client to really evaluate what the final product is going to look like.

The construction documents phase is the stage of the design during which the design details are finalized and all information required to perform the project is documented on both the plans and specifications. After this phase, the design is complete and the construction work can be bid. In a Cost-Plus Guaranteed Maximum Price contract, construction cost estimates are often prepared by the constructor once the construction documents are anywhere from 50–85% complete. The estimate is updated as the design continues to be finalized.

Construction phase service (or construction administration) is the final phase of the design effort. This stage occurs during actual construction. The constructor, subcontractors, and vendors normally submit shop drawings to depict the details of the materials, components, or installation. During this phase of the design, the architect and engineer must review the constructor's shop drawings and other submittals for materials and component and system details to verify whether the materials and details submitted are consistent with the original design. The design professionals also review and take action upon Requests for Information, change order proposals, and applications for payment. The role played by each party, and the specific nature of the construction phase services, may vary with the project delivery method. Usually in a Design-Build project, for instance, the designer is working for the prime design-builder and not for the owner. In that instance, the prime designer may be reviewing submittals of the company that engaged the designer to provide its services. The architect and engineer must also review the work that has been installed in the field, to ensure that the work is progressing consistently with the design.

Fast-Tracking

The term "fast-track" refers to any project or process in which there is overlap between two or more project phases. For instance, fast-track could apply to a project where construction work commences while the design work is still underway. When a project is fast-tracked, the designer provides design information to the constructor as that information is developed. The constructor, in turn, starts with the construction work even though the design is not complete.

This overlapping of phases allows the overall project timeline to be shortened. Many owners take advantage of this time savings and use fast-tracking as a way to accelerate their project schedules. On schedule-driven projects such as computer data centers and casinos, the benefit of this time savings and earlier project completion outweighs the potential risks of proceeding with construction of portions of the work prior to the completion of the entire design.

Fast-track is often confused with Design-Build, but, in fact, is not unique to Design-Build. On the contrary, fast-track efforts are most common in the Construction Management at-Risk delivery system. However, fast-track work cannot be accomplished under a Design-Bid-Build project with a single prime contractor, because the very nature of that delivery system is that the design is complete before contractors are permitted to bid upon it. Though it is rarely done, a fast-track process can be used with Design-Bid-Build if multiple prime contractors participate.

One problem with fast-track is that the speed of progress sometimes results in a need for rework or modification. Because the design is not finalized before construction begins, some portions of the work may be in place before the owner, designer, or constructor realizes that the design must be altered due to the sequence of activity.

Indemnification/Hold Harmless Clauses

An indemnity/hold harmless clause is a contractual risk-shifting mechanism between two or more parties. One party (the indemnitor) agrees to be responsible for any third-party claim or other hazard that might befall another party (the indemnitee). Historically, indemnities were used to transfer risk of loss to the party in the best position to insure against the risk(s) implicated. An indemnity need not be limited, however, to insured risks. Nowadays, many seek to increase the scope of risks for which an indemnity is sought so that the indemnity may be broader than what the indemnitor could cover with insurance.

Insurance

Insurance is a standard component of construction project risk management and risk-shifting. There are many different types and forms of insurance.

General Liability Insurance

General liability insurance is the most common form of insurance carried by constructors and others. It is sometimes called "comprehensive general liability" (CGL) insurance. This insurance provides protection against claims for personal injury and property damage caused by the operations of the insured party. Let's say a constructor has general liability insurance. Its subcontractor accidentally oversprays during fireproofing operations and causes damage to nearby cars. A claim by the owners of those cars would be covered by the general liability policy. (In that scenario, there may be coverage by general liability policies of both the prime contractor and the fireproofing subcontractor.) General liability insurance does not typically cover any damage to the ongoing work itself.

Builder's Risk Insurance

Builder's risk insurance is property insurance that covers against physical damage to the work while construction is in progress. The title is a misnomer; this insurance has historically been purchased by project owners (although there is no reason why a constructor might not obtain such insurance, and this is a fairly common practice in the public sector). Losses due to vandalism, theft, and fire, for instance, are normally covered by the builder's risk policy.

Professional Liability Insurance

Professional liability insurance is malpractice insurance, insuring against claims arising from the alleged malpractice of a designer. Traditionally available only to architects and engineers, in more recent years, professional liability insurance products have been made available to the constructor community. It provides protection to constructors of Design-Build projects and to those performing design work delegated to them under the construction documents.

Umbrella Liability Insurance

This insurance provides excess coverage, over and above the limits of insurance carried by a constructor for any other type of insurance. If, for example, the general liability insurance provides coverage for personal injury claims up to the amount of $1 million, then the umbrella insurance could provide coverage for damages incurred above that amount, up to the limits of the umbrella policy.

Automobile Coverage by Constructors

This insurance covers against claims involving the use of vehicles by the constructor's employees. For example, it would cover the damages if a project superintendent had an automobile accident on his way from the project to a vendor's place of business.

Workers' Compensation

Every state has workers' compensation laws that require employers to obtain and maintain insurance against injury to their employees on the job. The statutory schemes provide that employees are barred from suing their employer in the event of an injury but must be content with workers' compensation proceeds. However, an injured employee is not barred from suing other parties that may be responsible for the injury, and such suits are common for workers injured on a construction jobsite. (Such claims would be covered by a general liability insurance policy of the party that was sued.)

Workers' compensation laws are set by each state legislature. Although there is slight variation among the states, most of the fundamental concepts are the same. First, a worker who is injured on a project will be compensated for lost time and for medical expenses incurred as a result of the injury. This payment is paid directly by the employer.

Second, there is no need to demonstrate that the employer was negligent or at fault. Workers' compensation becomes effective upon the injury and nothing more.

Third, in exchange for this "no-fault" insurance, the employee is barred by statute from suing his or her employer for any damages or losses.

Owner's Liability Insurance

This liability insurance covers the same scope of damages as the constructor's liability insurance, except that it applies to claims arising from the actions of the owner.

Other Insurance Coverage/Issues

A number of other insurance issues arise on a regular basis.

Insurance by Subcontractors and Supply Contractors

Many prime contracts and subcontracts require the subcontractor to obtain the same level of insurance coverage as the prime contractor. Even if this is not expressly set forth in the prime contract, the subcontracts may have a similar provision. Constructors that are sensitized to this issue may seek a partial reduction in the coverage to be provided by subcontractors and suppliers.

Project Insurance

Project insurance is a multi-faceted policy that covers the interests of a number of the parties on the project. Parties that seek project insurance typically do so to minimize the possibility of argument over the extent of coverage in the event of a claim.

Self-Insurance

Most insurance policies have a "self-insured retention," or deductible. The insured must contribute the amount of the deductible in advance of any obligation on the part of the insurance company to cover a loss. For a general liability policy, the deductible (which varies among companies and insurance policies) can be as low as $1,000 or as high as millions of dollars. Some companies are "self-insured," which means that they must cover out of their own pockets any loss arising from a third-party claim. Often a self-insured company will, nonetheless, have an umbrella policy that covers catastrophic claims.

Wrap-Up Insurance

In wrap-up insurance, one party obtains several types of insurance coverage with a single carrier, or in a single policy. This minimizes the chance that an insurance carrier will seek to point the finger of coverage at another policy or coverage. There are two options for wrap-up insurance:

- **Owner Controlled Insurance Programs (OCIP)**—OCIPs are comprehensive insurance programs, with coverage of most or all risks, for the benefit of all companies and persons on the project. OCIPs also cover workers' compensation, general liability, automobile insurance,

PROJECT DELIVERY CONSIDERATIONS/RELATED AREAS

and the like. Under an OCIP, a claim by an injured worker for workers' compensation will be submitted to the OCIP carrier. The claim of any third-party person or company injured or harmed by the construction project will likewise be submitted to the carrier for resolution.

- **Constructor Controlled Insurance Programs (CCIP)**—The only critical distinction between an OCIP and a CCIP is the entity designated to procure and hold the insurance policies.

Lean Construction

The concept of "lean" was pioneered in the manufacturing industry and has widely been associated with automobile manufacturing. The basic philosophy of lean is centered on the idea of *eliminating waste*. As the concept of lean thinking has expanded to the construction industry, the term "lean construction" has evolved.

The application of lean construction is still evolving as the principles of lean (eliminating waste) are applied to many different aspects of the entire construction process. This includes one of the more popular areas—applying it to the planning and scheduling process with concepts such as Last Planner® developed by the Lean Construction Institute (LCI). However, lean construction can apply to any aspect of the construction process, either within a single organization or among the members of the team.

In recent years, Sutter Health, a Sacramento-based healthcare system widely considered one of the early owners to apply the principles of lean thinking, popularized a series of lean principles as their "Five Big Ideas"[1] and incorporated them in its multi-party IPD contract (Integrated Form of Agreement, or IFOA). Sutter's five big ideas are: 1) collaborate, really collaborate, 2) increase relatedness, 3) optimize the whole, 4) look at projects as a network of commitments, and 5) tightly couple action with learning.

Project teams working together can apply lean principles to their project's processes. In addition, there are an increasing number of firms applying lean internally within their own organizations. Tools such as Value Stream Mapping are used to identify existing processes and evaluate non-value adding activities that can be eliminated to streamline the process and thereby eliminate waste. There are many other examples such as "pull" (vs. push) where the user pulls when it needs something rather than always pushing things out to people in anticipation of when they need it.

AGC of America's Lean Construction Forum (www.agcleanforum.org) defines lean construction as "a set of ideas, practiced by individuals in the construction industry,

---

[1] Adopted by Sutter Health as the foundation of its lean initiative, the "Five Big Ideas" were developed and brought to the Sutter Health community by Hal Macomber and Greg Howell.

PROJECT DELIVERY CONSIDERATIONS/RELATED AREAS

based in the holistic pursuit of continuous improvements aimed at minimizing costs and maximizing value to clients in all dimensions of the built and natural environment: planning, design, construction, activation, operations, maintenance, salvaging, and recycling."

Another lean concept known as Set-Based Design allows a team to work together during the project formation state to evaluate multiple design solutions for the same problem and work collaboratively to carry that decision forward until the last possible moment in the design process that each decision must be made. This concept requires close communication as teams work together to identify multiple solutions and proceed with the design without finalizing the design based only on one particular solution.

Applying lean thinking to the field of construction is closely related to the discussion of project delivery. It can affect the delivery process so dramatically that some have referred to lean construction as its own delivery method. This textbook does not refer to lean construction as a delivery method but rather views lean as a philosophy that can be applied to any delivery method to enhance the collaboration, eliminate waste, and increase the value being provided by the project team.

Licensing

Architect/Engineer Licensing Requirements

Building codes in most states and municipalities require that the design professional preparing plans and specifications be licensed by a state licensing board. Licensing and registration statutes and regulations are established by each state, and there is some variation among the states. Most licensing statutes, though, require that a person seeking to become licensed as an engineer or architect demonstrate:
- Certain minimum college education in the applicable discipline (most often a bachelor's degree);
- Certain minimum experience, or a combination of education and experience; and
- Competence by passing a licensing examination given by the state registration board.

Licenses are held by individuals, not by companies, so that a company entering into a contract to furnish design services would need a licensed person as an employee or even as an officer of the company, depending on the particular state requirement.

Constructor Licensing Requirements

Constructor licensing varies widely among the states, and even among various political subdivisions of some states. A constructor wanting to perform work in a particular locale will need to investigate and determine whether a license is required. The purpose of most license requirements is to ensure that persons or companies that carry out construction work are doing so in a manner that is in compliance with building codes and with local, state, and federal safety laws. These requirements vary greatly from one jurisdiction to another, and there is little reciprocity. Thus, the constructor must go through the licensing process in each state or locale that has its own licensing requirement. To assist in the licensing process, the National Association of State Contractors Licensing Agencies provides information on license requirements in various jurisdictions.

Lien Waivers

The laws of most states permit those who furnish labor, materials, or equipment to a construction project to establish a "mechanic's lien" against the property as security for payment. If, for example, a duct supplier is not paid by the second-tier HVAC subcontractor that is performing the duct installation, the supplier can assert a mechanic's lien against the property. If the payment situation is not resolved, the supplier can seek a court order for a sale of the property to satisfy the lien. Due to the effectiveness of the lien security, such sales are very rare.

To avoid the prospect of a sale, owners require lien waivers during the course of the project. The lien waiver form is both a relinquishment of lien rights to the extent of the amount that has been paid and a record of the flow of funds down the chain from the prime contractor to subcontractors and suppliers. Most standard form contracts require lien waivers to be furnished in conjunction with each application or requisition for payment. Thus, the lien waiver documents the fact that the potential lien claimant has been paid for work performed through a specified date. The absence of a lien waiver, or the inability to obtain such a waiver from a supplier or subcontractor, on the other hand, is sometimes a signal that payments made to the constructor are not flowing all the way down to the company providing the materials, equipment, or labor.

The federal government and most state governments have retained their sovereign immunity with regard to public projects and do not permit contractors at any tier to place a mechanic's lien on public property. It would be inappropriate to grant the right to sell property owned by the public to satisfy a debt. This is particularly true when the property in question serves a public safety function, such as a prison, courthouse, police facility, or fire station.

The federal government promulgated the Miller Act to protect subcontractors and suppliers in this situation. The Miller Act requires all public works contractors to provide a payment bond that effectively serves as a substitute for a mechanic's lien. The Miller Act and several related statutes have specific release requirements and related certifications with regard to payments to subcontractors and suppliers. The failure to comply with these requirements can result in severe civil and criminal penalties.

Some states, such as New York, permit subcontractors and suppliers to file liens against payments that are due from government entities to a prime or principal contractor. Most states, however, preclude the filing of any type of lien on a public works project. Typically, these states have adopted "Little Miller Acts" that incorporate the release requirements set forth in the federal version of that statute.

Prequalification

Prequalification is the process by which qualifications of prospective designers or constructors are examined prior to those persons/companies being solicited to compete for the project. Persons and companies not having the appropriate qualifications are not permitted to compete for the work.

Prequalification typically focuses on the company's financial capability and project experience, and the experience of the company's key personnel. Analysis of the company's financial capability may focus on its bonding capacity or the maximum project size for which it can obtain performance and payment bonds. Analysis of the company's project experience will focus on past performance of projects and may include interviews with project representatives of those prior projects. Finally, the experience of the company's key personnel is evaluated to determine if they have the experience and skills necessary to perform the project at hand. Some owners require the designer or constructor to keep its "interview" personnel on the project.

The purpose of prequalification is to ensure—particularly when the contract award may be on the basis of Low Bid—that those designers or constructors competing for and bidding on the work are capable of performing that work. A secondary purpose is to "level the playing field" so that qualified designers or constructors are not attempting to compete with those who may not be qualified who may present lower prices or fees for the work.

Retainage

Retainage is money earned by the constructor but held by the owner pending completion of the project. The amount of retainage held is commonly in the range of 5–10% of the contract price (or 5–10% of costs incurred, if the contract is based upon the constructor's costs plus a fee). Most contracts provide that the retainage is to be released by the owner upon substantial completion of the project. The original reasoning for retainage was two-fold: 1) to provide for a "cushion" when estimating the amount of work completed for a progress payment and 2) to ensure that the constructor would complete the work. Currently, most owners consider retainage as simply an additional guarantee that the constructor will complete the work.

Prime contractors typically hold their subcontractors to the same retainage requirements as imposed by the owner on them. A subcontractor whose work is complete in the early stages of the project, such as a site excavator, may seek early release of retainage for its own portion of the work rather than waiting until the entire project is substantially complete.

Material and equipment supply contracts from distributors and manufacturers, on the other hand, do not typically provide for retainage. Suppliers are thus usually entitled to full payment upon delivery of the applicable materials, equipment, etc.

Safety

Safety programs are normally the province of the constructor. Under both standard contract risk allocation and statutes and common law standards, the constructor is responsible for means, methods, and techniques of construction. As such, the constructor is responsible for achieving a safe worksite. In the United States, safe practices are defined in detailed regulations issued by the Occupational Safety and Health Administration (OSHA). Those regulations also spell out, generically, which parties or companies are responsible for safety compliance on a jobsite. Most states have either adopted or follow the federal OSHA Act.

Standard Forms of Agreements

The contract, or agreement, between parties to a construction project defines the expectations and obligations of each party. Ideally, the contract should mirror the parties' relationship. Standard form agreements are in common use throughout the industry. Most owners, designers, and constructors either use standard forms or have custom forms that are modeled after the standard forms. The major purveyors of the standard forms are nationwide trade associations, including ConsensusDOCS (a coalition of 30+ leading industry associations including AGC of America), American Institute of Architects (AIA), Construction Management Association of America (CMAA), Design-Build Institute of America (DBIA), and the Engineers' Joint Contract Documents Committee (EJCDC). Other groups, including some owner organizations, also publish contract forms, but the five organizations just listed control, in combination, the vast majority of the market for standard forms.

Standard industry forms are in common use for two reasons. First, industry participants become familiar with the standard forms and thus are comfortable with the use of such forms as a model. They learn which terms are covered by those forms and in what manner. Second, standard forms have developed language for many situations and circumstances that has, over time, been tested and refined in the legal system. As a result, there is some certainty in how the clauses and terms will be applied. Many industry groups solicit endorsement of their model forms of agreement—and modify the forms to get such endorsement—from other groups so as to increase the acceptance and use of their forms. One family of forms, ConsensusDOCS, is unique to the industry because the forms are developed by a coalition of 30+ leading industry associations. This growing coalition represents all stakeholders in the construction process, including designers, owners, contractors, subcontractors, and sureties (DOCS). ConsensusDOCS are developed with best practices that represent the project's best interest, versus those of any particular participant. The forms are developed to fairly allocate risks and responsibilities to reduce adversarial negotiations and save all parties time and money.

Because standard industry forms are typically drafted by a committee, and not in the context of an actual project, they are intended as model forms and not as "one size fits all." As a result, parties may tinker with and adjust the language in the standard forms to meet their specific needs.

Allocation of common risks of design and construction is covered by the major standard forms in use. One using an industry standard form, such as ConsensusDOCS 200, "Standard Agreement and General Conditions Between Owner and Constructor (Lump Sum)," may have one article dealing with the payment process, another that deals with the allocation of responsibility for insurance coverage, and one delineating the areas of responsibility of the constructor. These are only examples, as the general conditions established by each of the associations noted previously cover a large number of issues. Use of industry standard forms thus minimizes the likelihood that the parties will neglect to consider and deal with a major issue.

Most government entities have developed their own contract forms, which may or may not be based on one of the standard industry agreements. When pursuing public work, industry participants are cautioned to carefully review the agreements before entering into a contract for services.

Subcontracts

A constructor or designer engaged by a project owner is often referred to as a "prime" constructor or designer. A subcontract, in turn, is the agreement between the prime constructor or designer and a constructor or designer hired to perform a portion of the prime's contract obligations. Thus, when a prime constructor engages another constructor to perform the work of clearing a building site and preparing the rough grading, the latter constructor is referred to as a "subcontractor" or a "trade contractor," and the agreement between the two constructors is a subcontract. Use of the term "subcontract" is universal when applied to agreements between a prime constructor and another constructor (subcontractor) that performs a portion of the project.

Likewise, when a prime architect engages an engineering firm to perform the structural engineering design, the engineering firm is a sub-consultant to the architect, and the agreement between the two is typically referred to as a "sub-agreement" or "sub-consulting agreement."

The term "purchase order" as used in the construction industry typically refers to an agreement for the purchase only of materials or equipment. Companies selling materials or equipment are usually referred to as "vendors" and are distinguished from "subcontractors" by the absence of any onsite workforce. A vendor simply furnishes pertinent equipment or materials, which are then installed by a subcontractor or the prime constructor.

One critical aspect of subcontracts and sub-agreements is that the obligations of the subcontractor to the prime constructor be consistent with the prime constructor's obligations to the project owner. Consistency of this obligation helps guarantee that there are no gaps between what the prime constructor owes to the owner and what the subcontractor owes to the prime constructor. Clauses creating this "flow-down" of rights and obligations are included in all major industry standard subcontract forms.

Surety Bonds and Other Forms of Security for Performance

Surety bonds are specialized tri-party agreements. Each bond involves three parties, one of whom may be a class of companies rather than an individual company. These parties are 1) the bond principal, who is the one obtaining and directly paying for the bond, 2) the bond surety, who is providing security for the performance of the bond principal, and 3) the obligee, who is the beneficiary of the surety's commitment to provide this security. The surety under a surety bond agrees that if the bond principal does not fulfill its obligation to the claimant, the surety will step up to the plate and do so.

Surety bonds are not insurance. There is no actuarial calculation as to anticipated loss. If the surety expends money under the bond, it expects to recover this money from indemnitors. A construction company seeking a surety bond will need to sign an indemnity agreement with the surety, agreeing to reimburse the surety in the event that any funds are paid out by the surety. In a closely held corporation, the indemnitors are likely to be the owner of the company and that person's spouse, in addition to the company itself.

Bond Underwriting

All potential surety bond principals must go through an underwriting process. In that process, the underwriters for the surety examine the financial picture and health of the company as well as the character of the company's management to assess whether the surety will agree to write bonds for that principal, and, if so, in what amount and at what rate.

Payment Bonds

A payment bond is a surety bond that secures a constructor's obligations to pay subcontractors, suppliers, and others lower in the hierarchy. Thus, if the prime constructor obtains a payment bond, then lower-tier subcontractors have recourse against the surety in the event that they are not paid by the principal, or by the subcontractor that hired them.

Performance Bonds

A performance bond acts as security for performance for the entity higher in the contracting chain than the bond principal. If a prime constructor obtains a performance bond, and is thereafter declared in default of the contract, the project owner has recourse against the surety to ensure that the constructor's obligations will be fulfilled.

In any bond scenario, when a demand is made on the surety to pay or to perform, the surety typically performs a due diligence review to ascertain whether the declaration of default was justified. If the surety determines that its principal was in default, then the surety must take action to complete the project, either on its own or by getting another constructor to complete performance. Instead of completing the project, the surety may choose to pay the penal sum of the bond and leave the completion of the project up to the obligee on the bond.

Bonding of Subcontractors and Trade Contractors

One risk management tool for prime constructors is to require performance and payment bonds from the subcontractors. Such a requirement has the net effect of reducing the constructor's risk because each subcontractor providing a bond will have a surety backing up its position. However, a surety bond is issued only after payment of a premium, so a widespread requirement for subcontractor bonds also increases the cost of the completed project.

Subcontractor default insurance is another alternative to subcontractor payment and performance bonds, which provides protection against the risk of subcontractor defaults. It is an insurance product, and the insurance policy includes coverage for both the direct and indirect costs resulting from a default in performance of any enrolled subcontractor. Such costs include the cost of completing unfulfilled subcontractor obligations, costs related to subcontractor replacement, and overhead and claim preparation expenses.

Although subcontractor default insurance and payment and performance bonds both provide protection against subcontractor default risk, there are differences between the two approaches. The primary difference is in the product delivery method. Payment and performance bonds are a three-party agreement, which requires a surety to guarantee the performance of a subcontractor to a third party (the general contractor). In the event of a subcontractor default, the general contractor files a claim against both the subcontractor and its surety. Subcontractor default insurance is a first party coverage where the general contractor purchases an insurance policy to protect itself from a subcontractor default.

Letters of Credit

Letters of credit are negotiable instruments under which the issuer (usually a bank) agrees to pay the holder of the note upon a written demand for payment or upon the occurrence of some other well-defined condition. This form of performance security is used in lieu of a performance bond. Where a letter of credit is used as performance security, it is typically issued in the amount of 10% of the contract value. When an owner makes a demand on the issuing bank, it may then use the funds for completion of the project to obtain a replacement constructor or for correction of defects. Letters of credit as performance security are more common outside of North America.

Sustainability

Sustainability is a term used to describe the application of sustainable practices to the design and construction process. Sustainable construction, green construction, or green building is the practice of designing and building facilities that are environmentally responsible; that is, these facilities minimize the impact to the natural environment and resources consumed both during construction and throughout the building's lifecycle. Characteristics of green-build facilities include efficiently using energy, water, and other resources; protecting occupant health and improving employee productivity; and reducing waste, pollution, and environmental degradation.

Multiple rating systems are available to measure and certify the level of sustainability incorporated into a project, but the most widely recognized is the system developed by the U.S. Green Building Council (USGBC). Founded in 1993 as a non-profit trade organization that promotes sustainability in building design, construction, and operation, USGBC works to promote buildings that are environmentally responsible, profitable, and healthy places to live and work.

USGBC is best known for the development of the Leadership in Energy and Environmental Design (LEED®) green building rating systems and benchmarks. LEED is a framework for assessing building performance and meeting sustainability goals, and the rating systems are currently available for new construction, existing buildings, commercial interiors, core and shell, schools, retail, healthcare, homes, and neighborhood development.

Through its partnership with the Green Building Certification Institute, USGBC offers industry professionals the chance to develop expertise in the field of green building and to receive accreditation as LEED Green Associates or LEED Accredited Professionals, along with various specialty designations.

Recent research, *Sustainable, High Performance Projects and Project Delivery Methods, A State-of-Practice Report*, sponsored by the Charles Pankow Foundation and The Design-Build Institute of America, September, 2009, looked at the link between sustainability and project delivery. More specifically, the research looked at the likelihood that a project team would achieve or exceed the original goal established for LEED rating based on both the delivery method and the procurement type used for that project.

The results showed that based on the metric of what percentage of projects achieved or exceeded their original LEED goal, CM at-Risk was highest at 94%, while Design-Build was 82%, and Design-Bid-Build was 77%. Conversely, measuring the number of projects that failed to achieve their original goal, CM at-Risk was 6%, Design-Build 18%, and Design-Bid-Build 23%. Regarding the impact the procurement process had on achieving sustainability goals, Qualifications Based Selection achieved or exceeded the original LEED goal 95% of the time, Best Value (Total Cost) was 87%, and Low Bid was 78%.

This research confirmed that there is a direct correlation between the delivery method and the procurement process with the ability to maximize sustainability. The explanation is most likely tied to the level of collaboration and the transparency resulting from the open-book contracts that are typically used on Qualifications Based Selections. In projects where owners place a value on maximizing sustainability and utilization of green construction techniques, the research indicates that consideration should be given to the choice of the delivery approach and the procurement process.

For a more complete discussion on green building, consult *Contractor's Guide to Green Building Construction*, published by AGC of America.

SUMMARY

In each of the chapters discussing a specific project delivery method (Chapters 7–10), in the section titled "Project Delivery Considerations," there is a discussion of the basic concepts noted above for the purpose of understanding how that project delivery method differs from others. Because the focus in each chapter is on the nuances of that particular project delivery method, only those basic concepts that are affected by the particular method are discussed.

Self Test

True or **false**:

1. Changes clauses are required only in the Design-Bid-Build delivery system and are not required in either Construction Management at-Risk or Design-Build.

2. "Partnering" in construction is a collaborative process.

3. The design for a construction project is typically performed by a licensed architect or engineer in conjunction with a constructor. The constructor assumes responsibility for the correctness of the design documents.

4. The term "fast-track" refers to any project and process where there is overlap between two or more project phases.

5. An indemnity is a risk-shifting mechanism between two or more parties and is used only on construction-related projects.

6. General liability insurance is the most common form of insurance carried by constructors and others. It is sometimes called "comprehensive general liability" (CGL) insurance.

7. Building codes of most states and municipalities require that the design professional preparing plans and specifications be licensed by a state licensing board.

8. The laws of most states permit those who furnish labor, materials, or equipment to a construction project to establish a "mechanic's lien" against the property as security for payment.

9. Prequalification is the process by which qualifications of prospective designers or constructors are examined prior to those persons/companies being solicited to compete for the project. Persons and companies not having the appropriate qualifications are not permitted to compete for the work.

10. There are four types of procurement: Low Bid, Best Value: Total Cost, Best Value: Fees, Qualifications Based Selection.

11. Retainage is money earned by the constructor but held by the owner pending completion of the project.

12. Safety programs are normally the province of the constructor, but the designer is responsible for achieving a safe worksite.

13. Standard form agreements are commonly used throughout the industry.

PROJECT DELIVERY CONSIDERATIONS/RELATED AREAS

14. A subcontract is the agreement between the prime constructor or designer and a constructor or designer hired to perform a portion of the prime's contract obligations.

15. Surety bonds are the same thing as insurance.

CHAPTER SEVEN

DESIGN-BID-BUILD

Introduction

Definitions in This Project Delivery System
- Design Specifications
- Spearin Doctrine and Owner's "Warranty of the Specifications"
- Bid Package
- Lump Sum Fixed Price
- Progress Payments
- Competitive Bidding
- Responsive Bid
- Responsible Constructor
- Risk Allocation in Design-Bid-Build

Delivery Method Overview/Structure
- Programming/Predesign Phase
- Design Phase
- Bidding Phase
- Construction Phase
- Commissioning
- Occupancy Phase

Defining Characteristics and Typical Characteristics
- Minimizing Construction Contract Price
- Independent Advice

Procurement and Establishing the Contract Amount
- Competitive Bidding
  - Low Bid
  - Best Value: Total Cost

Basis of Reimbursement Options
- Alternates, Substitutions, and Unit Prices
- Allowances

Roles and Responsibilities
- The Owner
- The Designer
- The General Contractor
- Specialty Contractors and Suppliers

Project Delivery Considerations
- Building Information Modeling (BIM)
- Changes
- Claims and Disputes
  - Partnering/Collaboration
  - Dispute Resolution Alternatives
  - Dispute Avoidance/Management
- Design Phases
  - Sources of Design Information
  - Design Process
- Fast-Tracking
- Indemnification/Hold Harmless Clauses
- Insurance
- Lean Construction
- Licensing
- Lien Waivers
- Prequalification
- Retainage
- Safety
- Standard Forms of Agreements
- Subcontracts
- Surety Bonds and Other Forms of Security for Performance
- Sustainability

Lesson Learned

Future Trends

Self Test

Case Study

INTRODUCTION

In this chapter, the term "Design-Bid-Build" is used to refer to a specific project delivery system. It refers here to a method of project delivery in which the owner procures a design and bid package from an independent designer, uses a competitive procurement process to get bid prices for all work required to build the project as specified, and then selects a constructor to build the project on the basis of either Low Bid or Best Value: Total Cost procurements.

There are many variations of this method. In some cases, the designer prepares less than a complete design or prepares multiple design packages for a multi-prime bidding process. Other variations use a pricing mechanism other than Lump Sum, like Unit Pricing, Guaranteed Maximum Price, or Cost Reimbursement. Each of these variations is applicable for particular projects.

An important feature of the Design-Bid-Build method is that it intentionally tries to separate the design phase, the bidding phase, and the construction phase so that each is performed independently. This has important consequences to the roles and responsibilities of the owner, the designer, and the constructor.

There is a sequential chain of events in Design-Bid-Build contracts. The owner first enters into a contract with a designer, who prepares contract documents. Next, the owner selects a general contractor through either a Low Bid or Best Value: Total Cost procurement process. The general contractor in turn selects subcontractors (usually through a similar process) to perform parts of the work. Subcontractors may employ sub-subcontractors for specialty work. General contractors, subcontractors, and sub-subcontractors may all provide labor, and they may all purchase materials from suppliers. The designer does not have a contract with the contractor but, rather, acts as the agent of the owner for design services and may provide contract administration during construction.

The Design-Bid-Build method of project delivery is among the most widely used in this country and abroad. It is popular in the private sector and often is mandated for use in the public sector. It brings the forces of competition directly to bear upon the cost of construction by soliciting a price for all work required by the plans and specifications issued for bidding. This is important because construction cost is a large portion of initial project costs.

The Design-Bid-Build method is attractive to private sector owners interested in securing low initial construction cost. It is important to public sector owners as an objective means of selecting constructors without the taint or suggestion of political pressure or influence.

DESIGN-BID-BUILD

DEFINITIONS IN THIS PROJECT DELIVERY SYSTEM

Design Specifications

The process begins when an owner, after determining the need for a project, enters into a contract with a designer to produce a complete set of drawings and written specifications of the proposed project. The designer prepares and delivers to the owner a set of detailed design drawings and detailed specifications that clearly state all the minimum requirements for all materials and labor to be furnished for the project.

The designer and owner have determined the materials, products, equipment, and other work that must be furnished by the constructor. This type of detailed design, utilizing drawings and specifications, is used to form a roadmap for the constructor to follow. These documents, along with addenda and approved change orders, are commonly referred to as "contract documents." The contract documents are so detailed that the constructor has no discretion in selecting materials or products for the project. These details are usually called "design specifications" or "prescriptive specifications." Prescriptive specifications designate the work the constructor is to perform. It might include products' or manufacturers' names and model numbers, or a specific description of the work to be performed and the materials to be used.

Spearin Doctrine and Owner's "Warranty of the Specifications"

In the Design-Bid-Build method of project delivery, the owner assumes the risk of defects in the contract documents, including the drawings and specifications. The owner, not the general contractor, accepts the risk of additional construction costs resulting from errors in the contract documents. While the contract documents need not be flawless, the owner represents to the general contractor that they are reasonably adequate for the task. The fundamental bargain is this: the general contractor agrees to follow the contract documents without substantial variation; if that is done, the owner agrees to accept the work. This often is called the owner's "warranty of the specifications" or the "Spearin Doctrine" after a 1918 Supreme Court decision concerning a federal government construction contract, *United States v. Spearin*, 246 U.S. 132 (1918). Spearin, a landmark construction law case, stands for the principle that as long as a contractor follows the plans and specifications provided by the owner, the contractor is not liable for loss or damage as a result of defects in the plans or specifications.

Contract documents used in the Design-Bid-Build method are not necessarily free of defects, as errors will always occur in the work of human hands. The owner may have recourse against the design professionals, particularly if the defects rise to the legal standard of negligence, but in this delivery method, between the owner and the constructor, the owner assumes the risks of errors in the contract documents.

In this delivery method, these design or prescriptive specifications are distinguished from "performance specifications" that state only the performance requirements set by the owner and give the constructor the freedom to select the materials and products to achieve the specified requirements. Such performance specifications often are used in other delivery methods, including Design-Build, but traditionally, prescriptive specifications are used in Design-Bid-Build.

Bid Package

A "bid package" is the group of documents issued by the owner to competing constructors so they can prepare bids. Typically, it is prepared by the designer and delivered to the owner upon completion of the design.

The bid package typically includes instructions to bidders, a bid form, contract forms, bond forms, and specifications and drawings. The bid package thus completely describes the proposed terms and conditions of the contract between the owner and the ultimate low bidder and also contains all technical requirements for the construction. In essence, the only information missing from the bid package is the bidder's price; once the bidder's price is added to the bid package, it becomes a complete contract between the owner and the constructor. All that is necessary to form a contract is the owner's acceptance of the bid offered by the constructor and the parties' signature on the contract.

Lump Sum Fixed Price

In the Design-Bid-Build method, the expectation is that bidders will compete against one another to offer the owner the lowest price. Each still must furnish all materials and labor necessary to complete the work required by drawings and specifications in conformance with the terms and conditions stated in the bid package. The lowest bidder will be selected to enter into a construction contract with the owner; the contract will limit the owner's cost of construction to the agreed upon price.

Typically the contract is for a lump sum or a "fixed price" for the scope of work described in the contract documents. The general contractor assumes the risk of increases in cost to perform the work required. Increased payments beyond that lump sum are allowed only through formal amendments (change orders) agreed upon by owner and general contractor.

Lump Sum pricing is not limited to Design-Bid-Build. It is sometimes used in Construction Management at-Risk and Design-Build arrangements. It also is frequently the method of payment in subcontracts and supply agreements in all project delivery systems. In all these situations, the constructor accepts the risk that it will complete the required work at a cost greater than the contract sum and have to cover any cost overrun (except for those costs due to change orders).

Terms related to Lump Sum include:
- "Stipulated Sum," a synonym for Lump Sum that is frequently used in contract language.
- "Fixed Price," a term favored by some owners. It means essentially the same thing as Lump Sum or Stipulated Sum, but it tends to be more broadly applied to other types of contracts, such as "Negotiated Fixed Price."
- "Hard Money," a colloquial term for any agreement wherein the constructor is at risk for a not-to-exceed fixed price.

Progress Payments

In most Design-Bid-Build contracts, the lump sum is a series of periodic payments (usually monthly) made by the owner to the constructor. These monthly payments often are called "progress payments" because payments are made as the work is completed in pre-established stages. The final payment is made after the completion and acceptance of the work.

Competitive Bidding

Competitive bidding is at the heart of Design-Bid-Build. Sealed bids are used in public work to demonstrate fairness and objectivity and are sometimes used in private work when the same objectivity is sought. Public bids are opened in public, and the entire process is subject to scrutiny by bidders, ordinary citizens, and other interested parties. Public bidding procedures must conform to legal and administrative regulations. Private owners set their own requirements for receiving proposals and base their decisions on whatever factors they believe to be relevant. Public and private owners that frequently build projects should employ fair, objective selection procedures if they hope to receive responsive bids.

Responsive Bid

In Design-Bid-Build, the construction contract is awarded to the lowest responsive bid submitted by a responsible bidder. A "responsive bid" is an unequivocal offer to do everything required by the contract documents, without exception. A bid must offer to perform all requirements of the contract documents so that the owner's acceptance of the bid forms a binding contract for the general contractor to perform the work as required by the contract documents. If a bid contains qualifications, conditions, or exclusions that differ from the requirements stated in the bid package, or if it is an equivocal offer, the bid is said to be "not responsive."

Responsible Constructor

A responsible constructor is one that can perform and complete the work required by the contract documents to the satisfaction of the owner. A responsible constructor must possess the necessary financial and technical capability to perform the work as well as the tenacity to do so, usually demonstrated by the constructor's past performance record. A responsible constructor must have the equipment, materials, and workforce—or the ability to obtain them—sufficient to complete the work. This usually is demonstrated by ownership of equipment (or suitable arrangements to rent equipment), and by the ability to purchase materials and hire personnel. Finally, a responsible constructor is expected to possess the integrity to perform the work. If a constructor has a history of serious violations of the law, the owner may judge it to be non-responsible.

Risk Allocation in Design-Bid-Build

Which party should carry the bulk of the liability, and thus carry the related insurance, is always a contractual issue. In Lump Sum contracting, most of the liability risk falls to the general contractor. If there are multiple prime contractors, each of them handles a share of the risk. Subcontractors and material suppliers are at less risk because they do not have direct contracts with the owner. The owner is the traffic officer of risk, having the capability to direct it to other parties or to absorb it. A good rule is that each risk should be handled by the party most able to manage that risk. The owner and owner's agents should consider risk allocation early, determine which party is best able to manage which risk, and make the proper allocations.

In some cases, the owner's wisest action may be to have the constructor carry most of the risk, provided the constructor has the ability to obtain adequate coverage. This makes accounting for total job costs easier. It is not wise, however, to allocate total risk to the constructor through broad form indemnity or hold harmless clauses, which shield the owner from any exposure. That would dramatically inflate the cost of insurance to the constructor, and such costs are passed on to the owner. Moreover, in some states such broad form indemnity may not even be enforceable.

The risk factors that need to be allocated in Lump Sum competitive bid contracting include:

- **Cost overruns**—The constructor, subcontractor, or supplier that has agreed to a Lump Sum contract accepts the risk.
- **Price escalation or shortages in materials or labor**—The affected constructor or subcontractor accepts the risk (and in some cases, suppliers, if they give fixed prices for materials).
- **Schedule overruns caused by the constructor**—The constructor is at risk for either liquidated damages or compensatory damages (i.e., losses claimed by the owner based on the actions or inaction of the constructor).
- **Schedule overruns caused by the owner**—The owner is at risk for a claim by the constructor for damages for delay, based on the fact that extended schedules increase constructor costs.

- **Problems with subcontractors, ranging from interpersonal relationship conflicts to subcontractor default**—The general contractor must accept the risk. In the case of subcontractor failure, the general contractor must complete the project by whatever means necessary, usually through agreement with another trade contractor or by self-performing the work at no increase in the contract price to the owner.
- **Quality problems**—The level of quality is determined by the specifications issued by the owner. The owner agrees to accept the minimum scope of work required by the specifications. This may lead to disputes if the owner does not understand this.
- **Casualty losses**—Usually carried by the one that owns the equipment, building, or materials lost. Typically, the materials already built into a building are considered the owner's property, and the owner is well advised to carry fire and casualty insurance—perhaps through a builder's risk policy—to cover potential loss up through project completion. At that time, the new building coverage can be incorporated into the owner's overall insurance program. The distribution of risk during construction may be contractually divided by different formulas within builder's risk or wrap-up insurance.
- **Safety**—This is the most crucial of the risks and each constructor, under federal OSHA laws and state safety and health standards, is responsible for the safety of all hired personnel. In addition, the general contractor has responsibility for the safety of workers and visitors, whether or not they are authorized to be on the property. Liability insurance can be obtained to deal with suits filed because of injuries. The owner is not completely free from safety risks. An injured worker or visitor will probably sue several parties for negligence. Workers' compensation insurance protects the immediate employer but not the other parties. There is no insurance coverage for the fines associated with safety violations, which may be significant.
- **Defects in the design and specifications**—The owner, rather than the general contractor, accepts this risk. The owner may have recourse against the designer for defects in the design. The constructor does not accept the risk of design defects and has recourse against the owner for additional costs caused by defects in design.

DELIVERY METHOD OVERVIEW/STRUCTURE

A major characteristic of this project delivery system is that the owner enters into a contract with the designer for a complete design and then enters into a separate contract with a constructor. The owner selects the constructor by competitive bidding on the basis of the complete design and specifications contained in the bid package.

This project delivery method must proceed in a linear fashion because the design must be completed before a constructor can be selected. Several phases make up this project delivery method.

Programming/Predesign Phase

The programming or predesign phase is the time during which the owner determines its needs so that those needs can be satisfied in the design. In this phase, the owner selects a designer and works with the designer to refine and determine its needs.

The owner typically selects the designer on the basis of qualifications and experience, rather than on the basis of competitive pricing. The designer usually serves as the owner's advisor during the programming/predesign phase and helps the owner determine its requirements. In the Design-Bid-Build method, the constructor does not participate in this phase, as the constructor is not selected until the design has been completed.

Design Phase

During the design phase, the designer works with the owner to prepare a design. The designer usually begins by discussing and presenting a conceptual design intended to meet the owner's requirements. Upon the owner's approval, the designer proceeds to prepare a preliminary or schematic design, again for approval by the owner.

Once the owner approves the preliminary or schematic design, the designer prepares a detailed design. The designer completes its work by producing and delivering to the owner final design and construction documents, including detailed drawings and specifications. The final design drawings and specifications then are combined with instructions to bidders, a bid form, and a contract form to produce a bid package to be issued to constructors. In the Design-Bid-Build method, the constructor does not participate in this phase, as the constructor is not selected until the design has been completed.

Bidding Phase

In this phase, the owner issues the bid package created by the designer and solicits bids from qualified constructors to perform the work required by the drawings and specifications in the bid package. The owner then selects one constructor and awards a construction contract on the basis of Low Bid or Best Value: Total Cost to perform all work required by the drawings and specifications.

To get the best price on a standard product—a particular model of car, for example—consumers get competitive prices from several different vendors. It makes sense to select a vendor on the basis of price, because the specifications for the car are set and the car is available immediately from all of them.

The Design-Bid-Build method is an effort to apply this concept to the construction market, even though each construction project is unique, by creating a mostly defined product. The product (or construction of a project) is defined by a complete bid package with designs, drawings, and specifications so that qualified constructors can bid to compete primarily on the basis of low construction price.

Thus, another typical characteristic of this delivery system, highlighted during the bidding phase, is its focus on low construction cost. Other project delivery methods may focus on other project issues and needs on which the owner might place a higher value. These include speed to market, coordination of design with construction, value engineering, innovative project financing, lifecycle cost, or overall lowest project cost. The Design-Bid-Build method focuses primarily on initial low construction cost.

Design-Bid-Build with the Low Bid procurement process also creates an objective way to select constructors. For this reason, the Low Bid procurement process often is used by public entities to select constructors for government contracts. Selection of a constructor solely on the basis of low price ensures the constructors a fair chance of winning a contract. The Low Bid procurement process also ensures taxpayers of a fair system reasonably intended to produce the lowest construction cost.

Construction Phase

In this phase, the selected constructor enters into a contract with the owner that includes the drawings, specifications, and terms stated in the bid package. The constructor then completes the work in accordance with those requirements, and the owner accepts and pays for the construction. The designer may or may not continue to serve as the owner's advisor during the construction phase to perform construction administration services. The scope of a designer's construction contract administration services is defined in the owner's contract with the designer. Likewise, the designer's authority on the project site is also defined in the owner's contract with the general contractor.

The owner's contract with the designer may define construction administration services in which the designer may monitor construction progress, review progress payment applications, issue a certificate when the construction is substantially complete, and create a "punchlist" of items to be completed. The designer may inspect the work upon completion, recommend that the owner accept the work when it is complete, and issue a certificate of final completion when the work is done. In performing construction administration services, the designer typically is charged with the responsibility of interpreting the drawings and specifications without bias toward the owner or the general contractor. The designer resolves any disputes concerning the contract requirements.

During the construction phase, it is important for the owner, designer, and general contractor to bear in mind that the constructor generally is free to select the means and methods by which the work will be performed. One premise of competitive bidding on the basis of completed drawings and specifications is that the owner will accept work that complies with those requirements, regardless of the means and methods used by the constructor. That is, the owner has agreed to allow the constructor to use its ingenuity to perform the work as quickly and inexpensively as possible—to earn as large a profit as possible—so long as the work satisfies the requirements of the drawings and specifications. During the construction phase, the owner may not have a basis to object if the constructor starts using means and methods it did not anticipate.

Commissioning

Prior to occupancy, the project's systems and equipment are tested and adjusted so that they perform as designed and satisfy the project's requirements. This process should be completed before the owner's final acceptance of the project. It is uncommon in this delivery method for the general contractor to have this responsibility, though it does occur. As in other delivery methods, contract requirements for commissioning can vary widely. The actual commissioning work may be done by a specialty contractor or commissioning consultant, and the designer may or may not have a separate professional on its staff involved on behalf of the owner.

Occupancy Phase

The designer's and the constructor's performance are complete upon the owner's acceptance of the construction work. In Design-Bid-Build, the contractor rarely performs post-occupancy services.

DEFINING CHARACTERISTICS AND TYPICAL CHARACTERISTICS

Defining characteristics uniquely distinguish one delivery method from other delivery methods. The following are the defining characteristics of Design-Bid-Build:
- Design and construction are separate contracts (versus Design-Build, where the contracts are combined).
- Total construction cost is a factor in the final selection of the constructor (versus CM at-Risk, where the total construction cost is not a factor in the final selection).

A defining characteristic of this method is that the design and construction are performed independently by different professionals. Thus, a premise of this project delivery method is that the project and the owner will benefit from this division of responsibility.

This project delivery method presumes that the owner can lower the construction cost through competitive bidding. It operates on the principle that the owner will get better and less expensive construction from a qualified independent constructor. This is because the constructor is free to select its own methods to maximize its profit, as long as the minimum requirements of the drawings and specifications are satisfied. This project delivery method uses the constructor's own profit motive and ingenuity to lower construction costs for the owner and to maximize the profit of the constructor.

The typical characteristics of having a nearly complete design and the sequential approach to design followed by construction with Design-Bid-Build results in the near elimination of collaborative input from the constructor during the design. This typically requires a significant percentage of design, if not the entire design, to be complete prior to the selection of the constructor that is going to be contracted to build the project. This, by definition, virtually eliminates any collaborative input from the builder during the design phase.

Minimizing Construction Contract Price

In a genuinely competitive marketplace, the Design-Bid-Build method should produce the lowest bid price for construction in accordance with the minimum requirements of the bidding documents. For example, in a contract awarded on this basis, the constructor accepts all risk of price and cost increases except for those specifically shifted to the owner in the contract—such as change orders and unanticipated site conditions.

This is important for owners in that, once the bids are received, it provides them with solid budget information (aside from the possibility of change orders). It also provides lenders with important protections.

This method also provides constructors with important incentives to improve their profits. The constructor is allowed to keep all savings from efficiency and favorable conditions. Thus, if things go well, the constructor can significantly increase its profit on the project without any additional cost to the owner.

Another feature of Design-Bid-Build and the Low Bid procurement process is that it permits the constructor to perform only the absolute minimum work required by the contract documents. This may not provide the level of quality desired for some projects, because the Lump Sum contracting approach typically does not provide an incentive to increase quality. An owner that insists on higher quality than that called for in the contract will be liable for the constructor's additional costs.

Independent Advice

The Design-Bid-Build method has other unique characteristics. It intentionally separates the design phase from the construction phase, using a separate independent professional in each phase. This allows the owner to obtain the assistance of an expert designer whose duties are solely to the owner. It also allows the owner time to consider, modify, and finalize the design before engaging a constructor.

PROCUREMENT AND ESTABLISHING THE CONTRACT AMOUNT

Competitive Bidding

The bidding process is how a contractor competes for a contract. For public work, the process begins when an owner, as required by law, asks for bids through an advertisement in a journal of public record. No such requirement exists for private work, but private owners are advised to follow formal procedures so that all contractors are treated the same, and so that the owner receives comparable bids. The procurement process for Low Bid is typically an Invitation to Bid, and for Best Value: Total Cost, the process is typically an RFQ/RFP process. For more discussion on both of these processes, see Chapter 2.

Low Bid

The selection process most commonly used to procure Design-Bid-Build is Low Bid. With Low Bid, the owner typically hires a design team (though some owners have the ability to do so in-house) to prepare documents to be used as the basis for competitive bids. This information is used by competing firms as the basis for preparing their bids. By definition, a project using a Low Bid competition would be awarded to the lowest responsive and responsible bidder.

Most government statutes also require public opening of bids for public work. While there is no such requirement for private work, the actual preparation of bids is similar.

First, constructors obtain contract documents from the owner or designer. Usually they must pay a deposit to do so. Deposits are more common in public work than private because of the larger numbers of bidders and greater size of documents (due to regulatory requirements).

Next, general contractors determine which parts of the job they will perform themselves and which parts to let for bids from subcontractors. The decision process

is based on the constructor's current capability and on marketplace circumstances. For any project, a general contractor should determine as early as possible:
- Which work to self-perform
- Which work to subcontract
- Which work could either be self-performed or subcontracted

General contractors then contact enough subcontractors to ensure they will receive an adequate number of bids in the second and third categories. If applicable, the general contractor should let subcontractors know that some of the work for which they are bidding may ultimately be performed by the general contractor.

Many general contractors have databases that help them set cost parameters for entire projects, enabling them to prepare reliable total estimates along with breakout costs of various segments of the work. An experienced general contractor will have a good idea of what most subcontractors' prices should be. General contractors should communicate with subcontractors during the bid period to be sure that the scope of the work is understood and agreed upon and that prices will be submitted when anticipated, in time for final review and submission of a bid to the owner.

General contractors usually have "plan rooms" for the convenience of subcontractors and suppliers. These help preclude the need for each bidder to obtain a set of documents and pay the deposit fee. General contractors may also issue memoranda to subcontractors with points of information that may be crucial to their bids.

Recently, the Internet and electronic plan rooms have become common means of distributing bidding packages for larger projects. A project website may be established where the owner posts the bid package for competing general contractors and subcontractors to download. Such project websites also may list competing constructors for the information of subcontractors and suppliers.

General contractors benefit from ongoing good relations with subcontractors. Subcontractors are not required to provide identical bids to all parties and tend to give better prices to general contractors that:
- Maintain open communication during the bid period
- Are always straightforward with subcontractors, refraining from bid peddling or bid shopping
- Manage projects efficiently
- Administer the subcontracts fairly
- Pay on time

Best Value: Total Cost

A second selection option to procure Design-Bid-Build is Best Value: Total Cost. With a Best Value: Total Cost selection, the owner makes a trade-off between price considerations and the other elements of the proposal. Many states have statutory laws that prescribe the manners in which capital projects can be procured. Some states refer to the Best Value: Total Cost selection process as Competitive Sealed Proposal (CSP) or some variation of this term.

After weighing all the factors, the owner determines which proposal offers the owner the best value in terms of price versus other factors. For example, the owner may select the firm that offers the most highly rated technical proposal if the owner determines that the price of that proposal is reasonable. On the other hand, an owner may select a lower-rated firm if the owner decides that the highest-rated offer comes at too high a price.

The owner may initially select several firms and then ask them to submit competitive proposals. The request usually is by a Request for Proposals (RFP) that describes the owner's requirements. Competitive negotiation is a means of selecting a firm based on a review of technical and price proposals. The firms compete on the basis of qualifications, experience, price, and possibly other factors, each weighted according to the owner's priorities. The owner may then enter into negotiations with one or more competing firms to select one firm for the project.

BASIS OF REIMBURSEMENT OPTIONS

As previously discussed, the Design-Bid-Build method typically uses Lump Sum pricing for the construction contract. Other pricing mechanisms, described in this section, are sometimes included to provide flexibility for certain items of work.

Alternates, Substitutions, and Unit Prices

Alternates, substitutions, and unit prices are means of inserting optional and conditional items into Lump Sum competitively bid projects. An owner that allows substitutions allows bidders to offer materials or work that may be better or less expensive than those specified.

Ideally, there would be few or none of these optional items. The best process would produce clear determination by owners and designers of all parts of the job. The documents would be completed accordingly, and the bidding would be simplified. However, in competitive bidding, owners like to hedge their bets by using optional extras to arrive at acceptable base prices plus itemized alternate costs.

An "alternate" is a separately priced item on a bid form that the owner, in its discretion, may include in the contract. Owners use alternates, particularly when there are budget concerns, to price non-critical items such as built-in furniture, carpets, and extra lighting fixtures, or to price upgraded material such as better quality curtain wall components, mechanical systems, doors, or wall finishes. Occasionally, deductive alternates are also used, such as when high quality systems are especially desired but lower quality will be accepted if the bids make it necessary. There is ongoing debate about the efficacy of deductive versus additive alternates, with most designers favoring the additive variety for better cost control. What most agree on is that there should *not* be a mix of both additive and deductive alternates because of the potential for confusion. In addition, it is important that the alternates be taken in sequential order and that the potential bidders be informed of the order in which the alternates will be taken to prevent "cherry picking" and other game-playing with the bidders.

Excessive use of alternates and unit prices can cause mistakes that increase costs. If the selection of certain options changes the low bidder, alternates may also set the stage for bid protests, which are allowed on public work in some jurisdictions. When alternates and unit prices are used, they should be kept to a reasonable minimum and should be clearly defined to allow for similar bidding by all competitors.

Unit prices are used to identify the costs of materials or activities when actual quantities can be estimated only prior to construction. Paying for work by the unit may minimize the need for contingencies to cover increased or decreased quantities. Unit prices are frequently shown for extra excavation and concrete work in case of soil problems not fully covered by contract documents. The objective is to know in advance the cost of labor, material, overhead, and profit for each extra cubic yard of soil removed or concrete placed. Unit prices may also be used for flooring, drywall, or any other readily described material with which variations in quantities may occur.

Allowances

Allowances are used for pricing materials or items not fully described in the specifications and which may be subject to later selection by the owner or designer. Examples may include brick, cabinetry, and carpeting. The quantities and configurations of materials are shown on the drawings, but the exact color or other characteristics will be chosen later. So an allowance price, representing the preferred quality level, is stated in the contract documents for all bidders to use. The overall contractual price is then adjusted when the selection is made based on the actual cost of the selected material. If actual price of the selected item is greater or less than the allowance, the contract price is adjusted appropriately.

ROLES AND RESPONSIBILITIES

The Owner

In the Design-Bid-Build method, the owner has separate contracts with the designer and the constructor. Those two contracts are governed by very different standards, and this can cause the owner to feel caught in the middle.

When the owner issues the bidding package to the constructor, the owner impliedly warrants that the design is correct and the specifications are reasonably sufficient for the constructor to follow and use to complete the project. When the owner issues the bid package to the competing constructors, the owner asks the constructors to assume that the package is correct and that they need not include contingencies for errors or problems with the design or specifications. If the drawings and specifications contain errors that cause the constructor to incur extra costs, the owner is liable for those extra costs. Thus, the owner is liable to the constructor if the constructor proves that the design contained errors and that those errors caused extra costs.

Although the owner warrants the design and specifications to the constructor, the designer does not warrant the design and specifications to the owner. Rather, the designer represents to the owner that the design was prepared with the degree of care and skill exercised by the architectural or engineering profession at large. If the designer makes a design error that costs the owner damages, the designer will be liable to the owner only if the error occurred because the designer failed to perform in accordance with the standard of care and skill applicable to the profession at large.

There are design errors that occur even though the designer performed in accordance with the requisite degree of care and skill. In those instances, the owner may be liable to the constructor, but the designer will not be liable to the owner. This leaves the owner caught in the middle. Some owners consider this to be a drawback of Design-Bid-Build. Other project delivery systems address this problem for the owner. The Design-Build method solves this problem by creating a single point of responsibility for both design and construction. The CM at-Risk method helps to guard against this problem by bringing in expert constructor assistance during the design phase to minimize the chance of error.

In the Design-Bid-Build method, the owner delegates the design to the designer and the construction to the constructor. That does not mean that the owner has no duties. The owner's duties are especially important because of the low competitive bidding typically used to select the constructor.

Some of the owner's most important duties are in the bidding phase. Although the designer may advise the owner about the bids received, only the owner can accept a bid and select a constructor.

The bidding documents tell constructors how the owner will select the constructor. Generally, the owner will award a contract to the responsible qualified constructor that submits the lowest lump sum price to complete the work in accordance with the contract documents. In public contracts, the owner must follow through and choose the constructor by applying those criteria to comply with statutes, regulations, and the terms of the bidding documents. Private owners have more latitude to depart from the selection criteria in the bidding documents because a constructor usually cannot force a private owner to award a contract in accordance with the bidding documents. But a private owner will lose credibility with competing constructors if it fails to follow the requirements of the bidding documents. That would prevent that owner from attracting vigorous competition in the future. Constructors would not have confidence that they may receive a contract even if they are the low bidder.

During the design phase, the owner is responsible for providing its requirements to the designer and for responding to the designer's submissions in a timely manner. Similarly, during the construction phase, the owner's duties include timely responses to the constructor's submittals, Requests for Information, and proposed changes and claims. In addition, the owner is responsible for correctly interpreting the requirements of the contract, drawings, and specifications. The owner must permit the constructor the freedom to perform the work using its own means and methods without improper interference.

The Designer

The designer's responsibilities are to the owner. The designer has a contractual and professional relationship with the owner and no contractual relationship with the constructor.

The designer's responsibility is to create a design that meets the owner's needs, is structurally sound, and complies with all applicable requirements of building codes and other government requirements. The designer owes the owner two types of duties—duties created by a professional standard of care expected of designers or engineers and a contractual duty established by the contract between the designer and the owner.

The designer's professional duty of care is to perform with the same degree of skill and care as may be expected of any member of the architectural or engineering profession. That professional duty of care is established by the profession itself, not by the government or by a contract.

The designer also must perform design services in accordance with the requirements of its contract with the owner. The contract may impose requirements concerning a schedule, cost, or approvals. These contractual duties may be in addition to the designer's professional standard of skill and care.

The General Contractor

In the Design-Bid-Build method, the general contractor has a contract only with the owner. The constructor has no contract with the designer. The general contractor's responsibility is to comply with the requirements of the contract with the owner.

It is important to note that the constructor's obligation is to satisfy the minimum requirements of the drawings and specifications. In the bidding process, the owner asks for the lowest possible price to perform only those things that are absolutely required by the drawings and specifications. Thus, the constructor is obligated only to satisfy those minimum requirements. Of course, the owner is always free to require additional performance by change order.

A general contractor will ordinarily have a direct contract with the owner to perform the entire project. The general contractor accepts the risk of completing the project within the lump sum price and is free to do so by its own means and methods.

Specialty Contractors and Suppliers

The general contractor often will use specialty contractors to perform portions of the work. These specialty contractors enter into subcontracts with the general contractor and have no relationship with either the owner or the designer. They are responsible only to the general contractor. The general contractor remains responsible for the work even when subcontractors perform it. The general contractor's contract covers all the work.

These contractual arrangements greatly affect decisions that must be made during performance of the construction work. The general contractor accepts direction from the owner. The designer may direct the general contractor only as authorized by the owner (and as provided in the general contractor's contract with the owner). It is up to the general contractor to communicate with its subcontractors; the owner and the designer are seldom authorized to give direction to subcontractors, except through the general contractor.

PROJECT DELIVERY CONSIDERATIONS

In Chapter 6, basic project delivery considerations were discussed along with risk issues common to all projects and various project delivery methods. Some vary from one project delivery method to another, while others remain the same. This section follows the same format as Chapter 6 and discusses those topics that are different for this project delivery method. Readers should review Chapter 6 for other basic considerations not discussed here.

Building Information Modeling (BIM)

The use of Building Information Modeling to improve the planning and design process can be valuable on Design-Bid-Build projects. There is potential benefit to improving the efficiency of the design process and providing benefits such as offering 3D visualization to users early in the process. Models can also be of great value to the eventual successful contractor during bidding and construction if the model is shared.

Model-enhanced collaboration between the primary parties, the design team, the contractor, and the owner is not as much of an advantage with Design-Bid-Build since the contractor is not engaged during planning and design. Lack of contractor involvement, however, does not preclude BIM use as a tool on Design-Bid-Build projects to enhance collaboration between the owner and the team.

Until the industry better understands the risks of using BIM, the contracts and insurance products addressing these risks will likely continue to be in flux. For example, digital models are more precise than traditional drawings, and there is less room for error. Contractors are able to compare designs more quickly and thoroughly, making it easier to identify design changes and possibly design errors.

ConsensusDOCS 301, "Building Information Modeling (BIM) Addendum," addresses the team's responsibilities as they relate to the model. The addendum was designed with the intention that it would work with any project delivery model, including Design-Bid-Build. Model sharing and the ability to rely on the information in the model with the Design-Bid-Build project delivery method are still evolving. In the case of Design-Bid-Build, where the contractor is relying on the information provided by the owner as the basis for its bid, all parties are still evaluating the trade-offs of sharing the full Building Information Models against the loss of the benefits from not sharing the information.

Changes

The owner can make changes during the construction phase, but because of the Lump Sum price structure, such changes may have financial consequences. The owner has agreed to accept only what is specified in the contract documents, and the constructor has given the owner its best price to perform only the work specified. When the owner makes changes to the work, that fundamental bargain is altered. Perhaps, for this reason, there have been more changes and disputes in the Design-Bid-Build project delivery system than in some others.

Claims and Disputes

Claims and disputes also may occur more frequently in this delivery system. One reason is that selecting the constructor on the basis of low Lump Sum price places tremendous pressure on bidders to bid only the minimum amount of work required by the contract documents. A claim or dispute may arise if an owner or designer disagrees with the constructor's interpretation of the contract requirements.

In this delivery system, the constructor must constantly be mindful of construction costs and productivity to manage performance within the contract amount. The constructor may notify the owner of a potential claim if its productivity or progress is impeded in an unanticipated way. This, too, may lead to more claims and disputes.

Change requests, claims, and disputes must be managed by the owner, leading to a higher cost of contract administration than in some other delivery systems.

Partnering/Collaboration

Partnering among the owner, constructor, and designer during the construction phase can help expedite project completion. Partnering is always possible and prudent, and it may be implemented with the Design-Bid-Build method. However, it may be more difficult to implement partnering successfully on a Design-Bid-Build project. For example, the constructor is not involved in the design phase and thus will not perform any constructability or value engineering reviews prior to setting the contract price. The emphasis on low price may also strain partnering if several disputes arise on the project.

Dispute Resolution Alternatives

All dispute resolution alternatives are available in this delivery method. The following are dispute avoidance and resolution processes:

1. An early meeting focusing on areas of possible misunderstanding. All parties identify questionable details, specifications clauses, site conditions, and unknowns and seek clarification and a checklist of information needs. A list of "watch outs" can develop from this.
2. "Problem seeking" sessions scheduled at weekly meetings. All parties try to envision what might go wrong in the next week, the next month, etc.
3. Parties agree to negotiate when problems do arise. A one-page agenda for such negotiation may be created to ensure that all aspects of problems are examined.
4. If these techniques are not successful, more formal procedures are required:
   - Mediation
   - Arbitration
   - Dispute Review Board

Dispute Avoidance/Management

As discussed in Chapter 6, communication is essential to avoiding disputes and resolving them at an early stage. This is especially important on Design-Bid-Build projects during contract administration. Typical dispute avoidance techniques on Design-Bid-Build projects during the construction phase include weekly meetings with representatives of the owner, the designer, and the general contractor, often followed by meetings between the general contractor and its specialty contractors.

Design Phases

Sources of Design Information

In the Design-Bid-Build method, the constructor is not selected until after the design and construction documents are complete. Thus, the constructor is not involved in the design process, as distinguished from Design-Build and most CM at-Risk methods.

Design Process

The design process is typically complete before bidding and selection of the constructor. This distinguishes the Design-Bid-Build method from Design-Build and CM-at-Risk.

Fast-Tracking

Fast-tracking is a means of accelerating project delivery to shorten the time from initiation of the design to completion of construction. To minimize overall project design and construction time, construction starts before the design is complete.

One of the characteristics of the Design-Bid-Build method is that it results in a longer overall project delivery time than some other project delivery systems. It generally takes longer to obtain a complete package of design and bidding documents than it does to award a Design-Build or Construction Management at-Risk contract. This may be partially offset by the use of multiple prime contractors performing different phases of the project (i.e., site work, foundations, etc.).

Fast-tracking is not possible in the Design-Bid-Build project delivery system unless multiple prime contracts are awarded. In this delivery system, the design must be 100% complete before the owner solicits bids, which lengthens overall project time compared to some other systems.

This longer time period can be beneficial to owners that want to finalize the project before engaging and becoming liable to a constructor. Conversely, it can be a drawback to an owner that needs to use the structure or project as quickly as possible.

Indemnification/Hold Harmless Clauses

There are no major differences in how indemnification/hold harmless clauses are managed on a Design-Bid-Build project, as compared to Design-Build or CM at-Risk. Further, it can be hard for the owner to have confidence that the design is adhering to the budget until the design is 100% complete and bids are received.

Insurance

There are no major differences in how insurance issues are managed on a Design-Bid-Build project, as compared to Design-Build or CM at-Risk.

Lean Construction

Lean construction, or the concept of eliminating waste, does not fundamentally change regardless of the project delivery method. However, the ability to integrate lean principles across the entire project and not just within portions of the project team is significantly enhanced by the existence of an open-book collaborative environment.

On Design-Bid-Build projects, the ability to integrate may be limited, but this delivery method by no means eliminates the ability of the owner and the design team to implement lean practices both within their own organizations as well in the execution of the design process. The contractor on a Design-Bid-Build project is also fully able to implement lean practices both within its organization as well as in the field on the construction project. The opportunity to increase productivity and improve efficiency is always available.

Licensing

Licensing usually is not a problem in a Design-Bid-Build project because Design-Bid-Build is the norm anticipated in the licensing laws in the states. The designer and engineer must be licensed. Many states license general contractors and/or specialty subcontractors. Normally firms already have the necessary licenses. While licensing can be a problem in some project delivery methods, it usually is not an issue in Design-Bid-Build.

Lien Waivers

There are no substantive differences in how lien waivers are managed on a Design-Bid-Build project as compared to Design-Build or CM at-Risk.

Prequalification

Prequalification is routine and relatively simple. Most private owners limit bidding to those constructors that have provided good service previously or that come well recommended by designers or other owners. Prequalification can be advantageous to all parties:
- The owner receives bids from only reliable, proven constructors.
- The designers, which usually help guide the prequalification process, recommend reliable constructors with which they could work effectively.
- The constructor knows, before investing the time and money to prepare a bid, whether there is a reasonable prospect of being selected.

A dilemma in prequalification is the possibility of excluding constructors that may be cost-competitive and perform quality work but do not yet have extensive track records. While wanting good quality and reliability, every owner also desires the best possible price. Consequently, good judgment may lead to including an up-and-coming constructor on the bid list. In any case, after once prequalifying constructors for a bid list, the owner should accept the lowest and best proposal and not unfairly qualify a contractor after the bid.

It is an ill-advised practice to reject a low bid after a prequalification process. It is unfair and unethical to expect a constructor to expend the time and effort to prepare a winning bid and then exclude that constructor for something that should have been determined by prequalification screening. Prequalification should be done early enough so as not to delay the bidding process.

In prequalification, owners and designers should realize the limits of any screening process. While the process may ensure the selection of qualified general contractors, it does not ensure the quality of subcontractors. On commercial and institutional projects, much of the work is done by subcontractors—including work in which quality is critical—from erection of structural steel to finishes. While it is expected that qualified general contractors will retain qualified subcontractors, those subcontractors are usually selected on the basis of price. General contractors may require bonds of certain subcontractors but may need to absorb the expenses of doing so. The owner has no contracts with those subcontractors, so it is incumbent upon the general contractor to be responsible for the entire project. In private prequalifications, general contractors may be asked to list a group of subcontractors from which final choices would be made. This is generally not allowed in public work because it could be viewed as an exclusionary practice. Occasionally in public work, however, a list of subcontractors is required by the owner soon after identifying the low bidder. The owner has the right to reject a subcontractor if the owner agrees to pay the constructor the difference in costs, if any, of selecting a replacement subcontractor.

Some private owners' groups have developed their own prequalification forms, procedures, and databases to assist both owners and constructors in streamlining the qualification process. Does prequalification increase the costs for owners by omitting possible low bidders? On projects of less complexity that may attract many bidders, the ultimate price may be lower without prequalification. Experience shows, though, that prequalification procedures provide better constructors that are adequately capitalized. This leads to projects with fewer disputes, better completion times, and fewer defaults.

Retainage

There are no substantive differences in how retainage issues are managed on a Design-Bid-Build project as compared to Design-Build or CM at-Risk.

Safety

There are no major differences in how safety issues are managed on a Design-Bid-Build project as compared to Design-Build or CM at-Risk.

Standard Forms of Agreements

There are a number of standard forms of agreement available for the Design-Bid-Build delivery system. Among the most well-known are the ConsensusDOCS 200, "Standard Agreement and General Conditions Between Owner and Constructor (Lump Sum)," and the ConsensusDOCS 205, "Standard Short Form Agreement Between Owner and Constructor (Lump Sum)." Both documents present a comprehensive agreement. The ConsensusDOCS 200 is the standard owner/constructor agreement, for use under the traditional general contracting Design-Bid-Build delivery method. Unlike the comparable AIA Contract Documents, which incorporate a separate set of general conditions (the AIA Document A201) by reference, the ConsensusDOCS 200 is a stand-alone document. Also unlike the AIA Document A201 (which inserts the project architect between the owner and the contractor for purposes of most communications), the ConsensusDOCS 200 encourages direct communications between the owner and constructor.

For public work, most government entities have developed their own contract forms, which may or may not be based on one of the standard industry agreements. When pursuing public work, industry participants are cautioned to carefully review the agreements before entering into a contract for services.

Subcontracts

One of the key differences in Design-Bid-Build and the "alternative" project delivery methods is the way that subcontractors are selected. In the other delivery methods, there may be an opportunity for the owner to have input in the selection of subcontractors. This is not the case with Design-Bid-Build, at least as it is defined in this book. In most circumstances, the selection of the various trade or subcontracts is left solely to the general contractor and is based almost exclusively on cost. The general contractor assumes full responsibility to the owner for the proper performance of all work, whether it is performed by its own employees or those of a subcontractor.

Surety Bonds and Other Forms of Security for Performance

Surety bonding tends to go hand-in-hand with Design-Bid-Build Lump Sum contracts. Most public entities are required by statute to have payment and performance bonds on public construction contracts. Therefore, to bid for public work, construction companies must satisfy the requirements of surety companies.

The typical procedure is to have a sequence of bonds purchased by the constructors selected to execute projects. These are:

- Bid bond (usually a percentage of the contract sum)
- Performance bond
- Labor and material payment bond

The bid bond is submitted by all competing firms, whereas the payment and performance bonds are typically submitted by the winning constructor upon award of the contract. The objective of all construction-related bonding is to mitigate the risk of work not being successfully completed. By agreeing to provide a bond, the surety company has taken on the responsibility for completing the project, should the constructor default, fail, or go bankrupt. Surety companies and agents carefully scrutinize candidates for bonds through the "three Cs" of capital, capacity, and character. Bonding ability represents a limited type of constructor qualification.

Private owners using Lump Sum contracting may or may not choose to bond their constructors. Bonding adds a level of assurance, but it also adds about 1% to the costs of projects. Corporations that carefully prequalify constructors usually do not require bonds. However, religious institutions, hospitals, and other private organizations frequently do require bonds because default would have a serious impact on their constituencies.

Sustainability

The difference of Design-Bid-Build on green building projects is that the contractor is typically not involved in the project until after the design is complete. It is difficult, after bidding on a completed design, to incorporate the contractor's ideas for reducing waste and increasing building efficiency during its operation. The project's green requirements must be stated in the contract documents issued to the bidders. These include how the contractor is required to handle construction waste, material storage and protection, indoor air quality during construction, and any documentation and tracking required to support any green certification.

Green requirements are often not exclusively the responsibility of the contractor and take close cooperation and communication among the entire team. The industry is still trying to fully understand the risks associated with green construction. For example, if a project is billed as achieving a certain third party's level of certification but fails to do so, whose responsibility is this? Is this failure the designer's or the contractor's responsibility? Does the owner have to take some responsibility? This is an area that many in the industry, particularly sureties and insurance companies that serve the construction industry, are watching closely.

The recent research, *Sustainable, High Performance Projects and Project Delivery Methods, A State-of-Practice Report*, September, 2009, sponsored by the Charles Pankow Foundation and The Design-Build Institute of America, examined the link between sustainability and project delivery. It looked at the likelihood of achieving or exceeding the original goal established for LEED® rating based on both the delivery method and the procurement type. The results depicted the metric as a percentage of projects that achieved or exceeded their original LEED goal; Design-Bid-Build was the lowest at 77%. Measuring the impact the procurement process had on achieving sustainability, Low Bid was the lowest at 78%.

This research seemed to confirm that there is a direct correlation between the delivery method and the procurement process with the ability to maximize sustainability. The lack of collaboration and transparency resulting from Low Bid selection and Fixed Price contracts is most likely a significant contributor to these results.

For a more complete discussion on green building, consult *Contractor's Guide to Green Building Construction*, published by AGC of America.

LESSONS LEARNED

The keys to successful Design-Bid-Build projects are straightforward:
- Because the quality of the documents is so critical in the Design-Bid-Build delivery system, owners should select and pay for capable designers, and designers must produce thorough, clear documents.
- Prequalification is important. Owners should employ appropriate prequalification where legally permitted, while ensuring that it is administered fairly and in the best interest of taxpayers.
- Open communication can overcome many problems. All parties need to understand the goals of the other parties and make special efforts to avoid serious disputes. The best strategy is to maintain continuous communication. The design representative needs to be on the job regularly to respond to the constructor's questions.
- Partnering has proven to be very effective in relieving many of the problems related to Lump Sum contracting. The partnering process, when well done, produces empathy among the parties and creates mutual understanding of what is required to complete the project to the satisfaction of all. It has greatly reduced disputes, formal claims, and litigation.
- Closely related to open communication and partnering is early negotiation of disputes. It is important to have a dispute resolution process in place that is quicker and more effective than arbitration or litigation. The process may be described in the contract, or it may be extra-contractual.

FUTURE TRENDS

The Lump Sum competitive bid system will remain popular in a large portion of public and private work. This system functions well when a project has clear parameters, and when sufficient time exists to prepare good documents and execute construction. It is perceived as the "safe" way for public agencies to contract for most construction. For large projects, such as prisons, convention centers, and air terminals, public agencies will undoubtedly also consider the Design-Build and Construction Management at-Risk delivery systems, but Design-Bid-Build can work on such projects if the owner allows ample time for programming and document preparation and if resources are available to manage the project.

Partnering and alternative dispute resolution will become even more prominent in Lump Sum contracts and will be encouraged by many owners as ways to avoid costly disputes and delays. Partnering is already being included in many public sector project solicitations.

The use of electronic procedures will continue to have a major impact on the construction industry. The use of "e-bidding," the process of electronically submitting a single responsive and responsible bid, will continue to increase because of the potential gains in efficiency. However, it may also serve to create more pressure on bid day. E-bidding is significantly different from, and should not be confused with, the process of "e-auctioning," which assumes that multiple bids will be placed by competing constructors up until a specified time limit.

The subject of project delivery is a field that is constantly evolving. For updated information and links to some of the latest information, see the Project Delivery section of AGC of America's website at: http://www.agc.org/projectdelivery.

Self Test

1. Design-Bid-Build is a:
   a. Construction project delivery method
   b. Project management system
   c. Method for ensuring the selection of the best constructor for the project

2. Defining characteristics for Design-Bid-Build are:
   a. Separate contracts with the designer and the constructor
   b. The only criterion for final selection is lowest total construction cost
   c. That a firm is paid a fee to provide a design service
   d. Both a and b

3. A "responsive bid" is:
   a. Limited to public construction projects and is never used in private projects
   b. Generally received by electronic media and after the closing time for bids
   c. An unequivocal offer to do everything required by the contract documents without exception

4. An "alternate" is:
   a. A separate system for providing mechanical equipment
   b. A separately priced item on a bid form that the owner, in its discretion, may include in the contract
   c. An opportunity for an owner to get work performed at no additional cost

5. From an owner's point of view, the most important aspect of the Spearin Doctrine is that:
   a. The constructor has access to legal counsel without cost
   b. The designer assumes the full responsibility for any errors in construction
   c. The owner assumes full responsibility for the performance of the designer

6. A common difference in Design-Bid-Build from the other delivery methods is:
   a. The designer has complete control of safety on the site
   b. The constructor has an incentive to increase the cost of the work beyond the contract price
   c. The constructor is typically not involved during the design phase

DESIGN-BID-BUILD

Case Study

The following is an example of a typical project. Evaluate the circumstances described and recommend how to proceed. Questions are offered for group discussion. Be prepared to explain and defend your recommendations.

A growing suburb of a large metropolitan city needed a new elementary school serving grades K–5. It had a project budget of $7.5 million for site, construction, fees, and related costs. State law required that the project be bid using Design-Bid-Build.

A local architect was hired and produced a design in a quick four months without any big surprises. The project was advertised and bid for the statutorily required period. Eleven general contractors purchased plans and began assembling their bids. For a variety of reasons, a number of contractors dropped out of the competition. The architect, who was managing the process, began to worry that not enough contractors were going to submit bids.

Bids were received at noon on the advertised date. A total of four bids were submitted for general construction. The bids were opened, immediately checked for responsiveness, and then read aloud. A clerk entered the bids onto a bid tabulation sheet. All bidders were determined to be responsive. Highlights from the bidding were:

The four general construction bids ranged from $6,222,000 to $7,089,000, approximately a 10% spread.

- The submitted bids were:

    General Contractor #1 . . . . $ 6,222,000
    General Contractor #2 . . . . $ 6,349,000
    General Contractor #3 . . . . $ 6,978,000
    General Contractor #4 . . . . $ 7,089,000

    From the low bidder, five of eight submitted alternates were accepted:
    Five alternates . . . . $ 472,500
    Note: The total of these five alternates from the second lowest bidder was $363,300.

    Related costs:
    Property. . . . . $ 485,500
    Design fees . . . . $ 257,500

Total costs at signing of contracts . . . . $ 7,437,500

This amount was within the original budget, so the city awarded the contract to General Contractor #1. Upon submission of a list of subcontractors, a time schedule, a schedule of values, and other required submittals, contracts were signed. The contract completion date was 10 months after contract execution, and there were no liquidated damages. The job proceeded slowly with a few issues:

- The fire inspector required a change in the number of exit signs after contracts were signed, causing an $11,520 change order.
- An error on the topographic survey provided to the contractor during the bidding process required an additional amount of fill material to be hauled in, resulting in a $30,780 change order.
- The owner decided to upgrade wiring for technology in the classrooms, causing a change order of $172,700.
- The owner was forced to add additional electrical work. The design team had left out electrical service to audio visual equipment that was being furnished by the owner and installed by the contractor. This led to a $61,475 change order.
- After the bids were turned in, the low millwork subcontractor withdrew its bid because it found a significant mistake in its estimate. The general contractor decided to pay the additional cost to go to the second bidder. No cost change was given.
- Several minor changes, such as partition locations and door openings, were executed without requests for extra payment.
- The constructor requested a change order for special waterproofing that he claimed was not covered by the contract documents. The owner rejected the request, saying that the waterproofing was clearly implied by the documents, and ordered work to proceed, including the flashing. The constructor sent a letter citing its position (request for extra money) and continued work.
- The owner agreed to pay the designer an additional $20,000 to incorporate all of the changes on the drawings and to provide more onsite assistance. The school was completed four weeks behind schedule, but the schedule did allow the school employees to occupy the building during final construction so they could prepare the school for the students. The punchlist consisted of 250 items, which again caused coordination problems.

The total project cost became:
At conclusion of bidding	$7,437,500
Total of all change orders, extra costs	+ 516,561
	= $7,954,061

At the dedication ceremony, the owner expressed satisfaction with the school building but dismay that the project ended up over its original $7.5 million budget. He did not seem to feel the reasons for this were entirely caused by the owner.

DESIGN-BID-BUILD

DISCUSSION ISSUES:

1. Do you think this project was typical of a Design-Bid-Build project? Why?

2. Why do you think some of the contractors dropped out during the bidding process?

3. What do the results of the four submitted bids indicate to you? Explain why you think it was or was not a "good bid."

4. Does the difference in the amount between any of the bidders mean anything?

5. Besides being responsible for the design, the architect had other roles on this project. What were they?

6. Was this a good application of the Design-Bid-Build delivery method? Is there additional information you need to answer this question? If so, what would it be?

7. Did the Spearin Doctrine, highlighting the owner's responsibility for the architect's performance, come into play on this project?

8. What is your reaction to the owner's thoughts at the end of the project?

9. What thoughts do you have about the low millwork contractor withdrawing its bid to the general contractor after bidding? Should the owner have had to pay the extra costs to use the next lowest bidder?

CHAPTER EIGHT

CONSTRUCTION MANAGEMENT AT-RISK

Introduction

Definitions in This Project Delivery System
- Conceptual Estimating
- Outline Specification
- Design Phase Contingency
- Construction Phase and Project Contingencies
- Savings
- Design-Assist Contractors

Delivery Method Overview/Structure
- Programming/Predesign Phase
- Design Phase
  - Schematic Documents
  - Design Documents
  - Construction Documents
- Bidding Phase
- Construction Phase
- Commissioning
- Occupancy Phase

Defining Characteristics and Typical Characteristics
- Independent Advice

Procurement and Establishing Contract Amount
- Procuring Construction Management at-Risk Services
  - Qualifications Based Selection
  - Best Value: Fees
- Timing of Establishing the Contract Amount
- Selecting the CM at-Risk Early

Basis of Reimbursement Options
- Guaranteed Maximum Price
- Cost-Plus a Fixed Fee
- Lump Sum

CONSTRUCTION MANAGEMENT AT-RISK

Roles and Responsibilities
- The Owner
- The Designer
- The Constructor
- Specialty Contractors and Suppliers

Project Delivery Considerations
- Building Information Modeling (BIM)
- Changes
- Claims and Disputes
  - Partnering/Collaboration
  - Dispute Resolution Alternatives
  - Dispute Avoidance/Management
- Design Phases
  - Sources of Design Information
  - Design Process
- Fast-Tracking
- Indemnification/Hold Harmless Clauses
- Insurance
- Lean Construction
- Licensing
  - Architect/Engineer Licensing Requirements
  - Constructor Licensing Requirements
- Lien Waivers
- Prequalification
- Retainage
- Safety
- Standard Forms of Agreements
- Subcontracts
- Surety Bonds and Other Forms of Security for Performance
- Sustainability

Lessons Learned

Future Trends

Self Test

Case Study

INTRODUCTION

Construction Management at-Risk (CM at-Risk) is a relatively new project delivery system that combines the skills and services of two different types of construction firms: the agent construction manager (CM) and the traditional general contractor (GC). By the 1970s, many owners did not feel they were getting the best use or value out of hiring these two different types of firms on projects, so they started looking for a better delivery system.

What has evolved is the CM at-Risk delivery method. In this method, the owner has separate contracts with the CM at-risk and the designer. The constructor, referred to as the CM at-risk, holds the trade contracts and takes responsibility for the performance of the work. The CM at-risk typically provides essential preconstruction services and guarantees the construction costs and schedule. The CM at-risk serves as the general contractor assuming the risk of the performance, either by its own crews or by specialty contractors and suppliers. Since this concept evolved in many different areas around the country simultaneously, it has many names that essentially mean the same thing. CM/GC, GC/CM, CMc, and CM at-Risk all are substantially the same, with minor variations on a regional basis.

The growth of both CM at-Risk and Design-Build has occurred in large part to help owners deliver their projects in shorter timeframes than were common with the Design-Bid-Build method. This led to the practice of "fast-tracking" projects by beginning construction while some design elements were not yet complete. CM at-Risk, like Design-Build, facilitates fast-tracking.

The terms "construction manager" and "CM" are some of the most confusing because they are used so differently from place to place. We can eliminate most of that confusion just by clarifying the context in which the term is being used. If the terms "construction manager" or "CM" are used in the context of a discussion about project *management* methods, then the CM being referred to is most likely an agent CM. If the terms "construction manager" or "CM" are used in the context of a discussion about project *delivery* methods, then the CM being referred to is most likely a *CM at-risk*. If the term "construction manager" is mentioned, take a moment to clarify the context—management or delivery. Ask which CM someone is referring to, agency or at-Risk? When either term is used in this chapter, it refers to CM at-Risk, the project delivery method. (For more information on agency CM, see Chapter 5.) The contractor in CM at-Risk is often referred to as the "CM at-risk," or the contractor.

CM at-Risk can be procured with either Best Value: Fees or Qualifications Based Selection (QBS). (If procured with Low Bid or Best Value: Total Cost, based on the definitions provided in Chapter 2, then the delivery method is Design-Bid-Build and not CM at-Risk.) As more owners have recognized CM at-Risk as professional service, it has become increasingly common to select a CM at-risk with Qualifications Based Selection.

DEFINITIONS IN THIS PROJECT DELIVERY SYSTEM

The following definitions are specific to this delivery system. They would also apply in other systems where preconstruction services are used and/or where the work is acquired on a Best Value: Fees or Qualifications Based Selection basis.

Conceptual Estimating

Conceptual estimating is a requirement of companies offering preconstruction services. An estimator compiles a relatively detailed estimate of anticipated costs by considering a historical database of similar projects. The estimator may have very little design input, other than basic schematic drawings. Frequently, the estimator will create an "outline specification" to define how the estimate was completed and what it includes and excludes.

Outline Specification

Early in the design process, the designer often has not had time to develop a set of specifications for the project. The initial drawings of the project are usually basic outline floor plans, simplified elevations, basic bridge or highway flow diagrams, and possibly a site plan. To define the pricing, the estimator must create a simple specification. At this stage, construction estimates should be based on more of a systems analysis approach, as opposed to the form and format that will be used for the final project specifications. Consequently, although the final plans and specifications will most likely follow the format of the CSI (Construction Specifications Institute) MasterFormat™, a system such as the CSI Uniformat II™ is more useful at this time. The estimates should be prepared so that the transition from a systems approach to the MasterFormat format is easily tracked.

Design Phase Contingency

The amount included in an estimate to represent the yet-to-be-detailed or defined portions of the contract documents is called a design phase contingency. It is identified during the initial estimates and is included in all budgets and estimates during the project. As the documents become more defined and costs are further identified (and shifted to the cost of the work or eliminated), the design phase contingency can be decreased.

Construction Phase and Project Contingencies

As the project moves into the construction phase, a construction phase contingency is usually identified and tracked separately from an owner's project contingency. The construction phase contingency is used to adjust for minor changes in the work, changes in economic conditions, or unanticipated problems. The project contingency is generally held by the owner and is used to account for major problems such as unforeseen subsurface conditions and scope changes.

Savings

Also evolving is the concept of "risk sharing" between the owner and CM at-risk. Often the two enter into an agreement to share any savings generated by bringing the project in under the Guaranteed Maximum Price. The purpose for this is to create a common goal, encourage all parties to seek timely decisions, and give the CM at-risk an incentive to be as economical as possible in completing the project.

Sharing savings between the owner and the CM at-risk enables the parties to capitalize on performance variables that were unrecognized at the time of contract information. There are numerous ways to structure a shared savings provision, although the public owner typically receives the larger share of any savings.

As an alternative to saving, other performance-based incentives such as "Incentive Award Fees" and "Satisfaction Fees" are used to further align the team's goals. Many public and private owners are uncomfortable with the concept of shared savings, feeling that it results in the CM at-risk furthering its own profits at the expense of quality in the project, but the use of these performance-based incentives has been found effective for both parties and allows greater collaboration and higher quality projects.

The Satisfaction Fee is developed during the negotiations of the project. The owner, working with the CM at-risk, places a negotiated amount of money aside as a Satisfaction Fee. This can be developed in any number of ways, but the amount should be significant enough to motivate both parties to participate fully in the process. Once the amount is established, the following is an example of how this process might work:

- Quarterly meetings are held throughout the life of the project and for one quarter past substantial completion. In these quarterly meetings, the owner and the CM at-risk discuss the concerns and frustrations of working on the project. The goal is to have candid discussions of how each party feels the other is performing.
- During the meetings, the owner reviews the CM at-risk's performance regarding the previously agreed upon criteria such as quality, schedule, budget, safety, or any other critical element of the project. The owner notes any concerns and discusses these with the CM at-risk. The owner

also discusses with the CM at-risk the overall score or rating it plans to award.

- The owner and the CM at-risk arrive together at a score relative to the satisfaction of the owner, or what the CM at-risk must do to improve the owner's satisfaction. This score is linked to a distribution amount for each quarter of the Satisfaction Fee. For example, if the owner is 90–100% satisfied with the performance of the CM at-risk, then the entire quarterly amount would be awarded. If, on the other hand, the owner is only 50% satisfied, only 0–50% of the Satisfaction Fee is awarded and the CM at-risk is given one quarter to correct the dissatisfaction in order to collect the other 50% or lose it all for that period.

The point of the Satisfaction Fee is not for the owner to keep the money. In fact, it is the opposite—the owner should expect and desire to award the full amount of the Satisfaction Fee to the CM at-risk. The purpose of the quarterly meetings is to communicate. Communication on the project is even more important than the savings derived by a shared savings clause. It is more important than holding back on the Satisfaction Fee. In the long run, these meetings will create a greater level of collaboration and trust that will pay huge dividends when real problems arise.

The use of financial incentives, whether with shared savings or with a Satisfaction Fee, is one way to align the parties' interests on non-multi-party, open-book contracts such as CM at-Risk or Design-Build.

Design-Assist Contractors

Design-Assist contracting for subcontractors is a term describing one method to support early involvement of subcontractors. It is used when the success of specific trades can have a major impact on the success of the overall project. Design-assist subcontractors can be procured with a QBS or Best Value: Fees procurement—similar to the process described above for the CM at-risk, in which a Request for Proposals is developed and the subcontractor responds with qualifications and sometimes a price.

Design-Assist can be done with a primarily Qualifications Based Selection with the expectation to work open-book providing preconstruction services collaboratively until a mutually agreed upon GMP for their scope of work can be established. The term Design-Assist also is used to describe the early involvement of subcontractors even when procured with a Best Value: Total Cost process or essentially a competitive pricing of their entire scope as part of their selection.

In contrast to the Design-Build subcontractor approach, Design-Assist is a process that allows the subcontractor to assist the design team through consultation without taking responsibility for the design. The Request for Proposals clearly spells out that the subcontractor will work as a design assistant to the design (architect's) team. They will collaborate and provide full cooperation and information to the design team on details, installation, fabrication, budget, and all aspects of the project. For this effort, the subcontractor is compensated the same as the contractor being reimbursed for preconstruction.

If, at the end of the Design-Assist phase, the subcontractor is willing to sign a contract for the agreed upon budgeted amount based upon its work, it will be awarded the subcontract. If, on the other hand, the subcontractor and design team are not able to arrive at the agreed upon budget, then the contractor has the right to use all the information developed by them and the designer to bid the project competitively.

The early involvement of key trade contractors has produced excellent results on projects. It can limit risk to the owner and provide added knowledge to the design professional in the design phase. To use the Design-Assist method of contracting, the owner should expect to pay for upfront consulting fees and for coordination. The owner should also expect savings later thanks to fewer change orders, delay claims, and chances of litigation.

DELIVERY METHOD OVERVIEW/STRUCTURE

Historically, agency construction management firms (CMa) have given owners and clients preconstruction advice on scheduling, budgeting, value analysis, and bidding. During the construction phase, the CMa continues to help the owner but does not take any risk in guaranteeing the price, schedule completion, or quality. Those risks remain for someone else to take. General contractors, on the other hand, have not historically provided preconstruction services to owners or clients, even though they usually have a better understanding of the risks.

During the 1970s, a new type of firm evolved. Most of these firms were general contractors looking to provide services, work as part of teams, and eliminate adversarial environments on projects. This raised construction to a higher level of professional practice. As this new system developed around the country, it took on different names that are practically synonymous: CM/GC, GC/CM, CMc, and CM at-Risk. These firms started providing preconstruction services (estimating, scheduling, value analysis, systems analysis, etc.), price guarantees known as Guaranteed Maximum Prices (GMP), completion commitments, and other services as needed by the owners and clients.

Since those early beginnings, CM at-Risk has become so effective at providing value that it is now a dominant delivery method in private industry. It is rapidly becoming acceptable nationwide in public construction. (For further information on its use in the public sector, please refer to the publication, *CM/GC Guidelines for Public Owners – 2nd Edition*, published jointly by AGC of America and the National Association of State Facilities Administrators). This system makes the whole construction process far more predictable for the owner and constructor. Because a CM at-risk is never selected based on a Low Bid (this would be Design-Bid-Build), it is inherently a "value-based" vs. a strictly "low-cost" delivery method.

Sometimes prior to selecting the designer or early in the design process (typically no later than the completion of the schematic design), the CM at-risk is selected using a Qualifications Based Selection method. Studies show that the owner gets the best value if it engages the CM at-risk and the designer at the same time. By doing so, the owner can start getting realistic feedback concerning budget and schedule. The later in the design process the CM at-risk is selected, the less value it brings to the project. Some public owners are limited by regulations as to when they can select the CM at-risk. In other instances, the owner may feel the CM at-risk could hinder the designer's creativity if selected too early in the process. In any event, once the CM at-risk is selected, its employees should start attending the weekly design meetings to add input.

Once the CM at-risk is selected, many teams like to choose some of the major trade or specialty contractors (e.g., mechanical and HVAC, electrical, fire suppression, and occasionally structural and glazing). This helps control costs and increases project predictability. Each specialty represents a large percentage of any project and can thus have significant impact on the cost, schedule, and quality. These, too, are either selected on the basis of their qualifications or on their ability to provide the best value for the general scope of the work, fees, charging rates, overhead, etc. Their contracts can ultimately be on a GMP or Lump Sum basis once the overall project GMP is set. Early selection of specialty contractor team members also allows them to provide their services on a Design-Build basis. The goal is to have the most economical design and system to meet the owner's needs. Like the CM at-Risk, these specialty contractors are involved on a daily basis in competitively pricing work. They have more knowledge of current trends in costs and efficiencies and can direct the design so that the owner receives the best value.

Programming/Predesign Phase

If already on board, the CM at-risk provides a square foot or unit price budget analysis. The CM at-risk develops a schedule that includes all preconstruction activities, designer activities, owner activities, and government activities, and sets critical milestones. The square foot or unit cost analysis is based on the CM at-risk's past cost experience with similar types of projects, as well as what is known about the site for the new building (whether import/export of earth is needed, utility availability, etc.). It may not be clear yet what the actual size of the project will be. Because there are so many unknowns at this stage, a large design phase contingency is included in the budget. The budgeting process determines whether the owner's most optimistic wish list can be met. Once the budget and the size and complexity of the building match, the designer moves on to the next stage.

Design Phase

The design phase of a project is normally made up of three parts:
- Schematic documents phase
- Design documents phase
- Construction documents phase

Schematic Documents

During this phase, the CM at-risk can update the budget based on actual drawings. The CM at-risk still benefits from experience as it determines what will be required by this project type, because many of these elements still are not shown on the drawings. However, much more definition is now available on materials and size, and that makes it possible to create a "tighter" budget.

Frequently, the designer has not had time at this point in the design to create a project specification. In this case, the CM at-risk will instead develop an "outline specification" that defines the assumptions made in the budget. For instance, it will define the amount of import/export of earth included in the estimate, what the concrete design will be, the type of structural frame, the quality of doors and hardware, the type of building enclosure skin, and the type of roof.

During this phase, the CM at-risk evaluates materials and construction systems (structural, mechanical, electrical, etc.) to advise the designer and owner of the most economical and best value alternatives available. The owner can then make informed decisions on cost vs. value based on its unique needs. An example could be structural systems. A cast-in-place (CIP) concrete frame might be more economical than a structural steel frame. The trade-off might be that the CIP would add two months to the construction schedule and would make the building less flexible to future tenant renovations. While only the owner can assess its future needs, owners should rely heavily on the advice of their team of designers and constructors.

An additional item that starts appearing at this time is a Value Analysis Report. This report, usually prepared by the CM at-risk, now tracks the options being considered. All cost-saving or better value ideas the team members can offer the owner are tracked in this report. It shows which ideas have been selected, which have been deferred, and which have not yet been considered. This report becomes one of the critical documents being developed as the design continues.

The CM at-risk also updates the schedule during this phase to show the impact of decisions on design, changes in the market for labor, specialty contractor availability, and material delivery.

Design Documents

As the design moves into the design documents (DD) phase, the CM at-risk updates the budget with much more detailed information, as more elements are now appearing on the drawings. The designer produces its own more detailed specification, which helps the CM at-risk create specific pricing for more and more individual items in the budget. Prior to this, the budget contained many "allowance" items. As the details emerge, the allowances become fewer, replaced with detailed items in the budget. The design contingency for the project is also reduced as the "unknowns" become fewer and fewer.

The schedule and the Value Analysis Report are steadily updated as well. As part of the schedule update during this phase of design, the CM at-risk identifies those materials and products that have long delivery times. If these are not procured prior to the completion of construction documents, project schedule delays could occur. Dates are set in the overall schedule for procurement of those items, and these become priorities for the designers, allowing them to integrate their design with the future construction and delivery requirements of the project.

At the end of this design document stage, the CM at-risk guarantees the price by providing the not-to-exceed Guaranteed Maximum Price and takes on the risk of the cost of the project. The price is a proposal based on the documents up to this stage and is accompanied by a Qualifications and Assumptions Statement. This guarantee, normally presented in a fairly detailed report, clearly defines the CM at-risk's assumptions, how the pricing is determined, any remaining allowances, and schedule-related issues. Once the proposal is accepted and a GMP is agreed upon, the cost risk transfers to the CM at-risk.

The CM at-risk guarantees that, if the scope of the project, assumptions, drawings, etc., do not materially change as the drawings and specifications are completed, the project will cost no more than this guaranteed price (commonly known as the Guaranteed Maximum Price (GMP)). In the future, should the costs exceed this price, and if the owner has made no changes, the CM at-risk will be responsible for the costs in excess of the GMP. This gives the owner an early price commitment for the project, rather than forcing the owner to wait until the design is complete before it knows the maximum price to be paid.

During the design process, the owner has received regular updates on cost, quality, and schedule, so the GMP should not come as a surprise. Sometimes, however, items slip into the design at the end of this stage. The owner may not be able to afford these additional items. The team will then make design and matching cost proposals to bring the project back into the budget range. Once the budget is adjusted and accepted, the design moves into the final phase.

Construction Documents

The most appropriate way to look at construction documents (CDs) is to view them as the designer's instructions to the constructor on how to build the project. They should contain all the information on connections, interfaces, specific locations for materials, required testing and observations, and specific performance criteria. None of this should be new information to the CM at-risk, as these documents should just be the completion and detailing of the design documents and previously discussed intents. Scope of work should not change. By the end of this phase, the more complex trades should have been selected by some competitive process and be participating members of the team. This would include mechanical, plumbing, electrical, and possibly structural and glazing specialty contractors.

Unfortunately, if all members of the team have not been working closely together, this is where the CM at-Risk process can fail. The estimate for this phase should be a confirmation of the pricing from the DD phase of design. However, it is usually found that there has been some "creep" in the design. As the designers are filling in the details for construction, they frequently find better solutions, identify additional problems, and in some cases, enhance the design. If these add to the scope of the work, the GMP should be increased to accommodate them. Usually, the CDs are complete enough that many items previously carried as allowances can now be priced. Additionally, the unknowns should be further reduced. As a result, the design contingency can be reduced. Generally speaking, the GMP can be reduced slightly upon the completion of CDs, as the risks and unknowns have been quantified and reduced. Normally, all design is completed during this phase. However, on a true "fast-track" project, completion of the interior finishes design may not happen until well into the construction phase.

During this phase, the CM at-risk defines the scope requirements by trade to allow competitive bidding and prequalifying. This helps the CM at-risk select potential specialty contractors that could bring the best value to the project. On projects requiring extremely fast-track efforts (often called "flash-track"), where the construction begins on certain components very early in the design, this competitive bidding process begins even earlier. Often this activity and the following bidding phase overlap.

Bidding Phase

Unlike Lump Sum public bid projects, the CM at-Risk method has an extended bidding process. It usually starts during the schematic phase and is not complete until well into the construction phase, when the interior finish documents are finally done. The CM at-risk puts together scopes of work by trade; carefully reviews the finances, experience, and capacity of interested specialty contractors; and then solicits bids from those with adequate prequalification status.

Unlike the Design-Bid-Build Lump Sum method, in which bidder selection is made in minutes, the CM at-risk takes the time to fully evaluate all bids from the specialty contractors, compare them to the budget and scope, and interview the low bidders to verify scope prior to making a recommendation to the owner. Also unlike the Design-Bid-Build method, it is typical for the owner to be very involved in the selection of all major specialty contractors for the project as part of the team.

Highly technical trades (those in the mechanical, plumbing, electrical, and sometimes the structural areas) may be selected through a competitive Qualifications Based Selection process of fees, overhead, and charging rates well before the design is complete. As in the relationship between the owner and the CM at-risk, the purpose is to get the trade contractor's input into the design to ensure best value based on its experience. Frequently, the mechanical, plumbing, and electrical trades (MP&E) actually come on board early (on a Design-Build basis) to provide this best value. Most of the rest of the trade specialty contractors become members of the team by pricing completed contract documents. Once agreement on the specialty contractors is reached, trade contracts are issued based on completed scopes of work.

Construction Phase

In the construction phase, the CM at-risk starts work on the project on site in the field. In fast-track applications, only the foundations and structural drawings may be available. They must contain enough information about the rest of the design to ensure that all penetrations and underground work are anticipated. This work must coordinate with future issues within the contract documents that complete the design of the project. The CM at-risk now operates to a large extent as a general contractor, coordinating specialty contractors, materials, and self-performed work. Weekly "owner, architect, contractor" meetings are held to resolve conflicts and to add or fill in missing information. The project schedule is updated monthly to determine overall status, and two-week look-ahead schedules are produced weekly. These focus on the micro activities of the specialty contractors and self-performed work. Budgets are updated to show where the project is ahead and behind, and change orders are processed to reflect the changing scope of the project.

Commissioning

Commissioning is the process used to validate that the design meets the owner's original design intent. This begins early in the design with design reviews. Also, later in the commissioning process but prior to occupancy, the project's systems and equipment are tested and adjusted to perform as designed. Often the CM at-risk's contract requires that this be done prior to the owner's final acceptance of the project. While the CM at-risk typically has this responsibility, contract requirements for commissioning can vary widely. The actual commissioning work may be done by the CM at-risk, a specialty contractor, or a commissioning consultant, and there may or may not be a separate professional on its staff involved on behalf of the owner.

Occupancy Phase

Because many CM at-risk projects operate on a fast-track basis, they often have a different occupancy schedule from the typical project in which occupancy occurs after "substantial completion." The fast-track project's early completion areas typically are those involving computers, communications, telecom, and conferencing. There is actually an advantage for the owner when certain portions of the project are completed earlier than the substantial completion date. The owner can bring in specialty contractors to tailor these areas before its employees move in. The employees can pack up their old office on Friday and be productive in their new office on Monday with no appreciable lost time. The ability of the CM at-risk to predictably accomplish phased schedule completions is one of the most important aspects of a firm's reputation and ability to acquire work in this product delivery method.

DEFINING CHARACTERISTICS AND TYPICAL CHARACTERISTICS

Defining characteristics uniquely distinguish a delivery method from the other delivery methods. The following are the defining characteristics of CM at-Risk:
- Design and construction are separate contracts (versus Design-Build, where the contracts are combined).
- Criteria for final selection does not include the total construction cost (versus Design-Bid-Build where total construction cost is a factor in the final selection).

Who holds the contracts and takes contractual responsibility for the performance of the work is a defining characteristic of all delivery methods. Because there is so much confusion between agency CM and CM at-Risk, the reader is reminded that the defining separation between the two is that CM at-Risk holds the trade contracts and is responsible for the performance of the project. Thus, taking the performance risk for the project (versus agency CM) is a defining characteristic of CM at-Risk.

Typical characteristics are attributes that are common and may occur on most CM at-Risk contacts but are not necessarily required under this delivery method. It is important to note that in CM at-Risk, a cost guarantee, usually in the form of a Guaranteed Maximum Price (GMP), is typically established during the design

CONSTRUCTION MANAGEMENT AT-RISK

phase. This is usually required on public sector projects, but it still is a typical characteristic rather than a defining characteristic.

The following are some other typical characteristics of this delivery method (though some apply only when selected with a Qualifications Based Selection):

- There exists a cost guarantee (in the form of a GMP) and a schedule guarantee. Without these guarantees, a debate on where the "risk" is in CM at-Risk usually ensues. The risk comes from the CM holding the trade contracts and taking the performance risk for the project. To avoid this debate entirely, many choose to use the term CM/GC in lieu of CM at-Risk.
- When the contract does provide for a GMP, it is usually provided before the completion of the construction documents.
- The CM at-risk is hired, usually by Qualifications Based Selection, early in the design phase to provide input on budget, schedule, quality, and systems. While the QBS method is the most used, selection can also be based on a combination of experience, staff, fees, general conditions, and a budget price for the project.
- The constructor's fee is generally a negotiated fee for services, with the project contingency being the focus of undefined risk instead of the constructor's fee.
- The CM at-risk operates on an "open-book" basis. All accounts relating to the project are open to owner review at any time during the project and up to three years after substantial completion. These review and audit rights are limited to those defined in the contract documents.
- The CM at-risk's preconstruction skills are as important as its ability to provide construction phase services. Preconstruction services are a typical characteristic.
- Ability to perform on a fast-track basis is a typical characteristic and is essential to success in this method.
- Success in acquiring work under this delivery system depends on proven experience in creating and participating in "team building," and on a history of win/win projects for all parties.
- It is the CM at-risk's responsibility to ensure that any specialty contractor or supplier requests for change orders are carefully reviewed to determine whether they are legitimate changes in project scope or caused by the owner's actions. If a change order is not legitimate, needs revision, or is improperly stated or priced, it should be returned to the specialty contractor or supplier.

Independent Advice

The CM at-risk, as in Design-Bid-Build, separates the design phases from the construction phase and utilizes a separate independent professional in each phase. This gives the owner the assistance of an expert designer whose duties are solely to the owner. It also allows the owner time to consider, modify, and finalize the design before engaging a constructor. In CM at-Risk, however, the constructor may be brought on board during the design phase to provide advice and assistance to the designer, which is not the case in Design-Bid-Build.

PROCUREMENT AND ESTABLISHING THE CONTRACT AMOUNT

Procuring Construction Management at-Risk Services

The procurement/selection process for CM at-Risk is more complex than in the Design-Bid-Build delivery method. By definition, the owner may select the CM at-Risk by either of two procurement options: Qualifications Based Selection and Best Value: Fees.

Qualifications Based Selection

In a Qualifications Based Selection procurement method, total construction cost is not a criterion for the final selection, and qualifications are the only criteria (total construction cost = 0% of the final selection criteria).

Best Value: Fees

In the Best Value: Fees procurement method, qualifications and the CM at-risk's fees are both factors in the final selection (total construction cost = 0% of the final selection criteria).

Some states, including Arizona, require CM at-risk selections to be based on qualifications. The following discussion is based on a typical CM at-risk with a Qualifications Based Selection process. While the QBS method is preferred, many hybrid selection processes have developed according to owners' requirements. The first step with either of these procurement options is typically a Request for Qualifications (RFQ), and the second step is the Request for Proposals (RFP). For more detail on both the RFQ and RFP Process, see Chapter 2.

Once the CM at-risk is selected, establishing the contract amount in the CM at-Risk delivery system is somewhat more complex than in the Lump Sum basis of reimbursement. Normally, the owner has a project budget. The construction costs are just a part of the budget, which also must cover land acquisition; design costs; testing; furniture, fixtures, and equipment (FF&E); interest carrying costs; owner contingency; and project administration. In the best situations, the owner is transparent about the amount allocated for construction costs. This allows the CM at-risk to be much more effective in budgeting and value analysis. It is also helpful if the owner is clear about its financial goals for the project. Is the intent to produce the project at the lowest reasonable cost or to utilize the budget to get the best value the budget will allow?

At some point, normally at the completion of the design development stage, the GMP discussed above is finalized. This sets the contract price for the project, including the CM at-risk's fee and reimbursable costs.

In some situations, the owner may want to use a hybrid of the process described above. Probably the most commonly used hybrid is converting the contract to Lump Sum. This occurs when the owner wants all the advantages of the preconstruction process but not the risk-sharing aspects of the construction phase. If it does occur, the lump sum amount theoretically will go up a bit higher than the GMP, as the entire burden for the price risk has shifted to the constructor, which should be adequately compensated for the increased risk.

The other commonly used hybrid is to convert the contract to a Cost-Plus delivery process at the end of the design process. This is used when the owner finds the costs so clear and complete that the owner does not fear cost overruns. With a Cost-Plus method, the overall price from the constructor can be reduced (contingency), as the owner has now taken on all the risk for cost overruns.

In other cases where the design has progressed to a substantial level, prior to the selection of the CM at-risk, the owner may wish to request a budget from each proposer as part of the selection process. Often this can become a very competitive pricing exercise on incomplete drawings. The owner needs to remain objective when evaluating the comparative budgets and not just take the lowest price. As the CM at-risk has the responsibility to carefully review specialty contractor bids for completeness, full scope, and ability to achieve the project's goals, the owner needs to be equally diligent in reviewing the CM at-risk's budget so as not to develop false expectations that cannot be fulfilled at a later stage in the project. The biggest risk of having what becomes a "competitive budget" at this stage is that those CM at-risk firms with the least experience may significantly underprice the project, creating false expectations and adding unnecessary adversarial aspects to the project as the construction documents are completed and the final GMP is established.

Timing of Establishing the Contract Amount

Of course, the parties can agree upon price at any time in the project. In Cost-Plus arrangements, parties agree at the beginning of the project to define reimbursable expenses, establish a means of presenting incurred costs for reimbursement, and establish a fixed fee.

A lump sum fixed price or a GMP may not be set until the design is complete (or at least at an advanced stage). This enables the CM at-risk to develop an understanding of the estimated costs of construction.

Contracts that require the CM at-risk to develop a GMP typically provide initially for payment on a cost-reimbursement basis, according to a preliminary project budget agreed upon by the parties. Such contracts require the CM at-risk to submit a proposed price at some defined point, such as completion of design. The costs incurred to date become part of the price, and the project proceeds on the basis of the agreed upon price. Because the parties must agree upon the new price, be it a lump sum or GMP, it is important for both parties to address in the contract what happens if they fail to agree upon a price.

Selecting the CM at-Risk Early

The typical Qualifications Based Selection (QBS) process on a CM at-Risk project is often to hire or select the design professional first, then to select the contractor or CM at-risk through a QBS process toward the end of the early design phase. This typical process does not result in a truly collaborative environment in which the contractor is fully invested in the goals established for the project.

Alternatively, by selecting the contractor or CM at-risk at the same time as the design team, or even selecting the CM at-risk first and allowing it to be part of the design professional's selection process, the team can develop a collaborative relationship from the very beginning. By selecting the CM at-risk early, designers and owners benefit from communication from day one on the project, but in addition, the owner benefits from the support in budget development, schedule management, and constructability reviews.

BASIS OF REIMBURSEMENT OPTIONS

Guaranteed Maximum Price

The establishment of the Guaranteed Maximum Price (GMP) is an important part of the CM at-Risk project delivery system. Many issues—such as when to establish the GMP, whether to fix the CM at-risk's fees, whether to establish an early GMP or use a progressive approach, etc.—exist with CM at-Risk.

With a GMP, overruns caused by the owner or the designer would be considered changes and not part of the original GMP. Note that this is an area where CM at-Risk and Design-Build contracts differ. In a GMP Design-Build contract, the category of overruns due to errors in design, after the establishment of the GMP, shifts from the owner to the design-builder and would not be considered a change to the original GMP.

Conversely, in CM at-Risk, design errors are generally the owner's responsibility (reference the Spearin Doctrine as discussed in Chapter 7) and are considered a justification for changes to the original GMP. There are some who question how much the owner's responsibility for the design may be eroded due to the early (preconstruction) involvement of the CM at-risk. The involvement of the contractor during the design phase has created an issue relative to how much, if any, responsibility the CM at-risk assumes for the design. There are many well established best practices for managing GMP contracts, and teams with limited experience with GMP contracts are encouraged to seek assistance.

The CM at-risk is typically paid by one of two methods. The first is based on a "schedule of values" and the second is based on "backed-up billing." Because of the need to promptly reimburse specialty contractors and suppliers, the schedule of values method is typically the CM's preferred method. At the beginning of construction on the project, the CM at-risk gives the owner a schedule of values that breaks the project costs down into its main elements. It normally follows the standards established by the Construction Specifications Institute (CSI), which are the same standards most design firms use in ordering and organizing the project plans and specifications. This produces a series of categories with the associated costs attached to each category, the total of which will add up to the GMP.

Once a month, the CM at-risk evaluates the percentage of work that has been completed by category. On major categories, such as mechanical, electrical, and structural areas, the CM at-risk may rely on specialty contractors' most recently submitted bills. That percentage by category will then be extended and applied to the dollars allocated to each individual category or line item. The total dollars derived by line are added together to represent the theoretical amount the project has cost up to that time. The schedule of values is then presented to the owner for approval. In almost all cases, the CM at-risk will submit lien releases for the entire billed amount, as well as lien releases from each major specialty contractor for the amount of its billing. Sometimes the owner will disagree with the amount of the bill, and the CM at-risk and owner will negotiate those line items on which they disagree to reach an agreed amount or percentage. The agreed upon amount is then paid to the CM at-risk, less those amounts previously paid and less the contractual retention amount. This method usually allows the CM at-risk to be paid within 30 days of submitting the agreed upon bill.

In the case of backed-up billing, the CM at-risk requires all specialty contractors and suppliers to submit all their costs for the month by a definite date, to be included in the next billing to the owner. The CM at-risk then assembles all those subcontractor costs, the costs the CM at-risk has incurred with its own forces and material and equipment purchases, all rentals, staff costs, copies of all invoices and bills (some owners will require original documents), lien releases from all specialty contractors, and the CM at-risk's own lien release. The CM at-risk prepares an invoice showing the total of all categories. It is a time-consuming method and generally means the bill will be submitted to the owner at a much later date than in the percentage complete schedule of values billing method. This gives the owner a more accurate bill for actual costs but significantly delays payment from the point the specialty contractors and suppliers submit their bills to the CM at-risk to the point they receive payment. As the specialty contractors and suppliers must wait longer for payment, they may increase their initial contract price to compensate for the extra time they anticipate carrying the costs of their work before being paid.

CMs at-risk, specialty contractors, and suppliers favor the percent complete method because it is much simpler and produces much quicker payment. Owners tend to favor the backed-up billing method, as they get more accurate bills and can better avoid being overbilled by the CM at-risk. On most projects, the CM at-risk and the owner find a hybrid approach that allows the CM at-risk to receive payment quickly while still ensuring that the owner is not significantly overbilled. In busy markets, it is important for an owner to find a method to provide timely payment to constructors, specialty contractors, and suppliers. Without prompt payment, contractors tend to avoid working with a particular owner, or to inflate the owner's costs to compensate for the slow payment, making the owner less competitive in the costs of the project. Ultimately, the owner and the CM at-risk should agree on the method of reimbursement as part of the contract negotiation.

Final payment on all delivery methods is generally similar. Normally, the project must be substantially complete, the punchlist must be finished, and all claims or disagreements settled. The project architect normally certifies substantial completion. At that point, the CM at-risk submits a final bill with final lien releases, which includes all costs and a request for all remaining retention.

Cost-Plus a Fixed Fee

A CM at-risk may be retained on a purely cost-reimbursement basis. The CM at-risk's fee is often a fixed amount so that the CM at-risk will have an incentive to minimize cost. This allows a completely open-book approach so that the owner can monitor project costs. This approach is common where the owner and CM at-risk have a high level of trust and confidence between them, whether through experience or reputation. It also is an appropriate choice for experimental or other high-risk projects and for projects in which cost estimates are not reliable.

Lump Sum

Though not very common, a CM at-Risk contract can be awarded on the basis of a Lump Sum Fixed Price contract if the parties agree. While parties can agree upon a fixed price at any point, they often wait until completion of preliminary or final design documents before committing to a price for the project.

ROLES AND RESPONSIBILITIES

The Owner

To get the most value out of this delivery method, the owner must select a knowledgeable CM at-risk early in the design process. The owner should also pick other team members who believe the CM at-risk is a fully participating member of the process. The owner will be the decision maker on options presented during the design process by the CM at-risk and in settling disagreements during the design phase between the CM at-risk and design team members. This is not a negative, but rather it is a natural result of having more information early in the design phase than some other methods provide. This is part of creating early predictability in budget and schedule. The owner will need to participate in setting milestones for project and design review that will be incorporated into the project schedule by the CM at-risk.

The Designer

The designer has the same basic responsibilities as in other delivery systems in which the design contract is between the designer and the owner. The designer's responsibility is to create a design that meets the owner's needs, is structurally sound, and complies with building codes and other government requirements. The designer's duty to the owner is two-fold— the duty created by a professional standard of care expected of designers or engineers and a contractual duty established by the contract between the designer and the owner.

The designer's professional duty of care is to perform with the same degree of skill and care as may be expected of any member of the design or engineering profession. The profession itself establishes this duty of care.

The designer also must perform design services in accordance with the requirements of its contract with the owner. The contract may impose requirements concerning a schedule, cost, or approvals. These contractual duties may be in addition to the designer's professional standard of skill and care.

The additional responsibility of the designer in the CM at-Risk delivery method is to allow the CM at-risk to be a fully participating member of the team during preconstruction. The designer needs to react and incorporate into the design those value analysis activities, constructability items, and system changes accepted by the owner once the team has offered input into the design of the project. The designer needs to commit to schedule dates that will be incorporated into the overall project schedule by the CM at-risk.

The Constructor

The prime constructor in this case is the CM at-risk. The CM at-risk's responsibilities have been defined and discussed throughout this chapter.

Specialty Contractors and Suppliers

Specialty contractors have their traditional roles in the project. Some of the more complex trades may sometimes participate early in the design process, bringing their particular expertise in construction to enhance the design and efficiency of the project. Those firms should possess the same high levels of conceptual budgeting and design evaluation for their trade as the CM at-risk brings to the overall project.

Early contractor involvement can be with either Design-Assist or Design-Build subcontracting. While the terminology works when you pass the Design-Build methodology down the line to the subcontractor, the industry trips when the CM at-Risk methodology is passed down the line. For the most part, the industry applies the term "Design-Assist" to describe when the same methodology used to select and contract with a CM at-risk is passed down the line to the subcontractor and the subcontractor assists with the design but does not take over the responsibility for the design.

With many CM at-Risk (or Design-Build) contracts, particularly those procured with Qualifications Based Selection or Best Value: Fees and contracted with an open-book GMP, Cost-Plus, or Target Price basis of reimbursement, the owner is able to actively participate in the subcontractor procurement process. This includes reviewing the scopes, pricing, and clarifications of each subcontractor as well as the evaluation, recommendation, and approval of each subcontract award.

Some owners' procurement rules require that the contractor procures under the same rules as the owner when it subcontracts the work, while other rules do not. Some rules require that all subcontracts be procured through Low Bid. It is critical that the owner understands this aspect of the buyout process and clearly explains the rules in the selection documents. This understanding will allow the contractor to procure the project with the greatest possibility for savings realized by the owner since the open-book GMP passes most, if not all, of this savings back to the owner.

An emerging practice is for owners to be able to encourage multiple selection options for the contractor to use on the project. Every project has unique elements the contractor must consider as it selects or procures its subcontractors. While this may sound like an unimportant area of concern for an owner, it is actually one that can result in great savings and fewer change orders if handled correctly. In theory, the same processes available to the owner are available to the contractor when selecting subcontractors. In addition to the Low Bid where subcontractors bid only the scope requested based on the documents that are provided, other successful selection processes have effectively reduced change orders and furthered collaboration.

PROJECT DELIVERY CONSIDERATIONS

Chapter 6 of this book discussed several basic project delivery considerations and risk issues common to all projects and various project delivery methods. Some considerations vary from one project delivery method to another, while others remain the same. This section follows the same format as Chapter 6 to discuss considerations that are different for this project delivery method.

Building Information Modeling

Since the CM at-Risk contract is most likely an open-book GMP, the benefit of collaboration from sharing Building Information Models among the primary parties—the design team, the contractor, and the owner—is available during the planning and design phases. BIM is used to improve planning and design and is of great value to CM at-Risk projects. In addition to the potential benefits of offering 3D visualization to users early in the process, CMs at-risk can use the model as a tool to assist in evaluating the design and providing input during the design process.

With the increased collaboration and involvement of the CM at-risk during the design phases, there is a whole new set of challenges. Who is modeling what and when? Who is using the model and how? With the team working together in an open, collaborative environment, BIM use during design and construction allows for better and more efficient analysis of design alternatives. It should also result in better coordination with the trade contractors and suppliers who can use models in addition (and perhaps, in lieu of) traditional shop drawings. The ability for the CM at-risk to build the building virtually prior to building it in the field allows for improved coordination and fewer issues in the field.

Like Design-Bid-Build, the industry is working to have a better understanding of the risks associated with the use of BIM on CM at-Risk projects. While the industry is addressing these risks, the contracts and insurance products will likely continue to be in flux for a number of years.

Model sharing and the ability to rely on the information in the model with the CM at-Risk project delivery method are still evolving. In the case of CM at-Risk, where the contractor is participating in the development of the design information, all parties are evaluating where the risks are and how and when risk is being transferred.

ConsensusDOCS 301, "Building Information Modeling (BIM) Addendum," addresses the team's responsibilities as they relate to the model. The addendum was designed with the intention that it would work with any project delivery model, including CM at-Risk.

Changes

Depending on the selection method and the resulting contractual relationship, the impact of changes under a CM at-Risk contract can be dramatically different.

Most often, if selected under a Qualifications Based Selection and then contracted under a not-to-exceed contract, the CM at-risk has a pre-established fee and general conditions. The close relationship defined by the contract requires the CM at-risk to operate in an open-book manner, always looking out for the best interests of its owner. The CM at-risk evaluates any changes and endeavors to incorporate them while simultaneously minimizing or eliminating any cost or schedule impact to the owner.

During the selection and bidding of specialty contractors, the CM is charged with ensuring that scopes of work are complete before awarding trade contracts. This reduces the likelihood of future change orders.

There are some who question how much the owner's responsibility for the design (see Spearin Doctrine discussion in Chapter 7) may be eroded due to the early (preconstruction) involvement of the CM at-risk. Holding separate contracts for design and construction still leaves the Spearin Doctrine in place; however, the involvement of the contractor during design has created an issue relative to how much, if any, responsibility the CM at-risk assumes for the design.

Change orders occurring during the project are strictly limited to owner-directed changes in the scope of the project. The CM also has an obligation to the owner to evaluate proposed costs from subcontractors for such changes.

If there is a conversion from a GMP to a Fixed Price contract after the original GMP is established, then the CM at-risk may no longer be required to operate in an open-book manner for the scope under the original contract. Changes at that point will be evaluated first for their potential impact to the CM at-risk, then for their impact to the owner. Even when the base contract is a fixed price, most contracts require an option to do an open-book on changes to the original contract.

Claims and Disputes

Partnering/Collaboration

An intrinsic part of the CM at-Risk process is building an effective team comprising the designer, owner, and constructor. One of the more effective methods has been the concept of "partnering." A partnering session helps the team understand the priorities, goals, and expectations of each participant. There are bound to be some disagreements among team members during the project, so it helps for them to have a common understanding of one another's point of view. These sessions establish a dispute resolution process that includes a progressive series of negotiations. A dispute is first considered by the onsite project team. If not resolved there, it goes up through the member organizations to increasingly higher levels of management. In this way, the partners aim to negotiate solutions rather than achieving resolution through more formal arbitration or litigation solutions.

Dispute Resolution Alternatives

If informal resolution fails, dispute resolution offers an alternative to litigation for resolving disputes. This delivery method encourages the use of processes other than litigation to solve disputes. Most contract forms recommend a notice timeframe for making claims. If a negotiated solution cannot be reached, the next step is mediation, generally using the construction industry rules of the American Arbitration Association. Other organizations have also published rules for mediation. If mediation is not successful, the next step is generally binding arbitration, also often using the rules established by the American Arbitration Association.

Dispute Avoidance/Management

The CM at-risk has an ethical responsibility to manage the project in such a manner as to avoid or at least minimize disputes. As a member of the owner's team, along with the designer, the CM should be proactive in working to eliminate problems. As the designer's standard of care does not require perfection, the CM should anticipate issues arising in the design documents. Most contract terms require the CM to inform the designer and owner of potential conflicts or errors. Early awareness of potential problems allows the team to find solutions before the problems create schedule and cost impacts on the project. This proactive approach to problem solving helps eliminate cost and schedule delays.

Design Phases

Sources of Design Information

One of the primary differences between CM at-Risk and Design-Bid-Build is the ability to bring the constructor on board during the design process. The CM's ability to affect the design depends on when the CM at-risk is brought onto the team. If brought on early enough, the CM can bring information in addition to what is provided by the design team. This information typically includes cost and schedule impacts of alternative solutions as well as input on the constructability of the design being created. This process gives the owner the information needed to make the most educated, informed decisions possible throughout the design process.

Design Process

Another difference between CM at-Risk and Design-Bid-Build is the way the design process is impacted by early involvement of the CM. In CM at-Risk, when the constructor is brought on board during the design phase, the constructor can be involved in determining which construction methods are more appropriate for the project. In addition, the constructor's market experience ensures more cost-effective design decisions.

Fast-Tracking

Like Design-Build, CM at-Risk facilitates the ability to fast-track a project. The ability to start construction before all design is complete lets the constructor deliver the project much more quickly. Generally, the designer produces the site and foundation package first. The constructor then prices that work scope, takes bids from specialty contractors, and starts work while the designer is working on the design of the shell or enclosure of the building design. Obviously, this phase of design needs to give the constructor the time to take specialty contractor bids, get owner approval of the new budget, and start work in such a way as to not have gaps in the schedule from the first phase of drawings. Then, while the constructor is proceeding, the designer completes the interior design, once again such that the construction process is not delayed waiting for design completion. This can easily reduce schedule duration by 15–20%, with the inherent savings of general conditions, interest carry costs on the project, and opportunities for early occupancy of the building.

Fast-tracking has another impact on the design process. During the design process for Design-Bid-Build, all components of the project are involved in each phase of the design (programming, schematic design, design development, etc.). This usually is not the case in CM at-Risk. Rather, each component of the project goes though each of the design phases, almost independently. For example, the foundation and structural components are in the construction documents phase before any of the other components. In this way, the requirements of the schedule are met. Plumbing design decisions (which in Design-Bid-Build are some of the last decisions to be made) must be made early in the process.

Although this difference in design phases is well known and axiomatic for fast-tracking, its consequences are not always fully understood. Design decisions are made in a different order than in Design-Bid-Build, and the input for those decisions comes from different parties. Failure to make correct, timely decisions can be extremely costly later. For example, in the Design-Bid-Build method, an owner may wish to change the location of the utility entrance. If this occurs late in the design phase of a Design-Bid-Build project, there is some cost and concern in the redesign of the project, but there are no major construction cost consequences. In a fast-tracked project, such a decision would have a significant cost and schedule impact.

Indemnification/Hold Harmless Clauses

The scope and nature of indemnity agreements with CM at-Risk does not vary in any significant manner from that expected in the traditional Design-Bid-Build method. Most CMs carry general liability insurance with high limits and, consequently, provide an indemnity for claims arising from the construction work to other members of the project team.

Insurance

Most CMs at-risk carry general liability, automobile, and other types of insurance to the same extent and with the same types and limits of coverage as traditional general contractors. The provision of builder's risk insurance on a CM at-Risk project is inherently no different than on a traditional Design-Bid-Build project. As a result, insurance considerations for CM at-Risk typically are the same as the traditional project delivery format.

Lean Construction

Lean construction, or the concept of eliminating waste, does not fundamentally change regardless of the project delivery method. However, the ability to integrate lean principles across the entire project and not just within portions of the project team is significantly enhanced by the existence of an open-book collaborative environment, which exists on CM at-Risk projects.

This collaborative environment increases the ability of the owner, the design team, and the CM at-risk to implement lean practices both within their organizations as well as in the execution of the design and construction process. The opportunity to increase productivity and improve efficiency is always available. In addition to applying lean at the CM at-risk level, it is also common to implement lean principles and techniques at the trade contractor level as well.

Licensing

Architect/Engineer Licensing Requirements

Although there usually is greater collaboration on a CM at-Risk project between the architect/engineer and the CM than there is on a Design-Bid-Build project, the owner nonetheless procures the design services. As a result, issues relating to architect/engineer licensing on a CM at-Risk project are the same as those on a Design-Bid-Build project.

Constructor Licensing Requirements

The CM at-risk is responsible for procuring a building permit. As a result, constructor licensing requirements pertaining to a general contractor will likewise apply to the CM. As noted previously, this is a matter of state licensing, and requirements vary from state to state. There are a few states that have approached the issue of requiring a license for construction managers, but with the increase in the use of CM at-Risk, it is quite possible that more states will adopt separate licensing requirements. To avoid future problems, the CM at-risk should check the status of CM licensing requirements in the project's state or commonwealth.

Lien Waivers

In all private construction projects, constructors, subcontractors, and vendors have the legal right to file liens. For public projects, most states follow the federal guidelines of the Miller Act for release of final payment and the waiver of claims. Similar to Design-Bid-Build, in the CM at-Risk delivery method, the constructor is part of the owner's team and has the contractual responsibility of keeping the project clear of liens or claims, if the owner has made timely payments for work completed. The CM should carefully evaluate all liens and claims for validity. If they are legitimate, they should be resolved. If not, there are many vehicles available to effectively remove the issues from the project (i.e., lien bonds, insurance guaranties, etc.), allowing their proper resolution.

Prequalification

Because the CM at-risk is typically not hired on the basis of total project cost, prequalification of potential CMs is critical to the CM at-Risk process. This prequalification, or "shortlisting," ensures that only those firms with experience in projects of the size and nature under consideration will be permitted to compete for the project.

Retainage

In CM at-Risk projects, retainage usually starts at 10% of the paid amount. As the CM at-risk may be representing the owner's interests, retainage is more flexible. Typically, 10% retainage is held until the project is 50% complete. From that point on, no additional retainage is held, such that at the end of the project, the retainage is equal to 5%. Also, it is normal practice to release all retainage on selected subcontractors that perform all their services early in a project.

Safety

On most CM at-Risk projects, the CM has overall responsibility for jobsite safety, much as a constructor on a Design-Bid-Build project. The CM at-risk may have an earlier opportunity to plan for safety operations and to encourage the designer to incorporate features that will facilitate safe methods of construction. Otherwise, there are no major differences between a CM and a general contractor with regard to safety.

Standard Forms of Agreement

There are a number of standard forms of agreement available for the CM at-Risk delivery system. One of the best known is the ConsensusDOCS 500, "Standard Agreement and General Conditions Between Owner and Construction Manager (CM At-Risk)" (where the basis of payment is a GMP with an option for preconstruction services). The ConsensusDOCS 500 is a stand-alone document that incorporates the general conditions.

For public work, most government entities have developed their own contract forms, which may or may not be based on one of the standard industry agreements. When pursuing work, all parties should carefully review the agreements before entering into a contract for services.

Subcontracts

A significant difference between CM at-Risk (when procured with a Qualifications Based Selection) and Design-Bid-Build is whether the owner participates in the review of the trade contractor bidding and award process. The CM at-risk, if under an open-book contract, will share all information regarding trade contractor bids with the other members of the project team. Trade contractors' bid clarifications and exclusions, alternates, and value engineering, etc., are available to the owner and the design team for review so that they may determine which proposal is in the project's best interest. The CM at-risk may be required to share all information about trade contracts with the owner. If the CM at-risk is under a Lump Sum contract, then the same information may or may not be available to the owner and the design team. Not having the contractual access to the original scope and costs could make evaluation difficult.

Surety Bonds and Other Forms of Security for Performance

As noted above, it is common for the owner and CM to discuss surety bonds to be obtained from various trade contractors. By contrast, it is less common for an owner to require performance and payment bonds from a CM, as an owner would from a constructor under the Design-Bid-Build method. Instead, the emphasis tends to be on security for subcontractor performance, so surety bonds from the trade contractors are common. For public work, however, most government entities will require bonds of the CM regardless of whether the various trade contractors are bonded. This is because in most jurisdictions, the CM, as holder of the subcontracts and of responsibility for the project, falls under the legal requirements for providing both a payment and a performance bond.

A key issue for owners is the relationship between a requirement for performance and payment bonds for the various trade contractors and the cost of the performance and payment bonds required of the CM. In fact, in some situations, the requirement for bonding of the trade contractors may be essential to the CM's ability to obtain a bond for the entire project.

Sustainability

CM at-Risk, which is typically procured with Best Value: Fees or Qualifications Based Selection, offers the advantage on green projects that the CM at-risk is involved early in the project's design. The CM at-risk is able to work closely with the owner during the design phase to collaboratively develop the green project requirements. The CM at-risk is also better positioned to provide input that should help assist in achieving the project's green goals. This input can result in better designs that meet the owner's criteria, better material and equipment selection, increased construction efficiency, and lower lifecycle costs for the project. The typical open-book process should also facilitate closer involvement of the trade contractors and suppliers in working to incorporate sustainable products and designs.

The disadvantage is that the owner may have to be in the middle between the designer's green responsibilities and the contractor's green responsibilities. For example, if a project is billed as achieving a certain third party's level of certification but fails to reach this standard, whose responsibility is this? Is this failure the designer's or the CM at-risk's responsibility? Does the owner have to take some responsibility? This is also a concern in Design-Bid-Build and is an area that many in the industry, particularly sureties and insurance companies that serve the construction industry, are watching closely.

The recent research, *Sustainable, High Performance Projects and Project Delivery Methods, A State-of-Practice Report,* September, 2009, sponsored by the Charles Pankow Foundation and The Design-Build Institute of America, examined the link between sustainability and project delivery. It looked at the likelihood of achieving or exceeding the original goal established for LEED® rating based on both the delivery method and the procurement type. The results were depicted according to the metric of what percentage of projects achieved or exceeded their original LEED goal. CM at-Risk was the highest at 94%. Measuring the impact the procurement process had on achieving sustainability, QBS was 95%, also the highest of the procurement methods.

This research seemed to confirm that there is a direct correlation between the delivery method and the procurement process with the ability to maximize sustainability. The higher collaboration and transparency resulting from the open-book contracts is most likely a significant contributor to these results.

For a more complete discussion on green building, consult the *Contractor's Guide to Green Building Construction*, published by AGC of America.

LESSONS LEARNED

CM at-Risk requires a constructor with a more expansive level of services and expertise than is required to be a lump sum or bid constructor. Growth in this method in project size and complexity is incremental, not exponential. Moving into this arena lacking the essential skills in conceptual estimating, full project scheduling, and value and systems analysis skills will create an unworkable situation. Projects initially will be underpriced, creating false expectations with the owner. Adversity could arise as the price goes up with each refinement in the design. The same will be true of schedule commitments if the new CM at-risk is unable to anticipate the complexity of design, owner review requirements, and government timeframes. Ultimately, the inexperienced CM may be terminated. The owner will be dissatisfied with the process; there may be substantial damages and litigation. None of these events advance the industry, the owner's needs, or the reputation of constructors in general.

Therefore, constructors that decide to participate in this delivery method need to have the skill sets, experience, and expectations to properly represent the owner's needs, be an effective partner to the designer during preconstruction, and deliver the finished product predictably as it relates to cost, schedule, and quality.

FUTURE TRENDS

The CM at-Risk delivery system has increased in popularity over the past several decades. With a growing need to be more efficient and sustainable, the convergence of major trends in the industry is likely to drive owners to look to more collaborative approaches to delivering their capital projects. There is also a growing trend to use CM at-Risk on horizontal projects such as highways and bridges.

The efficiencies gained by the use of new technologies such as Building Information Modeling (BIM), the drive to reduce waste and be green, and the application of lean philosophies are all converging. Collectively, they are having a significant impact on how construction projects are procured, contracted, and delivered.

In addition, the emergence of highly collaborative principles and contracts designed to incentivize a more integrated approach are evolving under the banner of Integrated Project Delivery (IPD). There is a growing trend to apply as many of these IPD principles as possible without having to use the relatively new multi-party contract. There is no industry consensus on what to call the approach of applying IPD principles to the more classic delivery methods such as CM at-Risk or Design-Build, but some refer to these approaches as "IPD-ish" or "IPD Lite."

Examples of IPD principles that are being applied without a multi-party contract include early involvement of trade contractors, co-location of project team members possibly in one location (a "Big Room"), and adding some pain/gain sharing and performance-based incentives to the contract.

As both private and public owners seek more collaboration, higher predictability, and a less adversarial environment, CM at-Risk provides an alternative solution. This is particularly true as projects are becoming more complex and managers are under pressure for speedy delivery and tighter budgets. By encouraging the concept of risk sharing, owners are seeking lower cost at the end of the project. The constructor has less need to use dollars to protect its risk.

The CM at-Risk method will continue to help owners be more comfortable with costs and schedule at an earlier phase in the process. Research has shown that the most important efficiency gains in the construction industry will be in the better use of non-adversarial team building. CM at-Risk is one of the ways available to achieve these efficiencies.

The subject of project delivery is a field that is constantly evolving. For updated information and links to some of the latest information, including a link to a map of the United States showing the ability to use CM at-Risk on both horizontal/highway and vertical/building projects by state, see the Project Delivery section of AGC of America's website at: http://www.agc.org/projectdelivery.

Self Test

1. Construction Management at-Risk is:
   a. A construction project delivery method
   b. A project management system
   c. An insurance program designed to control construction risk

2. The *defining* characteristics of Construction Management at-Risk are:
   a. A fast-track schedule, preconstruction services, a separate contract for design and construction, and final selection based only on lowest construction cost
   b. Preconstruction services, a separate contract for design and construction, and final selection based on factors other than just lowest construction cost
   c. A separate contract for design and construction and final selection based on factors other than just lowest construction cost

3. If a Construction Management at-Risk project includes a "GMP," this means:
   a. Guaranteed Maximum Profit for the construction manager
   b. All costs for the project will be subject to audit at the conclusion of the project
   c. Guaranteed Maximum Price for the project

4. If CM at-Risk is utilized on a "fast-track" project:
   a. The constructor will select the various trade contractors using a hard bid
   b. The constructor can begin construction before the completion of final construction documents
   c. The responsibility for design shifts to the construction manager

5. A true collaborative environment is most easily created when:
   a. All parties use the ConsensusDOCS standard contract forms
   b. Selection of the team members is based on criteria other than lowest cost
   c. The designer and the constructor share a common work space

6. The CM at-risk is typically paid by one of two different methods—the "schedule of values" basis or the "backed-up billing" basis. The method usually preferred by the CM is:
   a. The schedule of values basis
   b. The backed-up billing basis
   c. A hybrid of the two that includes payment advances

7. A major consideration for addressing changes in a CM at-Risk project is:
   a. The open-book relationship with the owner
   b. The trade contractor's markup on each change order
   c. Whether the design was approved in advance by the owner

8. Some owners prefer the CM at-Risk delivery method because of:
   a. The potential for major cost savings
   b. The ability to require the constructor to warrant the design
   c. The owner's ability to provide input on the selection of trade contractors

CONSTRUCTION MANAGEMENT AT-RISK

Case Study

The following is an example of a typical project. Evaluate the circumstances described and recommend how to proceed. Questions are offered for group discussion. Be prepared to explain and defend your recommendations.

The owner, a local board of education, has recently passed a school bond issue to finance a number of projects, both new construction and renovation of existing facilities. The owner has professional staff to maintain the schools and has used this staff in the past to renovate existing buildings. The size of the combined projects is too large for the in-house staff to construct, so the owner has engaged a program manager to assist them. Three of these projects are underway, all utilizing Design-Bid-Build, which is the method traditionally used by the owner. The State recently authorized counties to use Construction Management at-Risk and Design-Build if its Board of Education decides either is appropriate.

The project in question involves the renovation and expansion of a high school. It needs utilities replaced and an upgrade in the existing structure. A new structure is to be added to double classroom capacity. Also built will be sports facilities (two gyms and girls' and boys' locker/lavatory facilities) and additional educational facilities (one computer lab; one lab each for chemistry, biology, and physics; an auto shop and woodworking area; and a maintenance shop). The owner is concerned about the renovation portion of the project; the as-built documents may not be accurate, and the cost of renovation is a factor because a budget cap was set by the bond referendum. As is common with school projects, there is a need for the facility on a certain date, so speed to delivery is a major factor. The owner also wants to use the latest educational facilities design information and expertise and wants to be able to expand the facility.

The owner selects CM at-Risk with a program manager to facilitate requirements for the following reasons:
 a. The CM at-risk is to provide budget control and recommend adjustment of scope and design at the standard design phases to remain within the owner's budget.
    i. GMP to be set after design is in design development documents stage (2/3 through).
    ii. The CM at-risk and owner agree to adjust scope of work if the GMP is over the owner's budget due to design.
 b. The CM at-risk agrees to fast-track the project and to take responsibility for updating the budget and GMP during construction as the phases of design are completed.

c. The CM at-risk proposed a team that had:
      i. Worked together in the past on educational projects.
      ii. Had a good performance record from other school districts.
   d. The owner selected a designer and consultants with extensive educational experience, but the owner is new to the CM at-Risk delivery method.
   e. Although the owner has no experience with the CM at-Risk delivery method, the owner's judgment is that:
      i. The program manager will be able to draft owner's requirements.
      ii. CM at-Risk will permit flexibility during the renovation phase. The CM at-risk can respond to actual conditions in the old structure when they are encountered, and the team can judiciously use the contingency as needed.
      iii. As the CM at-risk will bid all the trade work, the school district will get the benefit of low bids on 80% of the work.

DISCUSSION ISSUES:

1. Was the owner's choice of project delivery system appropriate?
2. Did the owner overlook any relevant considerations? Which ones, if any?
3. Were the owner's expectations for the project delivery system realistic?
4. How/when should the owner make decisions and communicate them to the CM at-risk?
5. What authority should be given to the PM?
6. What authority should be reserved for the owner?
7. Should the PM/CM at-risk team consult with the owner's facilities staff?
a. During design?
b. During procurement of subcontractors?
c. During construction?
8. Should the owner involve the designer in the selection of the CM at-risk?
9. Should the owner select trade contractors or should the CM at-risk do so on its own, based on its experience?
10. How should the owner inspect the construction work?

CHAPTER NINE

DESIGN-BUILD

Introduction

Concept of Single Point Responsibility

Definitions in This Project Delivery System
- Design Phase Contingency
- Construction Phase and Project Contingencies
- Design-Build Team
- Bridging
- Teaming Agreement
- Design-Build Prime Contract
- Architectural/Engineering Subcontract
- Construction Subcontract
- Owner's Program
- Savings

Delivery Method Overview/Structure
- Programming/Predesign Phase
- Design Phase
- Construction Phase
- Commissioning
- Occupancy Phase

Defining Characteristics and Typical Characteristics
- Independent Advice

Procurement and Establishing the Contract Amount
- Selecting a Design-Builder and Procuring Design-Build Services
    - Qualifications Based Selection
    - Best Value: Fees
    - Best Value: Total Cost
    - Low Bid
- Timing of Establishing the Contract Amount

Basis of Reimbursement Options
- Lump Sum

DESIGN-BUILD

- Guaranteed Maximum Price
- Cost-Plus a Fixed Fee

Roles and Responsibilities
- The Owner
- The "Bridging" Architect
- The Project Criteria Consultant
- The Design-Builder
- The Design Subcontractor
- The Construction Subcontractor
- Other Specialty Contractors

Project Delivery Considerations
- Building Information Modeling (BIM)
- Changes
- Claims and Disputes
    - Partnering/Collaboration
    - Dispute Resolution Alternatives
    - Dispute Avoidance/Management
- Design Phases
    - Sources of Design Information
    - Design Process
- Fast-Tracking
- Indemnification/Hold Harmless Clauses
- Insurance
- Lean Construction
- Licensing
    - Architect/Engineer Licensing Requirements
    - Constructor Licensing Requirements
- Lien Waivers
- Prequalification
- Retainage
- Safety
- Standard Forms of Agreements
- Subcontracts
- Surety Bonds and Other Forms of Security for Performance
- Sustainability

Lessons Learned

Future Trends

Self Test

Case Study

INTRODUCTION

Design-Build is a method of project delivery in which one firm assumes responsibility for both the design and construction of the project. By combining these two functions from the outset, Design-Build can promote an interdisciplinary team approach throughout the entire duration of the project. Design-Build, which developed in the private sector and is used increasingly in the public sector, has increased in popularity in the last twenty years for many different types of construction.

Design-Build traces its heritage back to the ancient tradition of the master builder. The master builder was retained directly by the owner to produce the project in its entirety. While the owner defined the requirements for the project, the master builder was responsible for everything else: developing the design concept and aesthetic design; engineering; drafting; procuring labor, materials, and equipment; and the performance of all construction activities as well as interior design and construction. Master builders created many of the wonders of the ancient world, some of the largest and longest-lasting projects in history.

Design and construction gradually became separate disciplines as the arts and sciences flourished after the Renaissance. Architecture and engineering became separate professions, and construction became more specialized. In the United States, architecture and engineering came to be regulated in the interest of public safety. Many states established licensing requirements for architects and engineers and set minimum standards of education and training for applicants to qualify for such licenses.

The architect and engineer traditionally were retained by the owner to design the project and supervise the constructor during project construction. In the early twentieth century, some in the construction industry believed that ethical considerations prevented the architect or engineer from having a financial interest in the construction of the project. This position was premised on the indisputable proposition that the architect and/or engineer owe a professional duty of care to the owner and to the public in accordance with the approved specifications and public safety guidelines. It was thought that a designer's performance of this duty would be compromised if the designer also had a financial interest in the construction. The fear was that the designer might allow shoddy workmanship to achieve a profit on the project, contrary to the interests of safety and quality shared by the owner and the general public.

Since the 1960s and 1970s, such ethical barriers to Design-Build have slowly abated. Professional design groups, such as the American Institute of Architects, dropped ethical restrictions that had prevented its members from participating in the construction of the projects they designed. These developments sometimes were in response to antitrust and other legal issues. In general, however, there has been increasing acceptance in the United States of the notion that having a single entity both design and construct a project is not improper, and that owners should have the option to use this method of project delivery.

The growth of Design-Build also accompanied several other trends in the construction industry. Some owners required project delivery in shorter timeframes than were common with the Design-Bid-Build method. This led to the practice of "fast-tracking" projects by beginning construction while some design elements were not yet complete. Design-Build facilitates fast-tracking. Other owners had needs for expanded services from the project teams, including project financing or facility operation. Design-Build's multidisciplinary approach lends itself to delivery of such expanded services. The result is that Design-Build has grown from an alternative project delivery system to a mainstream delivery system popular with owners and industry alike.

CONCEPT OF SINGLE POINT RESPONSIBILITY

A design-builder is a single entity that accepts responsibility and control over the design of a project to the owner's requirements as well as construction of the project to that design. The owner thus contracts with one firm and holds that firm responsible for all aspects of project design and construction. This distinguishes Design-Build from both the traditional Design-Bid-Build and CM at-Risk project delivery systems, in which the design and construction are performed independently by different firms under separate contracts to the owner. In Design-Build, the owner has one single point of responsibility for the entire project—the design-builder.

The single entity that is the design-builder can take several different forms. It can be an integrated company with in-house architects, engineers, and construction professionals. It can be a combination of a design firm and a construction firm that come together for one project only or for a period of many years. Most commonly, Design-Build projects are delivered with a builder firm in the lead and the design subcontracted to architects and/or engineers, although designer-led Design-Build structures are also possible.

The notion that a design professional's responsibility to the owner flows through the contractor can be a difficult attitudinal adjustment for some designers, particularly for those trained with the belief that the architect/engineer's role is to protect the owner from untrustworthy contractors. Under this view, some fear that Design-Build can lead to a troubling diminution in the professional standing and function of the architect/engineer. While this perception may have validity in some circumstances, Design-Build does not necessarily reduce the design professional to a role of secondary importance. A well-structured Design-Build project should recognize and support the critical role of the A/E professionals, including appropriate access to and communication with the owner. The professional and ethical obligations of licensed design professionals to protect the owner and the public should be respected and supported in all delivery models.

Owners may hesitate to use Design-Build due to concern that their ability to control the outcome of the design process will be diminished. Owners are accustomed in other delivery models to being able to direct that whatever changes they desire be incorporated into the design by the A/E professionals who work directly for them. It is true that Design-Build diminishes to some extent the owner's direct control over the details of the design. In another sense, however, the owner under Design-Build can choose the level of control that it wishes to exercise depending on how it implements this delivery model. Specifically, the following are some of the techniques owners use under Design-Build to retain control over the design outcome:

- Select the design-builder based at least partly on qualifications. Be sure that those qualifications include a track record of achieving customer satisfaction on previous projects.
- Write effective performance specifications that hold the design-builder accountable to achieve the end result required by the owner.
- Incorporate prescriptive specifications selectively into the project criteria, limited to those elements where the owner knows precisely the design solution that it chooses to prescribe.
- Provide feedback during the design process either by requiring periodic interim design submissions for review and approval or by including owner representation within the integrated project team. If the feedback is provided early enough, the design-builder may incorporate the owner's preferences at no added cost.
- Negotiate trade-offs with the design-builder; that is, give the design-builder latitude to vary from the project criteria in a less important aspect of the project in return for accepting a no-cost change to satisfy owner preferences in another area.
- Incorporate financial incentives based in part on owner satisfaction or owner discretionary evaluation of the design-builder's performance.

DEFINITIONS IN THIS PROJECT DELIVERY SYSTEM

The Design-Build method is practiced in several different ways. It is helpful to define terms used in this method in order to discuss them.

Design Phase Contingency

This is the amount of money included in an estimate to represent the yet-to-be-detailed or yet-to-be-defined portions of the contract documents. A design phase contingency is identified during the initial estimates and is included in all budgets and estimates during the project. As the documents become more defined, the design phase contingency decreases as the costs are further identified and either shifted to the cost of the work or eliminated.

Because the design is generally assumed incomplete when using a Design-Build delivery method, the design phase contingency presents new issues. The selection process used to choose the design-builder, and the resulting contractual relationship, will affect the handling of the design phase contingency.

It becomes difficult to identify and track the design phase contingency if a design-builder is selected with a Low Bid and awarded a Lump Sum contract, then carries the design phase contingency. The design-builder will most likely keep any unused contingency. If a project is awarded with a Qualifications Based Selection and an open-book GMP contract, then the design phase contingency can more easily be identified, tracked, and managed. If the project is procured with Best Value: Total Cost, depending on the basis of reimbursement used, either scenario could result. Knowing whether the design phase contingency is being carried and how any unused contingency will be distributed is thus closely related to the selection method.

Construction Phase and Project Contingencies

As the project moves into the construction phase, a construction phase contingency is usually identified and tracked separately from an owner's project contingency. The construction phase contingency is used to adjust for minor changes in the work, changes in economic conditions, and unanticipated problems. The project contingency is generally held by the owner and is used to account for major problems, such as unforeseen subsurface conditions and scope changes.

The use of Design-Build does not have a material impact on how construction and project phase contingencies are handled, but the basis of reimbursement will again dictate how any unused contingencies will be distributed.

Design-Build Team

The design-build team is a group of design and construction professionals who deliver the project to the owner. They may all be part of one firm, called an integrated design-builder. They may also be members of different firms. The design-builder may be a constructor that subcontracts the design to a design subcontractor. On the other hand, it may design the project in-house and subcontract the construction. The design-builder may also be a joint venture of design and construction firms.

Bridging

Often with the Design-Build method, the owner may create a set of "bridging documents." This is common when selecting a design-builder with the Low Bid or Best Value: Total Cost procurements. Bridging documents are partial documents that are used by the owner as the basis of pricing when hiring a design-builder. Bridging documents can be preliminary (conceptual or schematic) or more complete (design development or partial construction documents). They can be prepared in-house if an owner has the design expertise available or by a consultant engaged by the owner. The consultant engaged by the owner to create a set of bridging documents is often referred to as a "bridging architect" or "bridging consultant." The bridging architect's responsibility is to assist the owner in developing its requirements or program and to help communicate those requirements to the design-builder. Using bridging documents can diminish some of the advantages of Design-Build. For example, bridging documents may limit the degree of innovation that can be exercised by the design-builder in developing a solution to the owner's requirements.

Teaming Agreement

A teaming agreement is an agreement between firms to jointly pursue an opportunity on an individual project and to perform the work if they are awarded the project. For example, a design firm and a construction firm may enter into a teaming agreement to compete as a team for a Design-Build project. They may agree that one firm will be the prime contractor and the other a subcontractor, or they may agree to be a joint venture. The "Design/Build Teaming Checklist," developed in 1999 by the American Institute of Architects and AGC of America, is intended as a convenient form for agreement among team members pursuing award of a contract for a single Design-Build project.

Design-Build Prime Contract

The Design-Build prime contract is the contract between the owner and the design-builder in which the design-builder agrees to design, construct, and deliver the project to the owner.

Architectural/Engineering Subcontract

In a constructor-led team or a Design-Build joint venture, an architectural/engineering subcontract is between the design-builder and the designer. Note that the owner does not contract directly with the designer in this agreement. Instead the designer contracts directly with the design-builder.

Construction Subcontract

In a designer-led team or a Design-Build joint venture, a construction subcontract is between the design-builder and the constructor to provide construction services.

Owner's Program

The owner's program is a statement of project requirements for the project. It may also be called the project criteria. It is provided to the design-builder so that its requirements may be satisfied by the design-builder's design and construction services.

Savings

The concept of savings in Design-Build is similar to that in CM at-Risk. Often the owner and design-builder enter into an agreement (as part of the contract) to share any savings they generate by bringing the project in under the guaranteed price. The purpose for this is to create a common goal, encourage all parties to seek timely decisions, and create an atmosphere in which the design-builder has an incentive to be as economical as possible in completing the project.

DELIVERY METHOD OVERVIEW/STRUCTURE

Programming/Predesign Phase

As in other methods of project delivery, in this phase the owner decides upon its project requirements and furnishes them to the design-builder. In Design-Build, the owner usually specifies the project requirements in terms of performance parameters. For example, on a project to construct a manufacturing facility, the owner's requirements may be stated in terms of the plant's output, such as units per shift. By stating requirements in performance terms, the owner allows the design-builder to use its own expertise and ingenuity to satisfy the requirements in a cost-effective way.

The design-builder will rely upon the owner's program in designing the project. Thus, it is especially important for the owner to determine its requirements accurately and to state them clearly. Clear requirements are essential to the success of the Design-Build undertaking.

Design Phase

The design-builder designs the project to satisfy the owner's requirements. In this phase, the design-builder designs in accordance with the owner's program and provides it to the owner for approval. The owner reviews and approves the design if it satisfies the program requirements.

During the design phase, the owner typically has the opportunity to revise its program requirements. However, such changes may be compensable under the contract.

The project design may be created by a subcontractor to the design-builder that has no direct contractual relationship with the owner. This is in contrast to the traditional Design-Bid-Build system and CM at-Risk, in which the owner is the designer's owner. The Design-Build approach permits the designer and constructor jointly to participate in the design phase, with the expectation that such a cooperative approach will benefit the project.

Construction Phase

Once the owner approves the design, the design-builder constructs that design. There are several differences in the construction phase between Design-Build and some other project delivery systems.

First, the drawings and specifications that govern the construction were developed by the design-builder performing the construction. The contract drawings and specifications may be less detailed than in the Design-Bid-Build method. Because the design and construction are under the control of a single entity, there should be fewer interpretational disputes concerning the construction documents than in Design-Bid-Build.

Second, the owner may not have the final word on interpretation of the construction documents. As such, if the owner disagrees with the design-builder's interpretation, assuming that the proposed design meets the owner's project criteria, the owner may have to make a compensable change to effect the change.

These differences demonstrate that in Design-Build, the owner does not have the same degree of control over the construction phase as in some other delivery systems. Remember, however, that the owner has engaged the design-builder to gain its experience and expertise with respect to the project.

Commissioning

Prior to occupancy, the project's systems and equipment are tested and adjusted so that they perform as designed and satisfy the project's requirements. Typically, the design-builder's contract requires that this be done prior to the owner's final acceptance of the project. While the design-builder usually has this responsibility, contract requirements for commissioning can vary widely. The actual commissioning work may be done by a specialty contractor or commissioning consultant, and there may or may not be a separate professional on its staff involved on behalf of the owner.

Occupancy Phase

The Design-Build method also lends itself to additional services after final completion of the construction work. Sometimes, these additional services include operation of the facility and maintenance under an incentive arrangement to minimize long-term costs. There are various terms for such arrangements, including "DBO" (Design-Build Operate) and "DBOM" (Design-Build Operate Maintain) (see Chapter 11 for more on this subject). While such services are not essential to Design-Build, the single point of responsibility can easily be combined with these additional types of services.

Sometimes a design-builder will guarantee that the facility will operate at specified performance measures. This is common in Design-Build projects for manufacturing or processing plants.

DEFINING CHARACTERISTICS AND TYPICAL CHARACTERISTICS

Defining characteristics uniquely distinguish one delivery method from another. The following is the defining characteristic of the Design-Build delivery method:
- Design and construction contracts are combined (versus both Design-Bid-Build and CM at-Risk, in which contracts are separate).

Single point responsibility is a fundamental characteristic of the Design-Build method. The owner signs one contract for the project, calling for the design-builder to design and construct the entire project. This distinguishes this delivery method from the Design-Bid-Build and CM-at-Risk methods of project delivery, in which the owner enters into separate contracts with the designer and the constructor.

On some Design-Build projects, the design-builder is selected long before a budget or price can be determined. In such cases, the design-builder is selected either with a QBS or Best Value: Fees competition. It is possible, however, to select a design-builder using a Best Value: Total Cost selection procedure or by Low Bid. If the cost of the work is a partial or sole consideration in the selection, the project must be more fully developed to avoid misunderstanding. This is typical on building projects, but in the case of horizontal projects such as highways or bridges, the RFP may provide only very conceptual design information or sometimes just performance specifications. Such information would then be the basis for the design-builder's response to the RFP.

Typical characteristics of Design-Build include the ability to fast-track and, depending on the procurement option, the use of an open-book contract with a GMP. Design-Build projects do not have to be fast-tracked; an owner could elect to finish the design before starting construction. Therefore, fast-tracking is a typical, but not a defining, characteristic.

Independent Advice

The Design-Build method does not separate the design phase from the construction phase or utilize a separate independent professional in each phase. If an owner wishes to receive independent advice during these phases apart from its own in-house resources, the owner must engage the services of a separate professional whose duties are solely to the owner.

If the owner has the in-house resources, it may designate a responsible person from its staff to verify quality during construction. The owner's amount of direct influence on how the quality is defined and verified depends upon the option chosen.

In every option, production of quality during the construction phase is the primary responsibility of the contractor, but the verification of that quality will vary between the options. The architect, as the owner's representative, is responsible in Design-Bid-Build and CM at-Risk. The owner assumes this role in Design-Build.

In the standard Design-Bid-Build delivery option, the definition of quality is heavily dependent upon the architect's ability to understand and translate the owner's needs. In the CM at-Risk and Design-Bid-Build delivery options, this task is still often assigned to the architect, though with assistance from the contractor. In Design-Build, the design-builder assumes these duties.

PROCUREMENT AND ESTABLISHING THE CONTRACT AMOUNT

Selecting a Design-Builder and Procuring Design-Build Services

As discussed in Chapter 2: Procurement Options, the owner may select the design-builder by one of several means, depending upon the relative weighting of qualifications and price. This distinguishes Design-Build from some other methods of project delivery, like Design-Bid-Build, in which the constructor is selected solely on the basis of low price.

Qualifications Based Selection

The owner may select the design-builder based solely on qualifications. Traditionally, designers have been selected by this method. A Qualifications Based Selection usually is accomplished by soliciting statements of qualifications from several firms, rating them by the owner's criteria, and selecting the firm rated highest by the owner. Public owners typically will issue a statement of their criteria so that firms can address them directly. The owner also may decide upon a shortlist of firms and then enter into negotiations with one or more of them to discuss project details, terms, or price.

Best Value: Fees

A design-builder could be selected based on its qualifications, fees, and possibly general conditions costs. This would be a Best Value: Fees competition if the price component that is competitively proposed does not include the total design and construction costs.

Best Value: Total Cost

With a Best Value: Total Cost selection, the owner consciously makes a trade-off between price considerations and the other elements of its proposal. After weighing all the factors, the owner determines which proposal offers the owner the best value in terms of price versus other factors. For example, the owner may select the firm that offers the most highly rated technical proposal, if the owner determines that the price of that proposal is reasonable. On the other hand, an owner may select a lower-rated firm if the owner decides that the highest-rated offer comes at too high a price.

The owner may initially select several firms and then ask them to submit competitive proposals. The request usually is by a Request for Proposals that describes the owner's requirements in terms of performance characteristics. Such a competitive proposal may include some preliminary design information and may also request a budget or ceiling price. Competitive negotiation is a means of selecting a firm based on a review of technical and price proposals. Typically, the owner will request Design-Build proposals from several competing firms. The firms compete on the basis of qualifications, design excellence, experience, price, and possibly other factors, each weighted according to the owner's priorities. The owner may then enter into negotiations with one or more competing firms to select one firm for the project.

A unique feature of Design-Build when selecting with a Best Value: Total Cost approach is that the selection could be "cost-based" or "solution-based." In a cost-based selection, the owner provides project criteria, and competing design-build firms state their most competitive price to complete the design. In a solution-based selection, the owner typically provides its budget along with its project criteria, and competing design build firms provide their own design solutions, trying to provide the best solution within the owner's stated budget.

Low Bid

A fourth option to procure Design-Build, though not as common, is Low Bid. In this case, the owner provides project criteria or bridging documents. This information is used by competing design-build firms as the basis for preparing their bids. By definition, a project using a Low Bid competition would be awarded to the lowest responsive and responsible design-build bidder. A number of challenges arise when using Low Bid procurement with Design-Build, including the responsibility the owner has to produce the design criteria.

Also, competitive Design-Build bids can often be problematic to compare to one another because each proposal might be based on different designs. As long as the owner is concerned only that the project criteria are met and not with how they are met, Low Bid is a viable option. One of the most critical challenges for the owner procuring with Low Bid is the difficulty of making changes after the time of the selection. This is an even more difficult issue than dealing with changes in the traditional Design-Bid-Build delivery method because, with Design-Build Low Bid, the design firm is no longer representing the owner as its primary responsibility.

Timing of Establishing the Contract Amount

Of course, the parties can agree upon price at any time in the project. In Cost-Plus arrangements, agreement typically is reached at the beginning of the project to define reimbursable expenses, establish a means of presenting incurred costs for reimbursement, and establish a fixed fee.

A lump sum or a Guaranteed Maximum Price may not be set until the design is complete or at least at an advanced stage. This enables the design-builder to develop an understanding of the estimated costs of construction.

Contracts that require the design-builder to develop a GMP typically provide for payment on a cost-reimbursement basis initially, based on a preliminary project budget agreed upon by the parties. Such contracts typically require the design-builder to submit a proposed price at some defined point, such as completion of design. The costs incurred to date become part of the price, and the project proceeds on the basis of the agreed upon price. Because the parties must agree upon the new price, whether lump sum or GMP, it is important for the contract to include or define what happens if they fail to agree upon a price.

BASIS OF REIMBURSEMENT OPTIONS

Lump Sum

A Design-Build contract can be awarded on the basis of a Lump Sum contract if the parties so agree. While parties can agree to establish a price at any point, often they wait until completion of preliminary or final design documents before committing to a price for the project.

Guaranteed Maximum Price

Depending on the procurement process and the subsequent contract chosen, establishment of the Guaranteed Maximum Price (GMP) is an important part of the Design-Build project delivery system. Many issues—such as when to establish the GMP, whether to fix the design-builder's fees, whether to establish an early GMP or use a progressive approach, etc.—exist with Design-Build.

An important distinction within Design-Build is that the cost of the design is a part of the GMP because the cost of the design (including the designer's fee) may be considered a cost of the work. There may also be a provision that creates an incentive for the constructor to minimize costs by allowing the design-builder to share in savings below the GMP.

Some fast-track Design-Build contracts require the design-builder to begin work on the project immediately, before there is a sound basis to estimate the project's cost. In such a case, the owner may agree to reimburse the design-builder's costs during the early stages of project design and ask the design-builder to propose a GMP at a later stage.

A GMP contract may contain a provision regarding any savings between the GMP and the project's actual cost. It may provide that the owner retains all such savings. Such provisions sometimes are criticized based on the theory that they do not provide an economic incentive for the design-builder to minimize costs. The design-builder may still have some incentive to hold costs down to diminish the chance that the GMP amount will be exceeded. To address this concern, some contracts provide for the design-builder to share in a portion of the savings.

With GMPs, overruns caused by the owner are considered changes and not part of the original GMP. Note that this is an area where Design-Build and CM at-Risk contracts differ. In a GMP Design-Build contract, the category of overruns due to errors in design, after the establishment of the GMP, shifts from the owner to the design-builder and would not be considered a change to the original GMP. Conversely, in CM at-Risk, design errors would generally be the owner's responsibility (reference the Spearin Doctrine as discussed in Chapter 7) and would be considered a justification for changes to the original GMP.

Cost-Plus a Fixed Fee

A design-builder may be retained on a purely cost-reimbursement basis. The design-builder's fee is often a fixed amount so that the design-builder will have an incentive to minimize costs. This allows a completely open-book approach so that the owner can monitor project costs. This is common where the owner and design-builder have a high level of trust and confidence between them, whether through experience or reputation. It also is an appropriate choice for experimental or other high-risk projects and for projects in which cost estimates are not reliable, such as in emergency repair situations.

ROLES AND RESPONSIBILITIES

The Owner

The owner plays an extremely important role in the Design-Build process, even though the design-builder accepts substantial risk and performs both design and construction. The owner must first establish its project requirements, review and approve the design, approve project budgets, and if required, review and approve price proposals. The owner's requirements must be stated clearly and accurately for the project to be successful.

The owner plays a different role in Design-Build than in some other project delivery systems. The owner does not have a separate contract with a designer. The design-builder may furnish the design, or it may subcontract the design to a separate firm. Although the design-builder and its subcontractors are responsible for meeting the owner's requirements, the owner may not be directly involved in overseeing the designer's work.

The "Bridging" Architect

A bridging architect or designer is one that assists the owner in developing its requirements or program and helps communicate those requirements to the design-builder. The bridging architect may also assist the owner by preparing specific design elements the owner wishes to describe within the project requirements. Then the bridging architect monitors the actual construction of the project to ensure that it is consistent with the requirements of the program. The use of the term "bridging architect" suggests that more extensive prescriptive design work is performed before selection of the design-builder. Contrast the role of the project criteria consultant (see below), which is focused more on performance criteria.

The Project Criteria Consultant

The project criteria consultant is hired by the owner to develop the owner's program, or project criteria, that are incorporated into the RFP. These become the standards which the design-builder must satisfy when it creates the design. Generally, these criteria are formulated as performance specifications rather than prescriptive specifications. For example, instead of defining the exact geometry and dimensions of a pumping system, the performance specifications will define the required output (gallons per minute) and leave the design-builder to determine how that performance will be attained.

Expertise in design is a helpful attribute for a project criteria consultant, but it does not follow that every design architect or engineer is best suited to this role. Some architects and engineers may be tempted to develop the design solutions themselves, whereas a skilled project criteria consultant understands that its function is to define the outcome desired by the owner and afford the design-builder enough flexibility to design an effective means to reach it.

The Design-Builder

Of course, with responsibility for both design and construction, the design-builder's role is to design the project to the owner's specifications and to construct the project in accordance with that design. The design-builder provides both preconstruction and construction services, so it can provide value engineering, constructability reviews, and design reviews that may eliminate potential problems and facilitate the construction work.

The design-builder may perform these responsibilities in several ways, depending on its in-house resources and structure. A firm that has in-house architecture, engineering, and construction resources will perform all responsibilities itself. Firms that lack some of those resources may combine to form a design-build entity as a corporation or joint venture established specifically to perform the Design-Build project at hand. Such a combination or joint venture of a constructor and designer may subcontract the design and/or the construction to the member firms.

The Design Subcontractor

In a constructor-led team, the design-builder often subcontracts the design to a design subcontractor. While that design subcontractor has duties to the owner, the design firm contracts only with the design-builder. This is a marked departure from the Design-Bid-Build method, in which the designer has a direct contract with the owner.

The Construction Subcontractor

In a designer-led team, the design-builder subcontracts the construction to a construction subcontractor. This also is a marked difference from Design-Bid-Build. The designer owes duties directly to the constructor under the subcontract. In Design-Bid-Build, the designer has a contract only with the owner, with no direct contractual duty to the constructor.

Other Specialty Contractors

Other specialty subcontractors play the same role they play in other delivery systems, like Design-Bid-Build and CM at-Risk, except that they are likely to have a contract directly with the design-builder.

PROJECT DELIVERY CONSIDERATIONS

Chapter 6 discussed basic project delivery considerations and risk issues common to all projects and various project delivery methods. Some risks vary from one project delivery method to another, while others remain the same. This section follows the same format as Chapter 6 and highlights the areas that are different in this project delivery method. Readers should review Chapter 6 for other basic considerations not discussed here.

Building Information Modeling

If Design-Build is procured with Low Bid or Best Value: Total Cost, then similar to Design-Bid-Build, the use of Building Information Modeling to improve planning and design can be limited by the lack of design-builder involvement in early planning and design development. Early model availability can be of great value to the eventual successful design-builder during bidding, design, and construction. When Design-Build is procured with Low Bid or Best Value: Total Cost, the benefit of enhanced collaboration between the primary parties—the design-build team and the owner—is not as much of an advantage because the design-builder is not engaged during planning and early design development.

If Design-Build is procured with Best Value: Fees or Qualifications Based Selection, similar to CM at-Risk, the Design-Build contract is most likely an open-book, not-to-exceed GMP. BIM use to improve the process is of great value on these projects.

When combining design and construction under one contract, some of the challenges that exist with CM at-Risk disappear, such as defining responsibilities and identifying handoffs between the designer and the contractor. Since the design-build team is combined and working with the owner in an open, collaborative environment, BIM use during design and construction allows for better and more efficient analysis of design alternatives. The ability for the design-builder to build the building virtually prior to building it in the field allows for improved coordination and fewer issues in the field.

ConsensusDOCS 301, "Building Information Modeling (BIM) Addendum," addresses the team's responsibilities as they relate to the model. The addendum was designed with the intention that it would work with any project delivery model, including Design-Build. Model sharing and the ability to rely on the information in the model with the Design-Build project delivery method are still evolving. In the case of Design-Build (Low Bid or Best Value: Total Cost), where the contractor is relying on the information provided by the owner as the basis for its bid, all parties are still evaluating the trade-offs of sharing the full Building Information Models versus the benefits lost by not sharing the information.

Changes

Theoretically, changes that are entirely the result of design errors and omissions should be eliminated as a risk to the owner because the same entity is responsible for the construction cost and the design. This is one of the most important benefits Design-Build provides to owners. The responsibility and the risk the owner undertakes with Design-Bid-Build and CM at-Risk as supported by the Spearin Doctrine (see Chapter 7) are essentially eliminated with Design-Build.

In Design-Bid-Build and CM at-Risk, the owner may change its requirements and modify its design prior to hiring the constructor without making a change to the construction contract. In Design-Build, however, depending on the procurement option and after the owner provides its requirements to the design-builder, any change in requirements may be a change to the design-builder's contract. That may entitle the design-builder to an increase in price or time. Evaluating changes can be more complex on a Design-Build project than on Design-Bid-Build or CM at-Risk, given the latitude the design-builder has in carrying out the owner's requirements. Sometimes owners will negotiate with design-builders for no-cost changes in exchange for relaxing other elements of the owner's project criteria.

Claims and Disputes

In Design-Build, claims and disputes between the designer and constructor will not affect the owner because the designer and constructor are on the same team and have a vested interest in resolving their differences. Further, the risk of additional construction costs arising from a design error rests with the design-builder, not with the owner.

Partnering/Collaboration

Partnering is as useful in Design-Build as in other project delivery systems. The collaboration inherent in Design-Build lends itself to partnering.

Dispute Resolution Alternatives

All informal dispute resolution mechanisms can be used in Design-Build to the same extent as in other delivery systems. Dispute review boards, mediation, and arbitration all have been used to resolve disputes on Design-Build projects.

Dispute Avoidance/Management

Surveys have shown that Design-Build produces fewer design-related disputes during the construction phase than Design-Bid-Build. One reason is the collaboration between the design and construction disciplines required in the Design-Build delivery system. Another reason is the single point responsibility and control inherent in Design-Build. Thus, Design-Build normally avoids design-related disputes involving the owner.

Design Phases

Because of the single point responsibility, there are some major differences between Design-Build and the other project delivery systems during the design phase.

Sources of Design Information

One of the primary differences between Design-Build and Design-Bid-Build is the source of design information. Once the owner's requirements are defined, design proceeds in Design-Build as in other delivery systems. Design documents may not be brought to the same level of completion as in the bid package in Design-Bid-Build, however. Design-Build encourages performance requirements rather than the detailed prescriptive design specifications common in Design-Bid-Build. This may be a concern to the owner unless a complete, final set of "as-built" or record documents are required as a part of the Design-Build agreement.

Depending on the selection type and contract, the owner may have less control over the details of the design as compared to other delivery models. The owner provides a program of requirements to the design-builder, which then transfers these requirements into construction documents. Many times these requirements are performance-based, not prescriptive. Consequently, the design-builder is expected to use its experience and knowledge to produce acceptable documents.

In addition, the designer of the project has no direct contract with the owner. Consequently, the owner cannot expect the traditional relationship with the architect/engineer and may not have as much direct access to the design professionals.

Design Process

Another difference in this delivery method is the way the design process is impacted. By definition, the constructor is on board during the design phase and can offer input. Depending on the delivery method and basis of reimbursement used, however, one of the key elements is the owner's ability to make changes in the design after design responsibility has shifted to the design-builder. For example, if the owner creates a set of bridging documents and procures the design-builder based on a Low Bid selection, the ability of the owner to affect design decisions without a change order may be limited.

Fast-Tracking

Design-Build facilitates fast-track project delivery. A design-build firm can begin design as soon as the owner's requirements are determined and can begin construction of early project phases even while later phases are being designed. Further, there is no waiting for bids to be prepared and evaluated after the completion of design, in contrast to Design-Bid-Build. The single point responsibility inherent in Design-Build facilitates project coordination. The higher degree of communication between designer and builder inherent in Design-Build helps to minimize any work that may have to be redone or altered as a result of proceeding with construction while the design is ongoing.

Fast-tracking has an impact on the design process. During the design process for Design-Bid-Build, all components of the project are involved in each phase of the design (programming, schematic design, design development, etc.). This is normally not the case in Design-Build. Rather, each component of the project goes though each of the design phases, almost independently. For example, to meet the requirements of the schedule, the foundation and structural components usually are in the construction documents phase before any of the other components. Plumbing design decisions, which are some of the last decisions to be made in the Design-Bid-Build method, must be made early in the process.

Although this difference in design phases is usually well known and axiomatic for fast-tracking, its consequences are not always fully understood. Design decisions are made in a different order from those in Design-Bid-Build, and the input for those decisions comes from different parties. Failure to make correct, timely decisions can be extremely costly later. For example, in the Design-Bid-Build method, an owner may wish to change the location of the utility entrance. If this occurs late in the design phase of a Design-Bid-Build project, there are no major construction cost consequences. In a fast-tracked project, such a decision would have significant cost and schedule impact.

Indemnification/Hold Harmless Clauses

Indemnification issues in Design-Build are generally the same as those in other project delivery systems, but the risk to the design-builder may be somewhat greater because of the single point of responsibility.

Insurance

The design-builder's design work is covered by professional liability insurance (errors and omissions insurance) while its construction services are covered by commercial general liability insurance and builder's risk coverage. The growth of

Design-Build has been matched by the increased availability of insurance policies tailored to the work of design-builders. Much of this insurance is now available to and procured by constructors or subcontractors that are performing or responsible for a portion (or all) of the design. This is the case even when the constructors or subcontractors are hiring out the design work rather than performing that work with registered professionals on their payrolls.

Licensing

Licensing has long posed challenges to design-builders because their work requires both a designer's license—for an architect and/or engineer—and a constructor's license. Licensing is regulated by the individual states, and states' requirements vary greatly. State licensing laws and practices are changing rapidly. It is always advisable to check a state's licensing laws prior to starting a Design-Build project.

Architect/Engineer Licensing Requirements

On a Design-Build project, the design must be produced by a licensed individual or firm in accordance with the law of the state where the project is located. Some states require that professional architect or engineer licenses be issued solely to individuals rather than to corporations or partnerships. In such states, a design-builder must ensure that the design is performed under the responsible charge of the individual who holds the license. Other states permit a corporation to be licensed, but only if the individual shareholders and directors of the corporation hold a professional license or a majority of the shareholders and/or directors are licensed. In these states, a Design-Build project often must have a separate corporation in charge of the design. In a few states, a corporation can undertake a contract requiring work by a licensed professional, even where the corporation does not have sole or majority ownership by registered professionals, so long as the design work is controlled by persons who are registered.

Constructor Licensing Requirements

Most states license general contractors and some subcontractors. Construction of a Design-Build project requires such licenses to the same extent as other projects. In designer-led teams, the design-builder may rely upon the license of the constructor. Some states prohibit a designer from holding a constructor's license.

Lean Construction

Lean construction, or the concept of eliminating waste, does not fundamentally change regardless of the project delivery method. However, the ability to integrate lean principles across the entire project and not just within portions of the project team is significantly enhanced by the combined contract of Design-Build.

If there is a collaborative environment, the ability of the owner and the design-build team to implement lean practices should be enhanced both within their organizations as well in the execution of the design and construction process. The opportunity to increase productivity and improve efficiency is always available.

Lien Waivers

As with all private construction projects, constructors, subcontractors, and vendors have the legal right to file liens. On Design-Build projects, there are a few unique issues with respect to mechanic's liens and, thus, lien waivers. First, in many states, design professionals are not entitled to lien rights. In such states, a requirement for lien waivers serves only the purpose of documenting amounts paid to consultants because there are no lien rights of those parties to be waived. On many projects on which there are no lien rights (e.g., public construction projects in some states), there may be no practical difference in administration for a Design-Build project than for the traditional Design-Bid-Build. Second, a lien waiver by the prime design-builder does not waive rights of the consultants or others without lien rights to be paid; therefore, such a lien waiver does not represent any verification to the project owner that all lower-tier consultants have been paid.

Third, the project owner is placed in the position of policing the lien waiver process because the design professional—engaged by the prime design-builder—will not be performing this role on behalf of the project owner. There is considerable debate on mechanic's lien rights, Miller Act protection, and lien waivers for hybrid entities such as design-build contractors and various types of construction managers. Again, this is a state-specific issue that is likely to evolve over time. Therefore, great care should be used in developing lien waivers, releases, and payment certifications under Design-Build contracts.

Prequalification

Design-Build firms may be prequalified or shortlisted. In the event of a Low Bid selection, prequalification becomes very important.

Retainage

In Design-Build projects, as with other methods, there is retainage. The key difference is the fact that, in this delivery method, the retainage includes a portion of the design fee. Release of the retainage may be postponed until the delivery of final, "as-built" design documents.

Safety

On most Design-Build projects, the design-builder has overall responsibility for jobsite safety, similar to a constructor on a Design-Bid-Build project. There is no real difference between a design-builder and a general contractor in this regard.

The early involvement of the constructor on Design-Build projects may help in planning how construction safety features, such as engineered tie-off points, can be incorporated into the design.

Standard Forms of Agreement

A number of standard forms of agreement are available for the Design-Build project delivery system. There are four primary industry standard sets of Design-Build agreements: ConsensusDOCS, AIA, DBIA, and EJCDC documents. While no contract form will capture the unique features of each and every project, the use of standard industry contract forms as a template or starting point in developing the contract is usually the most efficient way to accomplish these objectives and achieve consensus. One widely used Design-Build contract form is the ConsensusDOCS 410, "Standard Design-Build Agreement and General Conditions Between Owner and Design-Builder (Cost of Work Plus Fee with GMP)." The ConsensusDOCS 410, like all ConsensusDOCS forms but unlike some of the AIA contract forms, promotes, rather than prohibits, direct communications between the contracting parties, a key to avoiding and resolving misunderstandings and disputes.

Many owners develop their own contract forms, which may or may not be based on one of the standard industry agreements. Industry participants are encouraged to carefully review the agreements before entering into a contract for services.

Subcontracts

The concepts of design subcontracts and construction subcontracts are discussed above. During the construction phase, subcontracts are used in the same way they are used in Design-Bid-Build and CM at-Risk, although in Design-Build some of the subcontractors may have design obligations as part of their scope. These subcontractors would be referred to as design-build subcontractors and are distinguished from design-assist subcontractors by the fact that they accept responsibility for the design. The subcontract agreement for design-assist subcontractors must allocate responsibility for coordination of the design effort.

Surety Bonds and Other Forms of Security for Performance

The design-builder typically must obtain the same surety bonds as a general contractor. The design-builder must provide a performance bond to assure the owner that the project will be completed. It must also furnish a payment bond to ensure that subcontractors and suppliers will be paid.

In the past, performance bonds on Design-Build projects were written for only a portion of the contract. Care must be taken to ensure that performance bonds do secure design obligations in addition to the obligations for performance of construction activities. Even where the surety provides a performance bond with the penal sum equal to the Design-Build contract amount, that surety may take the position that it cannot be called upon to remedy any defects or defaults with respect to the design.

To obtain surety bonds, a firm must enter into an indemnity agreement with a surety company to reimburse the surety for any losses resulting from the bonds. The firm agrees to reimburse the surety for any claims paid on the bonds and pledges assets as security for that obligation. Design firms often lack the financial capability to pledge assets sufficient to obtain surety bonds. Thus, surety bonding can be a challenge in designer-led teams. Such teams usually rely upon the constructor-member's ability to obtain bonds.

Note: Underwriting, payment bond coverage, and the like do not vary on Design-Build projects from what one would expect on a Design-Bid-Build or a CM at-Risk project, except for the issue discussed in the "Lien Waivers" section above concerning the question of whether design professionals can be covered by a payment bond.

Sustainability

The disadvantage on Design-Build green building projects procured with Low Bid or Best Value: Total Cost, similar to Design-Bid-Build, is that the design-builder is typically not involved in the project until after the design is fairly well developed. It is difficult to incorporate the design-builder's ideas for reducing waste and increasing building efficiency during its operation. The project's green requirements must be stated in the contract documents issued to the bidders. These include how the design-builder is required to meet any green building criteria.

The advantage on Design-Build green projects procured with Best Value: Fees or Qualifications Based Selection, similar to CM at-Risk, is that the design-builder is involved early in the project's design. The design-builder is able to work closely with the owner during the early design phase to collaboratively develop the green project requirements. The design-builder procured in this manner is also better positioned to be sure the project's green goals are achieved. This input can result in better designs that meet the owner's criteria, better material and equipment selection, increased construction efficiency, and lower lifecycle costs for the project. The typical open-book process should also facilitate closer involvement of the trade contractors and suppliers in working to incorporate sustainable products and designs.

The benefit of the Design-Build's single point of accountability is that there is no possibility of the owner having to be in the middle of the designer's green responsibilities and the contractor's green responsibilities. However, there may be some ambiguity between the design-builder and the owner when a problem arises relative to certification. This is not the only ambiguity associated with green construction; the industry is still trying to fully understand the associated risks.

For example, if a project is billed as achieving a certain third party's level of certification but fails to receive this certification, is the owner or the design-builder responsible? This is an area that many in the industry, particularly sureties and insurance companies, are watching closely.

The recent research, *Sustainable, High Performance Projects and Project Delivery Methods, A State-of-Practice Report*, September, 2009, sponsored by the Charles Pankow Foundation and The Design-Build Institute of America, examined the link between sustainability and project delivery. The research looked at the likelihood of achieving or exceeding the original goal established for LEED® rating based on both the delivery method and the procurement type.

The results showed 82% of Design-Build projects achieved or exceeded their original LEED goal. This percentage fell in between CM at-Risk and Design-Bid-Build. Regarding the impact the procurement process had on achieving sustainability, Qualifications Based Selection achieved or exceeded the original LEED goal 95% of the time, Best Value: Total Cost 87% of the time, and Low Bid 78%.

Unfortunately, the study did not cross-tabulate by delivery method and procurement type. Thus, the research did not further the industry's understanding of the impact of Design-Build regardless of the procurement option. If the Design-Build projects were categorized by procurement type, it is reasonable to assume that the Design-Build QBS percentage would have been much higher, probably closer to 95%. Conversely, the Design-Build Low Bid would have been lower, probably closer 78%. The Design-Build Best Value: Total Cost would have been somewhere in between, most likely higher than the blended average of 82%. Perhaps future research will further analyze Design-Build's impact on achieving sustainability.

For a more complete discussion on green building, consult *Contractor's Guide to Green Building Construction*, published by AGC of America.

LESSONS LEARNED

Design-Build has proven to be a viable construction project delivery method in many circumstances, particularly when schedule is a controlling factor in the project. The process used for selecting and compensating the design-builder can have a major impact on the amount of information that is necessary prior to selection. If a Low Bid commitment is desired, the owner must develop a detailed program and should utilize either in-house staff or an independent party to monitor the design and construction to ensure that all the essential design elements are included. If Qualifications Based Selection is used, the relationship between the owner and the design-builder can take on a more collaborative quality.

FUTURE TRENDS

Design-Build has gained in popularity since its introduction, and many of the barriers to its use have now been removed. It is likely this trend will continue. Similar to the CM at-Risk delivery system, Design-Build has increased in popularity. With a growing need to be more efficient and sustainable, the convergence of major trends in the industry is likely to drive owners to look to more collaborative approaches to delivering capital projects. Over the last decade, the use of Design-Build on horizontal projects including highway, pavement, and bridge construction has become increasingly more common.

Efficiencies have been gained by the use of new technologies such as BIM, the drive to reduce waste and be green, and the application of lean philosophies to not only entire project teams but to each individual team member's firm as well. These efficiencies are all converging and making a significant impact on how construction projects are procured, contracted, and delivered.

In addition, the emergence of highly collaborative principles and contracts that are designed to incentivize a more integrated approach are evolving under the banner of Integrated Project Delivery (IPD). Today, there is a growing trend to apply as many of these IPD principles as possible without having to use the relatively new multi-party contract. There is no industry consensus on what to call the approach of applying IPD principles to the more classic delivery methods such as Design-Build, but some refer to these approaches as "IPD-ish" or "IPD Lite."

Examples of IPD principles that are being applied without a multi-party contract include early involvement of trade contractors, co-location of project team members possibly in one location (a "Big Room"), and adding some pain/gain sharing and performance-based incentives to the contract.

As both private and public owners seek more collaboration, higher predictability, and a less adversarial environment, Design-Build, if procured and contracted appropriately, can provide a solution. Project delivery is constantly evolving. For updated information and links to some of the latest information, see the Project Delivery section of AGC of America's website at: http://www.agc.org/projectdelivery.

Self Test

1. Design-Build is a:
   a. Construction project delivery method
   b. Project management system
   c. Method for ensuring competent design and construction of a project

2. The *defining* characteristic of Design-Build is:
   a. The use of a bridging architect
   b. That one entity assumes responsibility for both the design and construction of the project
   c. That a firm is paid a fee to provide a design service

3. The owner's role in Design-Build is:
   a. Limited to providing the funds to finance the project
   b. To first establish its project requirements, review and approve the design, approve project budgets and, if required, review and approve price proposals. The owner's requirements must be stated clearly and accurately for the project to be a success
   c. No different than in any other project delivery system

4. Surveys have shown that Design-Build produces:
   a. Fewer design-related disputes during the construction phase than Design-Bid-Build
   b. Cleaner, more attractive facilities
   c. Greater profits for the ultimate facility users

5. The single entity that is the design-builder can take several different forms. It can be:
   a. An integrated company, with in-house architects, engineers, and construction professionals
   b. A combination of a design firm and a construction firm, which come together for one project only or for a period of many years
   c. Designer-led
   d. Constructor-led
   e. Any of the above

6. The practice of creating a set of bridging documents is generally recommended when:
   a. Selecting a design-builder with Low Bid or Best Value: Total Cost procurement
   b. The Design-Build delivery method is employed
   c. The design-build team is constructor-led
   d. All of the above

DESIGN-BUILD

7. Design-builders can be selected using:
   a. A QBS procurement method
   b. A Best Value procurement method
   c. A Low Bid procurement method
   d. All of the above
   e. None of the above

8. Theoretically, with Design-Build, in contrast to Design-Bid-Build and the Spearin Doctrine, changes that are entirely the result of design errors and omissions should be:
   a. Totally the responsibility of the owner
   b. Eliminated as a risk to the owner because the same entity is responsible for the construction cost and the design
   c. The basis for major litigation between the designer and the constructor in the absence of a teaming agreement

Case Study

The following is an example of a typical project. Evaluate the circumstances described and recommend how to proceed. Questions are offered for group discussion. Be prepared to explain and defend your recommendations.

A large nationwide bank is consolidating more than 10 computer operation centers into one large center. Though the company has similar small facilities, the program for the large center is the first of its kind for the bank. It has a very large in-house design and construction group. Most of its experience is with regional offices and small branches, most of which have been built using a Design-Bid-Build approach.

The bank's information technology group (which operates the computer in the existing operations center and will operate the new one) estimates that the savings from operations will be tens of millions of dollars each year. Because the operational savings can be realized as soon as the larger center can be built, the need for the building is urgent. Premiums to accelerate the project (overtime, expediting delivery of major equipment, etc.) are pennies compared to the operational savings available to the bank.

The bank decides to fast-track and start building as soon as enough design is complete to support the process. This will result in a significant overlapping of the design and construction phases. Also, all areas where efficiencies are possible must be considered to support the decision-making process of the owner and the design team.

In-house resources were available to manage the project, but because of its limited experience with fast-tracking, the bank chose to use a Design-Build project delivery approach with Qualifications Based Selection procurement. Construction Management at-Risk was seriously considered, but the bank did not want to be responsible for the designer's performance, given the need for extraordinary speed and efficiency.

Using Qualifications Based Selection, the bank chose a constructor-led team with a constructor that had experience with the product type and aggressive schedules. To complete the Design-Build team, they encouraged the constructor to use a designer they had worked with for years.

The concern over losing control of the design was offset by the use of the Qualifications Based Selection process and a resulting open-book collaborative relationship. The bank was able to retain control over the design without taking the day-to-day responsibility for the designer's performance. Design and construction were well underway before the Guaranteed Maximum Price was established. The GMP included a contingency for schedule acceleration costs such as overtime.

DESIGN-BUILD

The bank decided to manage the project, including overseeing the construction, with its in-house staff. Verifying that the desired level of quality was delivered was the bank's responsibility. Onsite contract administration was handled by the bank's own staff.

The $75 million project was designed and built in 10 months. The project was completed below the GMP. Premiums to meet the schedule were estimated to be less than 5% of the total cost of the project. This was validated by comparisons to similar projects built in more traditional timeframes. The bank occupied the facility and is very satisfied that it was able to retain control over all the design decisions throughout the project.

DISCUSSION ISSUES:

1. Why did the bank decide to use Design-Build? Do you agree with its reasons?

2. Why did the bank use a Qualifications Based Selection? What would have been the pros and cons of using Best Value: Total Cost or Low Bid procurement?

3. Neither bridging documents nor a bridging consultant were used. Should they have been?

4. What was the bank's biggest reason for not using Construction Management at-Risk?

5. If the schedule requirement was such that more time had been available, would that have affected your recommendation of whether to use Design-Build?

6. The Design-Build entity was a contractor-led team. Could the Design-Build entity have been designer-led or an integrated firm? Would either have brought more benefits to the project?

7. Do you think that the Qualifications Based, GMP approach had any effect on the bank's ability to retain control over the design?

CHAPTER TEN

INTEGRATED PROJECT DELIVERY (IPD)

Introduction
- Levels of Collaboration

Definitions in This Project Delivery System
- New Phases
- Multi-Party Contract/Relational Contract
- IPD Principles—Contractual and Behavioral
  - Contractual
  - Behavioral
- IPD Contractors
- Target Price
- Shared Risk/Reward
- Set-Based Design

Delivery Method Overview/Structure
- Programming/Predesign Phase
- Negotiation Phase
- Conceptualization
- Criteria Design
- Detailed Design
- Implementation Documents
- Buyout
- Construction

Defining Characteristics and Typical Characteristics

Procurement and Establishing the Contract Amount
- Qualifications Based Selection
- Best Value: Fees

Basis of Reimbursement Options

Roles and Responsibilities
- The Owner
- The Designer
- The Constructor

INTEGRATED PROJECT DELIVERY (IPD)

Project Delivery Considerations
- Building Information Modeling
- Changes
- Claims and Disputes
- Design Phases
- Fast-Tracking
- Indemnification/Hold Harmless Clauses
- Insurance
- Lean Construction
- Licensing
    - Architect/Engineer Licensing Requirements
    - Constructor Licensing Requirements
- Lien Waivers
- Prequalification
- Retainage
- Safety
- Standard Forms of Agreements
- Subcontracts
- Surety Bonds and Other Forms of Security for Performance
- Sustainability

Lessons Learned

Future Trends

Self Test

INTEGRATED PROJECT DELIVERY (IPD)

INTRODUCTION

In recent years, a relatively new project delivery method known as Integrated Project Delivery (IPD) has emerged in the United States. With this method, the owner, the designer, the contractor, and other primary parties sign one agreement (referred to as a "multi-party agreement"). The term used to describe this type of contract is "relational" contracting as opposed to "transactional," which is used in traditional contracting. Early versions of this delivery method appeared in some projects around the world, particularly in Australia, under the name of "Alliancing." To date, the application of true IPD as a delivery method has been limited to a small number of projects, and its eventual widespread adoption is a subject of debate.

The appeal of this new form of contracting is that it leads to a higher level of collaboration among the project's participants. The early results are limited, but most owners who have used the multi-party contract believe that their organizations received a better value. IPD project participants who have been collaborating using CM at-Risk and Design-Build project delivery methods procured with Qualifications Based Selection and open-book (transactional) contracts—teams who have been working at a high level of collaboration for years—report that they have found themselves acting even more collaboratively and attribute this, in part, to the multi-party contract.

As more collaborative project delivery models increase in use, all owners may be increasingly tasked with evaluating how much integration or collaboration is appropriate or desired on their projects. Different owners on different projects are going to determine how much, if any, collaboration is desired. Some projects may not benefit much, if any, from having a collaborative contractual relationship.

Levels of Collaboration

The term "integration" is often used interchangeably with "collaboration." With the emergence of the term "Integrated Project Delivery," the term "integration" has been even more broadly applied. Most owners are determining on a project-by-project basis whether there is any benefit to trying to establish a higher level of integration and what the trade-offs might be.

The publication *Integrated Project Delivery for Public and Private Owners* describes a three-tiered approach to achieving collaboration. The three levels represent the typical spectrum through which owners move. Where on this collaboration spectrum any particular owner may fall depends on a number of factors including legislative restrictions, policy limitations, and cultural considerations.

The three collaboration levels are:

INTEGRATED PROJECT DELIVERY (IPD)

- **Level 1: Typical Collaboration**—The manner in which project teams have been collaborating for decades, most commonly with CM at-Risk or Design-Build project delivery methods.
- **Level 2: Enhanced Collaboration**—Level 1 collaboration enhanced with IPD techniques such as early involvement of trade contractors, co-location of project team members (the "Big Room"), and performance-based incentives. Incentives can be tied to performance goals, use of technologies (i.e., BIM), and incorporating lean principles to increase productivity and decrease waste.
- **Level 3: Required Collaboration**—Collaboration required by a multi-party contract that ties key team member's compensation to the overall project's achievement of collaboratively established goals and milestones. Use of IPD techniques, described as part of Level 2, are taken to even higher levels.

	Level 1: "Typical" Collaboration	Level 2: "Enhanced" Collaboration	Level 3: "Required" Collaboration
Level of Collaboration	Lower ⟵		⟶ Higher
Philosophy or Delivery Method?	Philosophy	Philosophy	Delivery Method
Also Known As…	N/A	IPD-ish; IPD Lite; Non-Multi-Party IPD; Hybrid IPD	Multi-Party Contracting; "Pure" IPD; Relational Contracting; Alliancing; Lean Project Delivery System™
Delivery Approaches	CM at-Risk or Design-Build	CM at-Risk or Design-Build	Integrated Project Delivery

Source: IPD for Public and Private Owners, NASFA, AGC of America, et al., 2010

Based on these levels of collaboration, IPD separates into two types:
1. IPD as a "philosophy" (Non-multi-party contracts, Levels 1 or 2 collaboration)
2. IPD as a "delivery method" (Multi-party contracts, Level 3 collaboration)

Many owners and their teams have been working at Level 1 collaboration for years. In the early evolution of the term IPD, applying collaborative methodologies to the traditional, transactional project delivery methods was also referred to as Integrated Project Delivery. In fact, many IPD techniques typical in Level 2 collaborations, such as early trade contractor involvement, are not new and have been employed by project teams for years as well. Level 2 collaboration was created to acknowledge the application of old and new IPD techniques to increase project team integration over the traditional manner of collaboration. Today, there is no industry consensus on names for Level 2 collaboration; thus, it is often referred to by a variety of nicknames, including "IPD Lite," "IPD-ish," or "IPD as a philosophy."

Relatively new, particularly in the United States, is the use of the multi-party contract or Level 3 collaboration. This chapter covers IPD as a delivery method (Level 3 collaborations), where the primary parties are signatory to a single multi-party contract. Chapters 8 and 9 discussed IPD as a philosophy, where integration techniques or IPD principles are applied to the traditional delivery methods. IPD as a philosophy, however, is not the focus of this chapter.

Along with the evolution of applying IPD principles to projects being designed and constructed under the traditional delivery methods (Level 2 collaboration or IPD as a philosophy) and the simultaneous emergence of projects using the multi-party IPD contract (Level 3 collaboration or the IPD delivery method), a debate has arisen in the industry. The debate centers on the question, "Can a project being constructed without a multi-party contract ever be as collaborative as a project using a multi-party contract?" In other words, can Level 2 collaboration ever be as collaborative as Level 3 collaboration?

There are two schools of thought to this question: 1) "Yes, a properly designed Design-Build or CM at-Risk contract with the right incentives can drive collaborative behavior to the same level as a multi-party contract" or 2) "No, a traditional, transactional contract will never be able to align the parties' interests and successfully direct the behavior of the team from shifting and avoiding risk to accepting and managing risks like a multi-party relational contract." The answer to this question is not known and likely will not be known for years.

DEFINITIONS IN THIS PROJECT DELIVERY SYSTEM

The following definitions are offered to further clarify the Integrated Project Delivery method.

New Phases

There is a general belief by many in the industry that the convergence of new technologies such as BIM, the drive to eliminate waste through lean practices, the desire to be more sustainable, and the need to increase value and drive down project costs is leading to a redefining of the project phases, particularly those involved in the design process. With highly integrated teams, there is an increasing ability to shift the design process forward and essentially replace the traditional design phases with new phases.

These new phases accommodate the ability to simulate the project with modeling technology as well as the ability to incorporate preconstruction input from the trade contractors, suppliers, installers, and fabricators. The industry is in a period of transition as more and more designers and integrated project teams become more efficient and eliminate much of the waste in the traditional design process.

AIA's *Integrated Project Delivery: A Guide* (2008) took the first pass at defining these new phases: conceptualization, criteria design, detailed design, implementation documents, agency coordination/final buyout, construction, and closeout. These new phase names are a reflection of the fact that project teams are now more integrated throughout. Time will tell whether these terms ultimately end up gaining wide acceptance as the names of the phases of design and construction, but this is a first step toward acknowledging that the process is going to look different going forward.

Multi-Party Contract/Relational Contract

A multi-party contract is a form of agreement where, at a minimum, the primary project participants comprised of the owner, the designer, and the contractor all sign one agreement. Although not required, it is also common to have other key members of the project team, such as major trade contractors or suppliers and certain design consultants (essentially those who can significantly impact the project's overall success), join in the multi-party contract. Such agreements focus on risk management at the project level, as opposed to shifting risk from one individual party to another. Additionally, IPD contracts contain language that promotes collaboration.

In addition to the shared risk and reward terms of the contract, another key element of some multi-party IPD contracts is a waiver of liability where all the parties agree that, with limited exceptions, they will not sue each other. Exceptions to this waiver might include a party's willful failure to perform. Many multi-party contracts actually executed on projects to date do not include a broad waiver of liability. Instead, some multi-party agreements have language that strives to create a "no blame" environment by eliminating risks at many of the classic places of risk conflict (cost, schedule, etc.). This highlights that even within Level 3 collaboration, there are degrees of collaboration and compromise that in turn affect the level of collaboration.

By definition, the use of a multi-party contract indicates that the delivery method is IPD, and multi-party IPD contracts typically include Target Price as the basis of reimbursement. Target Price is discussed in more detail later in this chapter and in Chapter 3. This chapter also includes a discussion of the industry's standard forms of agreement, and further information regarding contracts is included in the Appendix.

IPD Principles—Contractual and Behavioral

As described in *Integrated Project Delivery for Public and Private Owners* (2010), a range of fundamental principles can form the basis for a collaborative project. It is recognized that not all of these principles can be implemented in every project. Projects that implement some, but not all, of the identified IPD principles may still deliver much of the same value, with the notion being that the more IPD principles a project team implements, the greater the benefit to the owner.

These IPD principles are divided into two categories: 1) contractual principles (those that may be written into agreements) and 2) behavioral principles (those that are necessary for project optimization but are ultimately choice-based).

Contractual Principles

The following contractual principles, when embodied in the multi-party contract, are believed to contribute to a climate in which the project participants are better able to collaborate in the best interest of the project:

- **Key participants bound together as equals**—Whether it is a minimum of the owner, designer, and contractor, or a broader group, a contractually defined relationship as equals supports collaboration and consensus-based decisions.
- **Shared financial risk and reward based on project outcome**—Tying fiscal risk and reward to overall project outcomes encourages participants to engage in thinking and behaving in the best interest of the project rather than engaging in self-interested thinking and behaving.
- **Liability waivers between key participants**—When project participants agree not to sue one another, they are generally motivated to seek solutions to problems rather than assigning blame.
- **Fiscal transparency between key participants**—Requiring and maintaining an open-book environment promotes trust and helps keep contingencies visible and controllable.
- **Early involvement of key participants**—Projects have become increasingly complex. Requiring all participants essential to project success to be at the table early allows greater access to pools of expertise and better understanding of probable implications of design decisions.
- **Intensified design**—Greater team investment in design efforts prior to construction allows greater opportunities for cost control as well as enhanced ability to achieve desired project outcomes.
- **Jointly developed project target criteria**—Carefully defining project performance criteria with the input, support, and buy-in of all key participants increases the likelihood that maximum attention will be paid to the project.

- **Collaborative decision making**—Requiring key project participants to work together on important decisions leverages pools of expertise and encourages joint accountability.

Behavioral Principles
- **Mutual respect and trust**—Nurturing a positive environment requires deep appreciation for the motivations and concerns of all project participants. If they do not operate in an environment of mutual respect and trust, performance erodes and participants retreat to "best for stakeholder" behaviors.
- **Willingness to collaborate**—Collaboration is ultimately a behavioral choice. It is important to nurture an environment that supports and encourages participants to choose to collaborate.
- **Open communication**—Collaboration requires open, honest communication. If project participants are reluctant to share ideas or opinions, opportunities for innovation and improvement may be missed.

IPD Contractors

As indicated above, although IPD as a delivery method requires only that the owner, designer, and contractor sign a single multi-party contract, it is common to have other key project participants, specifically those whose contributions can most directly be tied to the project's success, also sign the multi-party agreement. This typically includes key trade subcontractors and design sub-consultants who, when they become part of the multi-party agreement, are referred to as "IPD contractors." Like the contractor and the designer, IPD contractors are typically procured with Qualifications Based Selection. Other project participants may be procured using more traditional methods, including Lump Sum and Design-Build with a GMP.

Unlike Design-Build and CM at-Risk, the ability to include trade contractors and suppliers as IPD contractors and parties to the shared risk/shared reward aspects of the multi-party contract allows an even more integrated involvement than does simply engaging them early as design-assist partners or, if the team decides, as design-build subcontractors. This deeper and at-risk role in the project allows IPD contractors to help contribute to overall project efficiency.

Target Price

As introduced in Chapter 3: Basis of Reimbursement, Target Price has emerged as a new basis of reimbursement that is almost exclusively tied to the relational multi-party contract type used in IPD projects.

With the Target Price basis of reimbursement, the project participants signatory to the multi-party contract collaboratively establish a target price for the project and then work together to maximize the value that the owner receives for that amount. The parties share in the burden of costs that exceed the target price and share in the benefits if the final project costs come in below the target price. Although there is no set formula for how costs and benefits are allocated in a multi-party contract, this "pain/gain sharing" is one of the main thrusts of the multi-party contract. The following diagram illustrates one method of structuring incentives for the parties to achieve or improve on the target price.

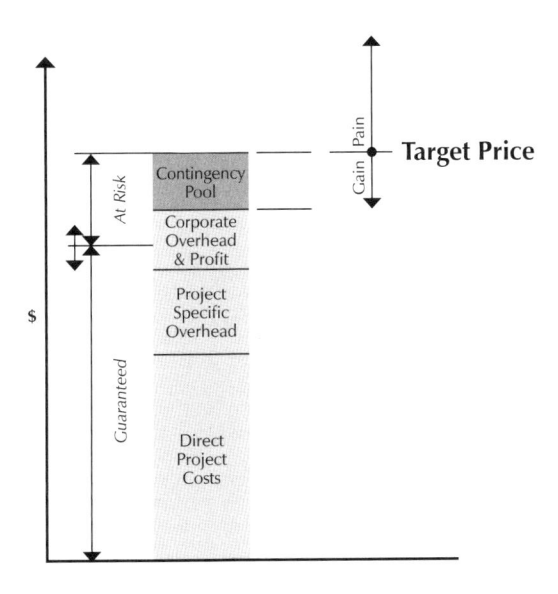

[Diagram: Target Price structure showing $ axis with components from bottom to top: Direct Project Costs, Project Specific Overhead, Corporate Overhead & Profit, Contingency Pool. "Guaranteed" portion covers lower section; "At Risk" covers upper section. "Gain | Pain" arrows around Target Price line.]

With typical Target Price contracts, the design team participates along with the owner, the contractor, and possibly the trade contractors in the risk/reward sharing and typically has a financial incentive if the project successfully hits the target price. This risk sharing often includes placing at least a portion of both the design and the construction team's compensation at risk. So now instead of referring to only the contractor's risk of cost overruns, when the IPD "team" is being referenced, this financial risk extends to all parties signing the multi-party contract. Though the designer's financial interest (and thus its financial risk) is often smaller in comparison to that of the contractor and owner, there is still benefit in having the design team take a direct interest in not only its own success but in the rest of team's success as well.

On projects using the Target Price basis of reimbursement, the owner agrees to reimburse the contractor for all of the actual direct project costs (cost of the work) and the project-specific overhead (general conditions). How each team member's profit is determined, including corporate overhead, varies on different projects. On some projects, the team's entire profit is placed at risk and tied to the project team's success with hitting the target price. On other projects, only a portion of the participants' profit is placed at risk. A third, less common approach is not to put any of the design and construction team's profit at risk, perhaps in exchange for concessions in the size of the overall fee.

To provide a buffer to the risk of losing some or all of their profit, IPD teams are often allowed to carry a pool of contingency within the target price. It is typical for the parties to pool their separate (and often redundant) contingencies, and this pool is then included in the target price and tied to the shared risk/reward portion of the contract. In this way, the team is able to reduce the amount of needed contingency, thus introducing an immediate cost benefit to the project.

If the project is completed for less than the target price, the contract provides a sharing of that savings in percentages agreed upon in the contract. In addition, multi-party IPD contracts typically include incentives for things such as safety, schedule, collaborative behavior, achievement of sustainability goals, and so on, all aimed at creating a collaborative, trust-based project.

If the project cost exceeds the target price, the contract also provides a sharing of that overrun in percentages agreed upon in the contract. Usually, the extent of exposure for everyone but the owner is limited to the amount of their profits. Once the overrun exceeds the target price plus the combined at-risk profits, the entire risk of cost overruns is the owner's.

Putting this risk of project overruns entirely upon the owner may be the limiting factor for many owners, particularly public owners, in their ability to use IPD multi-party contracts with the Target Price basis of reimbursement. Again, some owners who have been willing to accept this potential risk have shared anecdotally that they have received a better value both through time savings and completed projects that better meet the user's needs, while remaining within the target price. In practice, owners who want collaboration benefits but also require a GMP have tended to use integrated varieties of CM at-Risk or Design-Build rather than a true IPD delivery model.

The timing of setting the target price may have an impact on how well the IPD project team will work collaboratively. The best time to set the target price has not yet been fully established as a best practice. If set too early, the project scope may not be defined well enough to narrow the target to an accurate number and may stifle creativity. If set too late, the opportunity to drive proper behavior during the design process could be limited, particularly if there is a target price incentive tied to a design milestone. The target price is probably best established after a validation process has occurred, while still early enough in the detailed design phase for the team to feel confident that the range of accuracy is within the amount of at-risk profit and pooled contingency.

Shared Risk/Reward

The two concepts that are at the heart of IPD as a delivery method are the relational contract and shared risk/reward. When combined, the goal of the relational contract and shared risk/reward aim to create a culture that drives the parties to the multi-party contract to focus their energies and resources on the project's best interest.

The Target Price basis of reimbursement is the primary mechanism that facilitates the sharing of the project's risks and rewards. By guaranteeing the actual project costs, the owner eliminates the need for the team members to include redundant contingencies and to engage in defensive behavior. The pooling of the team's contingencies along with sharing any of the unspent pooled contingency and linking at least a portion of the participants' profits to the project's overall target price provides significant incentives for the team to work together.

Set-Based Design

The application of Set-Based Design (or concurrent engineering) theory is identified in lean construction theory as a tool to evaluate and prioritize multiple design options. With Set-Based Design, when creating a product, the team develops multiple versions simultaneously, each version being a "set." Eventually, the designs will "compete" against one another and ultimately be consolidated to contain the best and most appropriate design elements from each set.

The main point of Set-Based Design is to make expensive design commitments at the last responsible moment without delaying the project. In theory, this helps the project team achieve the highest quality design. The main negative is that, to succeed, the owner must have the ability to delay final design decisions and then very quickly finalize the design. The ramifications of waiting too long to make a decision can end up being very costly if the team has to go back and make corrections.

DELIVERY METHOD OVERVIEW/STRUCTURE

The services provided throughout the IPD process are not dramatically different than with the other collaborative delivery methods. It is not "what" is getting done (for the most part, this is very similar to CM at-Risk or Design-Build when procured with a QBS or Best Value: Fees selection process and contracted with an open-book GMP contract). The design team is still taking the lead for the design, and the contractor is still supporting the design process and then taking the lead for the performance of the construction. The differences are *how* this is achieved in the environment and the behaviors that are created and incentivized by the multi-party contract.

By creating the shared risk/reward model tied to overall project success and not to the success of individual team members, the manner in which the services are provided in each phase can be quite different. Assigning blame to another team member no longer shifts the financial downside. In fact, it can hurt the bottom line for the member that is seeking to assign blame if, for example, the result is an unnecessary costly delay.

BIM technology and lean practices become catalysts throughout the entire project and are often so intertwined with the IPD project delivery process that debates ensue over which ingredient is most critical to team integration: the multi-party agreement, the technology platform, or lean processes.

Programming/Predesign Phase

In this phase, as in other methods of project delivery, the owner decides upon its project requirements and furnishes them to the IPD team. The owner usually specifies the project requirements in terms of performance parameters. By stating requirements in performance terms, the owner allows the integrated team members to use their own expertise and ingenuity to satisfy the requirements in a cost-effective way.

Negotiation Phase

IPD contract negotiations differ from traditional contract negotiations. Partially because the contract approach is relatively new, but also because negotiating an IPD agreement requires a new way of thinking and addressing issues, contract negotiation has taken significantly longer than most traditional contract negotiations. Negotiations of some multi-party contracts have taken six months or more.

The negotiation of the multi-party contract is itself the IPD team's first opportunity to collaborate. A significant portion of the process of negotiating a multi-party agreement is determining how risks and rewards will be shared among the multi-party contract participants. Generally speaking, the amount of risk a party is taking is directly correlated to its share of the incentives.

Issues that must be negotiated include: the identification of the team members, each member's compensation and corresponding percentages, milestones for triggering incentives, the group decision-making process, the procedure to establish and validate the target price, the contingency pool, and how risks are going to be shared. Because incentives are often tied to project milestones, they must be clear and specific—unlike many of the classic milestones tied to the traditional design phases. Once negotiated, the IPD agreement should enhance the IPD project and implementation of IPD principles.

As the industry gains more familiarity with these agreements, much of the extensive negotiation should become easier and shorter, but because much of the negotiation is unique to the project and the chosen participants, the negotiations will probably always take longer than with the other delivery methods.

Conceptualization

In the conceptualization phase, teams develop project goals concerning the desired outcomes of a successful project. Even at this early stage, BIM is utilized to begin to conceptualize the project scope linked to both schedule and cost information. Costs are more detailed than is typical at this stage and are also detailed by system.

Communication methodologies including BIM protocols, levels of detail expected at each phase, acceptable tolerances, and other standards for sharing information wherever possible are agreed upon. Goals and plans for sustainability are also established during this phase. The team works closely, suggesting potential ideas for how to achieve the project goals as effectively as possible.

The use of lean techniques such as collaborative planning and pull scheduling of the entire project team's processes is almost expected on IPD projects. Co-location of key project personnel in the same room (the "Big Room") has proven to be essential in improving communications, promoting information flow, reducing waiting, and resolving questions that would otherwise become inefficient Requests for Information (RFI).

Criteria Design

The criteria design phase generally combines the traditional schematic design and design development phases. The significant difference with IPD is that the contractor and IPD trade contractors are not only providing input, they are integrally involved in the decision-making process. Since everyone has a financial incentive to optimize the entire project, there is a much higher level of ownership, not only of each separate discipline of work but also for how those separate disciplines combine into an overall project that maximizes the value the owner receives for its investment. For example, the mechanical engineer is incentivized to work closely with the mechanical subcontractor to find a solution that satisfies the heat load criteria with the least impact to the building structure, envelope, and architecture.

Also identified during this stage are potential opportunities to pre-purchase equipment and scopes of work that can be prefabricated. Prefabrication is one of the few "quadruple wins" where an owner is able to 1) save money, 2) save time, 3) get a higher quality product, and 4) do so more safely. The close integration of the engineers, subcontractors, and fabricators allows a higher level of trust and confidence. There is an increasing level of confidence in the data from the modeling technology, and IPD project teams are often given the right to rely on the model, a risk that is not yet commonly accepted as a standard practice in other delivery models.

Detailed Design

This phase involves much of what, in the traditional design process, is done as part of the construction document phase. During this stage, the project scope becomes well-defined, coordinated, and validated by the entire team. Building systems and all major elements are fully engineered and coordinated. Levels of quality and acceptable tolerances are established. Portions of the scope have been tagged for prefabrication and have possibly been pre-purchased. Both the cost estimates and schedule, including sequencing, have been established with a high level of accuracy.

Because all signers of the IPD contract and possibly other design-assist trade contractors and suppliers have been involved during the design process, their continuous feedback allows the owner to make highly informed decisions throughout. Detailed models are developed jointly and provide benefits to every member of the team. The owner can offer visualization to the ultimate users of the project, who likely are not familiar with reading construction documents. The model also provides analysis assistance to the code officials.

Implementation Documents

Integration pays great benefits during the implementation documents stage. This is the stage where the team completes the documentation of how the design will be implemented. The traditional shop drawing process is melded into this stage and, in many cases, is bypassed entirely or at least replaced by a model coordination process that connects the design process directly to the fabrication process. This phase is often overlapped with the detailed design phase and is shorter than the traditional construction documents phase.

Because the key members of the construction team have been engaged throughout the project process, the design already reflects a scope that has been reviewed for constructability as well as means and methods. Prefabrication of some scope can commence if it has not already done so.

Buyout

The buyout phase on IPD projects is significantly reduced since many of the trade contractors and suppliers are already on board as either IPD contractors or as early awarded design-assist contractors. The early trade contractors often represent well over 50% of the project cost, and the balance of the scope is usually procured with either a Low Bid or Best Value: Total Cost selection process. Since much of the work is already contracted, the IPD buyout phase is shorter than with the other delivery methods.

Construction

The construction phase on an IPD project is very similar to a highly collaborative CM at-Risk or Design-Build project, again with the exception that the IPD project team members may work more collaboratively to execute the project plan. This collaborative behavior includes not only looking after their own areas of work and responsibility but also anticipating how they can assist others with theirs. Since the participants are not at risk for the actual cost of the project, they are free to look at the project costs through the eyes of the owner and find ways to save time and money. For example, team members may share hoisting and scaffolding and coordinate work and sequencing activities so that everyone's work—not just their own—can be installed efficiently.

DEFINING CHARACTERISTICS AND TYPICAL CHARACTERISTICS

IPD as a delivery method has one defining characteristic: the use of the multi-party contract for the owner, designer, and contractor (at a minimum). Regardless of the number of additional parties signatory to the contract, the specific terms included, or the IPD techniques implemented, a capital project delivered under the terms of a multi-party contract is IPD.

Typical characteristics of IPD include fast-tracking, early involvement of trade contractors, collaborative decision making, the use of BIM technology, application of lean principles, and shared financial risk and rewards.

PROCUREMENT AND ESTABLISHING THE CONTRACT AMOUNT

As discussed in Chapter 2: Procurement Options, the owner may select the primary parties of the IPD team by one of several means. By far the most common option to procure IPD is Qualifications Based Selection.

Qualifications Based Selection

The owner selects the designer and the contractor based solely on qualifications. A Qualifications Based Selection usually is accomplished by soliciting statements of qualifications from several firms, rating them by the owner's criteria, and selecting the firm rated highest by the owner. The owner may also decide upon a shortlist of firms and then enter into negotiations with one or more of them to discuss project details, terms, or price.

Best Value: Fees

For those owners required to include price as an element of their selection processes, an IPD team could be selected based on its qualifications, fees, and possibly general conditions and reimbursable costs using the Best Value: Fees procurement option.

In theory, there is nothing prohibiting the use of competitions based on total cost (Low Bid or Best Value: Total Cost) with IPD. However, because these types of selections require some level of design to be developed and typically foster a more adversarial risk-based relationship, it is very difficult, if not impossible, to use either of those selection options with this delivery method. The whole premise of risk sharing is difficult after one member of the team is already locked into a total price and is expected to hold onto this risk.

BASIS OF REIMBURSEMENT OPTIONS

The most common basis of reimbursement with the IPD multi-party agreement is Target Price. The Target Price basis of reimbursement effectively aligns the parties' economic interests and their collaborative management of risk rather than prompting the traditional shifting and avoidance of project risk. Properly done, this approach is believed by some to be the catalyst for an actual reduction in project risk.

Another reimbursement option that can address this risk is a not-to-exceed GMP. However, once the GMP is implemented, the existence of a GMP will immediately affect the behavior of the entities providing the GMP. Instead of having everyone on the team focused on the project's best interests, the GMP creates a disincentive to this collaborative behavior. Those parties responsible for the guarantee are now at risk and are much more likely to focus, at least in part, on protecting their own interests, thus creating the very behavior that the multi-party contract strives to eliminate.

ROLES AND RESPONSIBILITIES

All of the parties signatory to the multi-party contract have the responsibility to participate in the collaborative decision-making body, which is critical to an IPD project's success. However, the owner, who is funding the project, retains a veto right in this decision-making process.

The Owner

The owner has an even greater responsibility in an IPD multi-party contract than with traditional contracting to provide leadership to the project team and to lead by example. For instance, if the owner expects the team to adopt lean thinking and lean principles, it is important for the owner to adopt these principles in its own organization.

The Designer

The design team's role in an IPD multi-party contract shifts from a focus solely upon the design responsibility to a focus on the overall success of the project. The design team is incentivized to do so by having its own financial performance directly linked to the project's performance. Because there is a shared responsibility for the project's overall success, the designer has a higher level of interest in the efficiency, cost, and effectiveness of the construction.

Some in the industry might prefer IPD over integrated Design-Build based on a perceived difference in the designer's role. In Design-Build, the architect/engineer typically is a subcontracted member of the design-builder's team. The notion that a design professional's responsibility to the owner flows through the contractor can be a difficult adjustment for some designers, particularly those accustomed to a more adversarial approach to project delivery in which part of the architect/engineer's role is to protect the owner from untrustworthy contractors. Under this view, Design-Build can lead to a troubling diminution in the professional standing and function of the architect/engineer. IPD, by contrast, is perceived as allowing the lead design entity to come to the table as an equal with the owner and the contractor.

The Constructor

The constructor's role in an IPD multi-party contract also shifts from a focus on supporting the design process and then assuming primary responsibility for the construction performance to a focus on the project's overall success. The constructor is incentivized to do so by having its own financial performance directly linked to the project's performance. As with the designer, the constructor has a shared responsibility for the project's overall success and, thus, a higher level of interest in the efficiency, cost, and effectiveness of the design.

Just as the designer's role is expanded in IPD to include potential input into means and methods aspects of a construction project, the contractor's role (historically limited to those means and methods) is expanded under the IPD delivery method to include what have traditionally been considered design functions. While this already existed with the preconstruction services provided by the CM at-risk and the design-builder, respectively, the contractor is, as a rule, even more involved in design under IPD.

This raises the question of whether anything remains of the contractor protection created under the Spearin Doctrine. Under this doctrine, the contractor is not liable to the owner for loss or damage resulting from errors or omissions in such plans and specifications. This, of course, assumes that the contractor has not had a role in the preparation of the plans and specifications. With IPD, the constructor is taking an active part in all design phases of the project and, thus, potentially may begin to challenge the protection of Spearin for design problems. As with many of the uncertainties surrounding this new project delivery method, the industry will not know the answer to this question for some time.

PROJECT DELIVERY CONSIDERATIONS

Chapter 6 of this book discussed several basic project delivery considerations and risk issues common to all projects and various project delivery methods. Some vary from one project delivery method to another, while others remain the same. This section follows the same format as Chapter 6 but focuses on the IPD delivery method.

Because the IPD project delivery method is still relatively new and rapidly evolving, in the case of many of these issues, particularly the business-related ones (e.g., indemnification, insurance, surety, retainage, etc.), best practices have not yet emerged. Readers should keep this in mind when reading this section.

Building Information Modeling

Is BIM essential to a properly managed IPD project? No, but if the entire premise of using a multi-party contact is to contractually drive the team to work collaboratively and look for ways to optimize the project, then expecting the team to use the latest collaboratively-based technological tools is imperative. BIM, especially employed in a collaborative setting, can greatly enhance information sharing and streamline project design and construction; therefore, it is integrally tied to IPD.

On IPD projects, teams collaboratively decide early in the process the best way to develop and use the model. If key trade contractors and design consultants are involved, they also participate in model development during the design process. In addition to the potential benefits of offering 3D visualization to users early in the process, IPD participants can use the model as a tool to assist in evaluating and providing input to the design.

As discussed in Chapter 8, using BIM under the CM at-Risk model introduces a whole new set of challenges. Who is modeling what and when? Who is using the model, and how are they using it? Who owns the model, and who ultimately is responsible for any flaws? In contrast, IPD teams are able to address these challenges early and eliminate some of the potential difficulties that arise when project participants share in the preparation, interpretation, transmission, and use of model information. With the team working together in an open, collaborative environment, the use of BIM during design and construction allows for better and more efficient analysis of design alternatives and their cost and schedule implications. IPD contractors and suppliers use the models for the purpose of preparing and managing (and perhaps, in lieu of) traditional shop drawings. The IPD team's ability to build the building virtually prior to building it in the field enhances coordination and reduces issues in the field.

As with CM at-Risk and Design-Build, the industry is still working to better understand the risks of using BIM with multi-party contracts. The strategies to address these risks, as well as the related contracts and insurance products, will likely continue to be in flux for a number of years. ConsensusDOCS 301, "Building Information Modeling (BIM) Addendum," addresses the team's responsibilities as they relate to the model. This addendum is structured to work with any project delivery model that involves early involvement of the constructor, not just IPD.

Model sharing and the ability to rely on the information in the model with the IPD project delivery method are still evolving. Where the key members are all participating in the development of the design information, all parties are sharing some, but not all, of the risks. Fully understanding how and when risk is being transferred in IPD projects in which the responsibility for developing the model is shared will take years.

Changes

As previously explained, IPD is different from CM at-Risk and Design-Build using Qualifications Based Selection and open-book contracts; IPD is approached in a much more collaborative manner, and team members are looking after the project's best interests rather than focusing strictly on their own.

The big difference in the area of change management on IPD projects using a Target Price basis of reimbursement is that the owner is not placing the team at risk for the actual cost of the work but is holding the team accountable to a target price for the entire project. This, in addition to the pooled contingency and the joint decision-making process, creates a much different environment for evaluating and incorporating changes. An IPD contract often stipulates that there are no change orders except for specific conditions such as owner-initiated changes, site conditions, changes in laws or regulations, or termination.

The IPD team evaluates any changes and endeavors to incorporate them while simultaneously minimizing or eliminating any cost or schedule impact to the client. Though not definitively established by available research, case studies and anecdotal research have indicated that the higher level of collaboration created by the multi-party contract provides correspondingly higher levels of incentives for the team not just to focus on the project's best interest because it is the right thing to do (as with open-book contracts in either CM at-Risk or Design-Build), but to do so because there is a financial benefit to the IPD parties.

Claims and Disputes

Some multi-party IPD contracts include a clause under which the IPD participants, with limited exceptions (such as willful default), waive their rights to make claims against each other. Driven in large part by a contract structure that eliminates, or at least minimizes, many of the areas where the classic conflicts occur (i.e., cost risk, scope changes, and indemnifications) and incentivizes the team to resolve issues collaboratively, the early experience on completed IPD projects has been a very low occurrence of any major disputes. When disputes do arise, most IPD contracts provide a process wherein they are resolved among the project participants at the lowest possible level and then taken to higher levels of project team decision-makers before being taken outside the project team.

Design Phases

The IPD project delivery method provides new ways of viewing and describing the design phases of a capital project. As mentioned earlier, AIA's *Integrated Project Delivery: A Guide* (2008) defines these new phases: conceptualization, criteria design, detailed design, implementation documents, agency coordination/final buyout, construction, and closeout. These phases are a reflection on the fact that the teams are now more integrated throughout.

Fast-Tracking

Like CM at-Risk and Design-Build, the ability to overlap the design and construction phases is facilitated well by the IPD delivery method as long as the procurement process of all parties is done early enough to support fast-tracking.

Different from Design-Build and CM at-Risk, though, is the ability to include trade contractors and suppliers as parties to the multi-party contract. This opportunity could allow an even more integrated involvement, going beyond the involvement of a design-assist subcontractor. Earlier involvement and sharing of project-wide risks and rewards could allow IPD contractors to further improve their ability to overlap design and construction.

Indemnification/Hold Harmless Clauses

The multi-party contracts currently in use all contain indemnification clauses under which the IPD participants indemnify one another and hold each other harmless from the same sorts of claims covered by indemnifications in traditional contracts. However, to a greater extent than what is seen in the more traditional contract forms, the multi-party contract seeks to limit or mitigate the impact of the indemnifications through, for example:

- Waivers of claims among the parties to the multi-party contract (with certain exceptions that vary from form to form) while leaving in place third-party claims
- Safe harbors under which the parties waive claims for decisions made collectively by the IPD project team
- Limits of liability pegged to the amount of required insurance
- No-questions-asked access to a project contingency for liabilities that might otherwise fall within the indemnification (for claims arising due to simple negligence, for example)

To the extent a multi-party contract waives outright, or even limits, the parties' liabilities to one another and mitigates their liability for third-party claims through jointly managed contingencies and project-specific insurance, these contracts can be viewed as moving toward a "no blame" environment in which parties are encouraged and incentivized to act in the best interest of the project rather than strictly in their own best interest.

Insurance

Traditional liability insurance is based on holding the party at fault financially accountable. An IPD project dramatically alters this approach by defining shared risk for various project issues. The tension between the traditional fault-based system and the different philosophy represented by IPD has yet to be fully resolved.

Generally, although the lines between the parties' traditional responsibilities become blurred in a multi-party IPD delivery method, most parties are, for the time being, continuing to carry the same insurance coverage they carry under the other delivery methods, with some adjustment to the policies in recognition of the unique IPD model. Just like the CM at-risk, who is providing preconstruction Design-Assist services, a contractor participating in the design phases of an IPD project is taking on potential third-party design liability. Insurance products already exist for contractor design liability insurance, and in the absence of project-wide coverage protecting all of the parties from this liability, the IPD contractor would be well advised to obtain it.

It is increasingly common on IPD projects to use an Owner Controlled Insurance Program (OCIP) as a form of project-wide liability coverage; however, professional liability for the designer must still be obtained as an add-on. Builder's risk claims are typically waived among the IPD parties, as is also true in the other delivery models. Unless the subcontractor itself is a party to the multi-party contract, it is also common for the contractor in an IPD project to carry subcontractor default insurance because it is the contractor who enters into the direct contracts with the subcontractors.

Given the relative newness and lack of claims history with IPD multi-party contracts, the insurance industry is still evaluating the best risk management approach. At least one insurance carrier has developed IPD-specific insurance for designers. A comprehensive OCIP product for IPD projects (an "IPDCIP") is expected to become available in the future. If IPD projects continue to reach completion without producing the types and numbers of claims among the project participants that have been seen in traditionally procured projects, one would expect that the cost of insurance for IPD projects would be less than for traditional projects.

Lean Construction

The application of lean construction techniques and principles, which are focused primarily on the concept of eliminating waste, does not fundamentally change regardless of the project delivery method. However, while lean practices are optional under the other delivery models, they are practically a universal feature in the IPD projects that have been performed to date.

The ability to integrate lean principles across the entire project and not just within portions of the project team is enhanced by the existence of the typical multi-party contract. This collaborative environment increases the ability of the IPD participants to agree upon and implement lean practices.

Licensing

Architect/Engineer Licensing Requirements

Architect/engineer licensing requirements on an IPD project are the same as those on projects using other delivery methods.

Constructor Licensing Requirements

Constructor licensing requirements pertaining to a general contractor will likewise apply to the contractor in an IPD contract. This is a matter of state licensing, and requirements vary from state to state.

Lien Waivers

As with all private construction projects, constructors, subcontractors, and vendors have the legal right to file liens if they are not paid, and this is not affected by the multi-party contract. Similar to the other delivery methods, the providing of lien waivers should be made a part of the payment procedures provided in the contract.

Prequalification

Because IPD participants are typically not hired on the basis of total construction cost, prequalification of potential IPD participants is critical to the delivery process. This prequalification, or shortlisting, ensures that only those firms with experience in projects of the size and nature under consideration are permitted to compete for the project.

Retainage

Retainage is not typical in IPD projects, at least not among the parties signatory to the multi-party contract. This is due in part to the fact that the parties are paid for actual costs only as the project proceeds and do not receive their profit until project success is determined. With respect to project participants who are not parties to the IPD contract, the IPD team will work collaboratively to determine on a case-by-case basis which trade contractors and suppliers should be subject to retainage, as well as how much and for how long retainage should be held.

Safety

On IPD projects, the contractor has overall responsibility for jobsite safety similar to the other delivery methods. Compared to Design-Bid-Build, the contractor and any IPD parties have an earlier opportunity to plan for safety operations and to encourage the designer to incorporate features that will facilitate safe methods of construction. Moreover, the fact that the project participants' financial success is tied together may well provide an incentive for them to look after one another's safety in ways they might not otherwise under traditional delivery methods.

Standard Forms of Agreement

There are two primary industry standard forms of the multi-party agreement, one each from the ConsensusDOCS and the AIA families of documents. There are a growing number of custom form multi-party agreements being developed in the United States, some of which are variations of Sutter Health's Integrated Form of Agreement (IFOA).

ConsensusDOCS 300, "Standard Form of Tri-Party Collaborative Agreement for Integrated Project Delivery," was the first standard IPD agreement published in the United States. The owner, designer, and constructor all sign the same agreement, binding them to collaborate in the planning, design, development, and construction of the project. This agreement incorporates lean principles to minimize waste and inefficiencies throughout the design and construction process. A core team at both the project management and project development levels is created to make consensus-based project decisions (including project incentives and risk-sharing) to increase project efficiency and results.

AIA C191-2009, "Standard Form Multi-Party Agreement for Integrated Project Delivery (IPD)," is a standard form multi-party agreement through which the owner, architect, contractor, and perhaps other key project participants execute a single agreement for the design, construction, and commissioning of a project. C191-2009 provides the framework for a collaborative environment in which the parties operate to further cost and performance goals that the parties jointly establish. The non-owner parties are compensated on a cost of the work basis. The basis of reimbursement model is also goal-oriented and provides incentives for collaboration in design and construction of the project. Primary management of the project is the responsibility of the project management team, comprised of one representative from each of the parties. The project executive team, also comprised of one representative from each of the parties, provides a second level of project oversight and issue resolution. The conflict resolution process is intended to foster quick and effective resolution of problems as they arise.

AIA has another form of IPD agreement, C195-2008, "Standard Form Single Purpose Entity Agreement for Integrated Project Delivery (IPD)," where the parties actually form a legal entity for the purpose of a specific project. This form has not seen widespread use so far.

Subcontracts

A significant difference with IPD is the ability to bring select trade subcontractors and design consultants into the multi-party agreement as IPD contractors. These subcontractors will be members of the integrated, at-risk IPD team.

With regard to the rest of the trade contracts, as with CM at-Risk and collaborative Design-Build, the owner has the ability to participate in the review of the trade contractor bidding and award process. The multi-party contract's required transparency will result in information sharing regarding trade contractor bids with the other members of the IPD team. Trade contractors' bid clarifications and exclusions, alternates, and value engineering, etc., are available to the owner and the design team for review so that they may determine which proposal is in the project's best interest.

Surety Bonds and Other Forms of Security for Performance

Because there is no contract price, it is difficult to establish the basis for a payment or performance bond. There is also a much higher level of trust that is presumed with IPD contracts, and similar to highly collaborative CM at-Risk and Design-Build projects, it is increasingly common for owners not to require any surety bonds from their IPD participants. This is another area that is being closely reviewed and will probably take years to fully evaluate.

For public work, however, most government entities will typically require bonds of the contractor regardless of whether the various trade contractors are bonded.

How this is accomplished on IPD projects may be one of the hurdles for public owners in trying to use multi-party IPD contracts.

With regard to bonding of trade contractors, as noted above, it is common for the contractor to provide subcontractor default insurance in lieu of bonding the eligible subcontractors. In cases when bonds on trade contractors are considered, it is typical for the owner and the IPD team members to discuss surety bonds to be obtained from various trade contractors. A key issue typically for owners is the relationship between a requirement for performance and payment bonds for the various trade contractors and the requirement of the performance and payment bonds required of the contractor.

Sustainability

Earlier discussions and referenced research has clearly indicated that there is a direct correlation between the level of collaboration among the project team and likelihood of achieving or exceeding sustainability goals on projects. The natural extension of this thought is that the higher level of collaborative behavior inherent with IPD should lead to even higher success in achieving or exceeding goals for sustainability.

IPD projects offer the advantage on green projects that the IPD team is involved early in the project's design. The team is able to work closely with the owner during the design phase to collaboratively develop the green project requirements. The team is also better positioned to provide input that should help ensure the project's green goals are achieved. This input can result in better designs that meet the owner's criteria, better material and equipment selection, increased construction efficiency, and lower lifecycle costs for the project. The involvement of IPD contractors also enables the incorporation of sustainable products and designs.

Unlike with CM at-Risk, if a project is tasked with achieving a certain third party's level of certification (LEED® for example) but fails to do so, the responsibility belongs to all parties to the contract. The likely result will be the forfeiture of the financial incentive that is tied to that goal. This does not solve the problem that this creates for the owner, so the question of liability waivers and their breadth and enforceability come into play. Many in the industry, particularly sureties and insurance companies that serve the construction industry, are watching this area closely.

For a more complete discussion on green building, consult *Contractor's Guide to Green Building Construction*, published by AGC of America.

INTEGRATED PROJECT DELIVERY (IPD)

LESSONS LEARNED

Though IPD as a delivery method has not existed long enough to offer best practices, the following are some of the lessons learned from successful IPD projects:

- **Engagement of an "IPD consultant"**—IPD contracts involve a number of new issues that present new challenges. Until such time as the majority of participants have had experience with the IPD contract, it is a good idea to hire someone to orient the IPD team and guide their development of the project's goals, incentives, decision-making structure, and contract negotiations.
- **Participation in negotiation workshops**—Because IPD contracts are relatively new, participating in a workshop helps the team learn how to address issues within the IPD contract framework.
- **Early involvement and greater participation in the incentives**—Have more trade contractors and design consultants participate as IPD contractors so that they are incentivized to achieve the owner's goals.
- **Jointly developed and validated cost targets**—In addition to determining the right time to set the target price, it is critical to have the IPD participants involved in determining the right value for the target price and validating that the scope is appropriate for the established target.
- **Utilize co-location**—Nothing seems to tear down the walls that separate the typical project participants more than literally removing the walls.
- **Engage in an IPD pilot project**—Prior to trying to change your organization's project procurement policies outright, it is recommended to try IPD on a pilot basis and proceed with the understanding that there are many lessons to be learned.

Results from successfully completed IPD projects as characterized by the owners themselves include: higher quality, fewer non-owner initiated changes, significantly fewer RFIs, less construction administration, fewer injuries (helped by more prefabrication), earlier completions, designs that better address their user's needs, and project participants energized about the desirability of working in a highly collaborative environment.

FUTURE TRENDS

The expectation is that the use of IPD as a delivery method will increase, but it is unclear whether it will ever be used anywhere to the degree of CM at-Risk or Design-Build. There are those who believe that IPD offers inherent advantages that will lead to its eventual widespread use, while others are skeptical that IPD will ever receive acceptance in the public sector or among any but a few specialized private sector owners. Only time will tell us the answer to this question, but chances are, the end result will be somewhere in between these two views.

INTEGRATED PROJECT DELIVERY (IPD)

Some compare IPD as a delivery method to Design-Build because it contractually brings the design and construction teams together, and others compare it more closely to CM at-Risk because separate firms with their corresponding resources and leadership are brought together for the purpose of designing and constructing the project. Regardless of which comparison is more appropriate, the reality is that at the heart of IPD as a delivery method is a significant departure from how design and construction are traditionally contracted and how risks and benefits are allocated and shared.

There currently are not any well known examples of an IPD project having gone seriously wrong. Eventually, there will likely be one, but most predictions are that this will be the exception and not the rule. IPD advocates believe that future IPD projects will actually be less risky than traditionally delivered projects and that the perceived additional risks embodied in the IPD approach are not really new risks but rather risks that the owners are addressing already. The biggest foreseeable downside to IPD is that it is unclear how an owner will obtain relief if a project goes bad. With no price or schedule guarantee and limited, if any, ability to hold the other participants responsible through legal channels due to waivers of claims, how is an owner to obtain relief in a legal system that is not yet familiar with the collaborative concepts inherent in the IPD model?

There is no "perfect" project delivery method, certainly, and the current question is whether IPD will become accepted widely enough to be considered one of the common options available to most owners.

The subject of project delivery is a field that is constantly evolving. For updated information and links to some of the latest information, see the Project Delivery section of AGC of America's website at: http://www.agc.org/projectdelivery.

INTEGRATED PROJECT DELIVERY (IPD)

Self Test

1. Integrated Project Delivery is a:
   a. Project delivery method
   b. Project management approach
   c. Basis of reimbursement option
   d. Procurement option

2. Which level of collaboration is based on a multi-party agreement?
   a. Level 1
   b. Level 2
   c. Level 3
   d. None of the above

3. Which of the following is not a common nickname for IPD as a philosophy?
   a. IPD-ish
   b. Pure IPD
   c. IPD Lite
   d. Hybrid IPD

4. Which IPD principle is considered a behavioral (vs. a contractual) principle?
   a. Collaborative decision making
   b. Early involvement of key participants
   c. Shared risk and reward
   d. None of the above

5. Which of these is the most common procurement option for selecting IPD participants?
   a. Qualifications Based Selection
   b. Best Value: Fees
   c. Best Value: Total Cost
   d. Low Bid
   e. Target Price

6. True or False: Trade contractors who are signatory to the multi-party agreement are referred to as design-assist contractors.

7. On a typical IPD contract, which of the following would be an acceptable reason for a change order?
   a. Owner-initiated changes
   b. Costs exceeding the target price
   c. Conflicts found with the Building Information Model
   d. The amount of the changes is greater than the amount of the pooled contingency

CHAPTER ELEVEN

DELIVERY METHODS INVOLVING FINANCING OR OPERATIONS AND MAINTENANCE

When Financing or Operations Become Part of the Project
- Financing Construction Projects
- The Impact of Financing on the Project Delivery Process
- The Impact of Financing on the Procurement Process

Financing Public Construction Projects
- Typical Varieties of Financing Structures
- Taxes
- Bonds
- Certificates of Participation
- New Parties and Their Roles When Financing Is Included

Financing Commercial Construction Projects
- Typical Varieties of Financing Structures
- Debt Financing
- Loans
- Other Financing Options
- New Parties (and Their Roles) When Financing Is Included

New Roles for the Original Parties

Public/Private Partnerships
- Elements of Public/Private Partnerships

Strategies for Offering Financing Services

Agreements Involving Financing

Operations and Maintenance
- The Lifecycle of a Facility
- The Impact of Operations on the Procurement Process
- Performance-Based Contracting
- New Parties and Their Roles When Operations Is Included

DELIVERY METHODS INVOLVING FINANCING OR OPERATIONS AND MAINTENANCE

- New Roles for the Original Parties When Operations Is Included
- Strategies for Offering Operations and Maintenance Services
- Agreements Involving Operations and Maintenance
- Privatization—Combining Financing and Operations

Summary
- A New Definition of "Total Cost"
- Project Delivery Becomes More Complex

DELIVERY METHODS INVOLVING FINANCING OR OPERATIONS AND MAINTENANCE

WHEN FINANCING OR OPERATIONS BECOME PART OF THE PROJECT

To develop a capital asset or improve an existing asset, several significant issues must be addressed before the delivery of the design and construction phases. A funding source must be identified, as must a physical site for the project and the resources necessary to operate and maintain the physical asset once it has been developed. On most projects, these phases are managed independently from the delivery of the design and construction phases. Though the trend is still not predominant, more and more projects are combining either the financing or the operation of the facility, or both, into the project delivery process.

When project financing or facility operations become part of the design and construction process, the number of variables can increase significantly. This becomes most apparent during the selection process, when factors such as lease rate, lease duration, and operating expenses are factored into the evaluation of competing offers. Because multiple financial transactions are rolled into one or more contracts, combining these phases can become very complex.

One method is to look to the design and/or build entity to help secure funding or operations/maintenance management. Increasing pressures (e.g., limited resources for funding, corporations focusing on their core competencies, and the need for faster facilities delivery in a globally competitive marketplace) are driving owners and users of facilities to consider combining different elements of the lifecycle.

Examples include student and military housing projects, wastewater treatment plants, correctional facilities, and toll roads. More of them are combining the funding, real estate, or operations and maintenance with the responsibility for facility delivery. This allows each organization to focus its efforts on the facility's intended use and not on the facility itself. In this way, a university that needs housing for its students no longer must obtain the funding from its legislative body, acquire the land, or administer a design and construction process. Even responsibility for maintaining the facility is turned over to a private firm.

Terminology can become even more confusing when financing and/or operations are combined with the delivery of the design and construction. For example, the term "turnkey" is often used when the entire responsibility for delivering a project belongs to a single entity such as a developer. The developer could obtain the real estate, arrange for financing, and take responsibility for the design, construction, and possibly the operation and maintenance of the completed facility.

If the tenant or user of the facility already owns the land and intends to operate and maintain the facility, then the turnkey developer would be arranging for the financing and the design and construction (a common occurrence). These same services—financing, design, and construction—could be provided by a design-builder that also arranges for financing. Thus, the line separating a turnkey entity and a design-build finance entity is very thin. It is important to clearly define the required services and avoid terms such as "turnkey" without additional explanation.

The first part of this chapter provides a brief overview of construction project funding. Next, we will examine financing as an added element of project procurement and how that affects the project delivery process. The second part of this chapter addresses the impact of blending the operations and maintenance responsibility into the project delivery process.

Financing Construction Projects

Every owner must find ways to fund its capital improvement programs. Funding is necessary for real estate acquisition, construction, and operations/maintenance. Obtaining funding is always a challenge, whether it be temporary financing to fund the project during the heavy cash flow period of construction or permanent financing to carry the cost of building or operating the facility.

Funding for a capital project typically includes the following:
- Funding the purchase of the real estate
- Funding the project development, including planning, design, and construction
- Funding the operation of the project after construction is complete

How are these basic funding needs being met? Given the many ways to structure financing and the corresponding legal instruments, this fundamental question must be answered on every project.

"Public projects" generally include all projects for use by the public. This includes public libraries, schools, office buildings, firehouses, prisons, civic centers, sewer treatment plants, military facilities, etc. "Commercial projects," as defined here, include not only privately developed projects such as office buildings, hotels, retail, etc., but also residential and multi-family projects.

This distinction is important because project financing methods differ depending on whether the project is public or commercial. Though many principles of project financing are the same for both, there are significant variations in types of financing available, players involved, and applicable laws.

Usually the funding of a construction project comes in the form of cash or borrowed money. If the funding is borrowed, it often is referred to as "debt financing." There are many types of debt financing, but money borrowed is generally categorized as either temporary (short-term) or permanent (long-term) financing. Sources of cash may be donated funds, cash reserves, or operating revenue.

Short-term or temporary financing is used to pay for the costs up through construction completion. Long-term or permanent financing is similar to a mortgage on a home. Long-term financing allows the borrowed cost to be paid over an extended number of years while the facility is used. The long-term financing may incorporate the costs for all or part of the real estate or development costs, depending on the amount of cash available to reduce the amount borrowed.

Because there are myriad of ways to handle the financing of the project, it helps immeasurably to engage the services of someone who is familiar with both construction and financing. Real estate professionals, or major accounting and law firms with experience in real estate, often provide these services. If time and resources permit, it is best to use consulting services independent from the providers of the project's financing or development services. Legal instruments such as leases and ownership partnerships can be tricky and have long-term consequences.

Though the tax implications of the project are separate from the financing decisions, they are closely related. Complicated tax laws vary from one locale to another. How a project's financing is contractually established can have major consequences for tax and total expenses throughout the life of the project. Thus, it is best to seek help from an accountant or tax lawyer familiar with the federal, state, and local tax laws.

Especially in the public sector, it is critical to determine who will provide the financial guarantees for the project. If money is borrowed, is the user of the facility or public entity tied in any way to the financial guarantees on the project? For example, are there loan guarantees or lease payments that the public entity can be held responsible for repaying? If the answer is yes, all parties should be sure they understand what the risks are, both short-term and long-term, before proceeding with the project.

"Off balance-sheet financing" is a term that refers to whether the ownership of the facility is required to be carried on the using entity's financial balance sheet as an asset. How the project ownership is structured is subject to generally accepted accounting rules that determine how the project is treated from a tax standpoint.

One simple determination often overlooked is the total maximum dollars available for the project. Breaking the available dollars down early in the process and identifying the total available funds for construction is a critical first step in any project delivery process. Public project finances are a matter of public record. Hence, information about the project should be shared regardless of the financing option used.

Given the complexity of combining financing into the project delivery process, it is important to realize that the lead party often changes. Individuals with financial backgrounds, rather than construction backgrounds often assume the lead role on these projects, but management of project development should be assigned to individuals experienced with managing real estate, planning, design, and construction.

The Impact of Financing on the Project Delivery Process

The extent to which the scope of the project delivery will need to be expanded will depend on which type of funding is needed: the real estate, the development, or the operations. The primary consideration would be the owner's knowledge and experience with construction financing. An owner with an ongoing building program (such as a large university) probably has a business officer familiar with numerous creative approaches to obtaining funding. On the other hand, a small religious institution owner might have little experience with obtaining financing for a new place of worship.

It is important for the owner to identify what it is looking for on each project. Usually, the initial advertisement and Request for Proposals should clearly indicate the scope of the desired services. Does it seek short-term financing? Long-term financing? Both? Is there an expectation that ownership will be transferred? If so, when? Will there be a lease? If yes, how long should the term of the lease be? Without this clear direction, responses from proposers will vary so significantly that they may be difficult, if not impossible, to compare.

For example, if an owner of a future building already owns the real estate but cannot finance the development, it may then need someone else to arrange for the permanent financing. In this example, the owner does not require real estate financing but does need temporary financing through the development, plus an arrangement of permanent financing. This owner is likely to become a "tenant" occupying the building and paying for its use in the form of lease payments. This is analogous to someone renting an apartment that is owned by someone else.

Project delivery in this example could be handled in a number of ways. One approach would be for the owner to hire a firm to be responsible for the financing while the owner directly handles the design and construction. An alternative would be to ask the designer and/or builder to bring the financing as part of its responsibility and then "sell" the building to another entity at the completion of the project. The new owner would then lease the facility back to the original owner. If delivered by combining the design and construction responsibilities (i.e., Design-Build), the resulting project delivery method would then be referred to as "Design-Build Finance."

Funding of the real estate, the development (including planning, design, and construction), and the operations of the facility must be accounted for on every project. What differs on many projects is who is providing the funding for each of these functions. The result is numerous hybrids of project delivery methods: Turnkey Development, Design-Build Finance, Design-Build Operate, and Design-Build Operate Transfer, to name just a few. The rest of this section addresses the basics of project financing and how financing affects the project delivery process.

DELIVERY METHODS INVOLVING FINANCING OR OPERATIONS AND MAINTENANCE

The Impact of Financing on the Procurement Process

If the procurement of design and construction was not already complicated enough, combining the financing of all or part of the project almost ensures that the procurement process will exceed the expertise of most organizations. Determining who to hire first, who to assign which responsibilities, which criteria to use as the basis for selection, and whether to assemble the team or let the team assemble itself are just a few of the major decisions an owner makes, sometimes without realizing it.

Who to hire first? There is no easy answer to this question when financing is involved in the project. But if we categorize owners into three broad categories, common approaches begin to appear.

1. **An owner with the knowledge and resources to arrange for financing.** This category of owner often also has the ability to manage the development and operations. Therefore, each of these can be procured separately with the procedures already established for the delivery option chosen. This first category of owner can simultaneously pursue the financing while beginning the development process with any of the project delivery options.

2. **The owner that does not have either the available resources or time to obtain funding for the real estate or development but does have the resources to manage the operation of the facility.** This category of owner will often turn the entire project over to a third-party entity, such as a program manager or agent CM. That entity can then provide the necessary services through construction, including the financing for the real estate and development. The third-party entity may have the expertise in-house to provide all or part of the services necessary, or the third-party entity may have the expertise to coordinate all of these services but will go out-of-house to perform some elements of them.

3. **The owner that does not have the time or resources available for the real estate or development.** This category of owner also does not have the resources to manage the operation of the facility. Similar to the second category, this owner will often turn over the entire project to a third-party firm that may or may not have the expertise in-house to provide the services. The difference with this third type of owner, though, is that it also needs the third-party entity to provide the resources to operate and maintain the facility. The "Operations and Maintenance" section of this chapter discusses this third category in more detail.

In the second and the third categories, it is most common for the owner to hire the third-party entity first to either provide all the services necessary or assist with assembling the firms necessary to provide the required services. Developers

DELIVERY METHODS INVOLVING FINANCING OR OPERATIONS AND MAINTENANCE

traditionally were called upon to fill this role of the third-party firm, but as more and more expertise evolves in the financing field, many different types of firms (including contractors, design-builders, and even design firms) are able to take on this responsibility as well.

Deciding which criteria to use as the basis for the selection is very similar to deciding which criteria to use when selecting between Low Bid, a Best Value approach, or Qualifications Based Selection. The difference, of course, is that now financing is part of the equation. Great care must be taken because now, in addition to having the typical variable of the project scope definition and costs, there are financing terms that vary as well. Financing concerns such as length of financing, rate of interest, amount being financed, and balance after the term of loan is over—all have an impact on the project cost. It is difficult enough to evaluate the criteria of procurement when the scope of services is just design and/or construction, but trying to evaluate competitive bids or proposals that include financing makes comparisons of bids very difficult.

With the project delivery processes discussed in the earlier chapters, the owner has the option of using any management method to facilitate the development of the project. When financing becomes part of the project delivery process, the owner still has the option of hiring a separate entity to represent it. Often, the line separating the owner's representative and the third-party entity that takes responsibility for the financing along with the project becomes easily blurred. Many times the owner uses the same entity providing the financing as its representative for the project. This can be a perfectly acceptable option as long as the responsibilities are clear and the risks (primarily the cost, schedule, quality, and delivery risks) are well understood by all parties.

FINANCING PUBLIC CONSTRUCTION PROJECTS

Financing public improvement projects is typically accomplished with tax revenues, the sale of bonds, or both.

It is critical to determine who will be providing the financial guarantees for a public project. Is the user of the facility or public entity tied in any way to the financial guarantees on the project? Can the public entity be responsible for repaying any loan guarantees or lease payments? If the answer is yes, all parties should be certain they understand both the short- and long-term risks before proceeding with the project.

Typical Varieties of Financing Structures

A decision to provide financing should include a thorough analysis of all project risks. What are the project's risks and who is assuming them? Among the many risks associated with a construction project are construction risk, management risk, demand risk, operating risk, environmental risk, and various political risks. The greater the risk, the more difficult securing the financing will be. At a minimum, even if the financing can be obtained, the greater the risk, the more expensive the financing will be.

On public projects there are many typical sources of funding. These include taxes from the public entity's general funds, loans, bonds, and a special type of bond referred to as a Certificate of Participation.

Taxes

There are a number of ways for a public entity to use taxes for capital improvement projects. For instance, special purpose taxes are approved for funding specific projects.

Bonds

Bonds are securities issued by a private company or public governing body to secure funding. They are backed by a promise to pay a certain interest in installments during the term of the bond. Bonds are often used to secure financing for real estate projects. While "corporate" bonds are sold by businesses to raise capital, bonds sold by a public governing body are usually referred to as "municipal" bonds.

There are many types of municipal bonds, including general obligation bonds, revenue bonds, and development bonds. Each is used for a different purpose and is backed by different guarantees.

- **General obligation bonds**—These are used to finance municipal improvement projects such as schools, streets, sewers, parks, and other general public use projects. General obligation bonds are guaranteed by the taxing power and full faith and credit of the community.
- **Revenue bonds**—These are used to fund a specific improvement project and are repaid from the revenues generated by the project.
- **Development bonds**—These are issued by private investors to finance a public improvement. A developer that can show that the project will enhance the community's welfare can take advantage of the tax-exempt feature of these bonds.

Most transactions involving the sale of bonds involve several entities and can be complex. Also, the ability to issue bonds for public projects requires full disclosure to the public and often requires the approval of the taxpayers. Municipal bonds can qualify for tax-exempt status, allowing the interest paid to the bondholders to be exempt from some or all taxes. Tax-exempt status allows them to be sold with a lower interest rate, so they are less expensive to repay. For example, a public housing project can obtain less expensive financing and pass that savings along in the form of more affordable rents.

Certificates of Participation

A Certificate of Participation (COP) is another form of lease-purchase financing often used to finance capital projects. A COP evidences ownership of a proportional interest in the right to receive payments provided for in a lease-purchase agreement. It is generally used for larger and more complex projects or when the public entity does not have a need for a public referendum.

The process is much the same as a municipal bond underwriting. The lease-purchase financing agreement is underwritten and marketed with certificates commonly offered for retail distribution to the general public. This type of financing may also be marketed as a private placement.

A lease agreement or a lease-purchase agreement is the primary instrument signed between the lessee and the lessor. The lessee can be any qualified political subdivision (states, counties, city districts, universities, hospitals, etc.). Payment is made from annually appropriated funds from the lessee, so the agreement is not considered long-term debt.

A bank or trust company acting as the trustee receives the lease agreement upon assignment from the lessor. The trustee issues Certificates of Participation in the lease, which grant to the investor a proportionate right to receive a share of principal and interest in the lease payment stream. These certificates are offered as fractional shares in denominations of $5,000 and closely resemble municipal bonds. In many instances, a Certificate of Participation uses the credit-worthiness of the public entity and often provides the lowest cost of funds available for the financing of essential capital projects.

New Parties and Their Roles When Financing Is Included

A number of new parties can enter into the project team when financing becomes part of the project. These include the lender, the lender's underwriter, a financial consultant, a developer, foundations, and authorities. A brief introduction to these parties and their roles follows:

- **Bond trustee**—A bond trustee is an intermediary in the controlling of the funds being raised and received relative to the bonds. The trustee receives the bond proceeds from the investment banker after the bonds are sold. The trustee distributes the bond funds to the party managing the project development. This is usually either the developer or design-builder. The bond trustee collects the payment from the entity responsible for repaying the bonds. On private sector projects, this is usually the owner of the project; on public sector projects this could be the owner or a not-for-profit foundation. The trustee then distributes the payments to the bondholders, including interest at the rate stated on the bond.

- **Bond investor (or bondholder)**—A bond investor purchases bonds from the bond underwriter. The money paid by the bond investors is referred to as the bond proceeds and is the money that is used to pay for the project.
- **Investment banker/underwriter**—The investment banker/underwriter prepares the project financing plan and underwrites the project bonds. By underwriting the bonds, an investment banker takes responsibility for providing the funds to purchase the bonds or Certificates of Participation from the trustee. The underwriter, in turn, sells the bonds or certificates to the investors.
- **Not-for-profit 501(c)(3) foundations**—Not-for-profit organizations meet the federal requirements for status as a "not-for-profit." This status brings numerous benefits to the organization, including an exemption from some taxes. This allows the entity to borrow money and keep exempt from some taxes the interest paid to the holders of the bonds. The result is the ability to borrow money at a lower interest rate than would otherwise be available.
- **Special authorities or tax districts**—Special authorities or tax districts are legal entities that exist for a special purpose. Usually created by a public entity, they have the ability to raise funds or collect taxes for a specific purpose.
- **Construction inspector**—The construction lender's inspector is employed by the lender to verify that the money being distributed in the periodic draws is appropriate.

FINANCING COMMERCIAL CONSTRUCTION PROJECTS

Financing for commercial projects can come from a variety of traditional and non-traditional lenders. Fiduciaries (banks, thrifts, insurance companies, pension funds, and credit unions) all lend money to finance real estate acquisition and construction. Semi-fiduciaries (mortgage brokers and investment trusts) also are sources of funds for real estate projects. Other sources include individuals and private loan companies.

Combined, these sources create a market that allows borrowers and lenders to be matched based on their specific needs and goals. Numerous products are offered to meet the various needs that arise in today's real estate market.

Typical Varieties of Financing Structures

As stated previously, the greater the risk, the more expensive the financing will be. In addition, almost every project requires some level of equity to be included in the project financing. The higher the risk, the higher the amount of equity required.

DELIVERY METHODS INVOLVING FINANCING OR OPERATIONS AND MAINTENANCE

Debt Financing

Short-term financing pays for the costs of planning, designing, and constructing a project. If short-term financing is borrowed in the form of a loan, it is often referred to as a construction loan. The lender will typically disburse the funds in increments (draws) tied to the completion of the work performed. To ensure that the lender does not lend more money than the value of the work performed, and to monitor how the borrowed funds are being used, the lender often hires a construction inspector to verify that the work is being completed as agreed upon and that the incremental draw on the loan is appropriate.

Loans

Loans for commercial projects are fundamentally similar to loans for public projects. "Construction loans" or short-term financing are common on commercial projects. Money borrowed at the beginning of construction is used to pay for the design and construction costs during construction. The amount borrowed is tied to an appraisal of the proposed project and to estimates provided by the owner's development team (including its designer and constructor).

The money is disbursed as needed, similar to borrowing money from a line of credit. With the outstanding balance gradually increasing as the project proceeds, interest is paid on the outstanding balance—typically on a monthly basis. Cash flow projections, showing how much money and when it will be borrowed, throughout a construction project are a very important part of the project budgeting process. Carrying the cost of construction during the work often leads to substantial interest payment costs. This is just another reason owners often look toward alternative project delivery methods that allow them to shorten the construction schedule and lower their interest costs. This is especially true when interest rates are relatively high at the time.

The construction loan is due for repayment upon final completion of the project. Prior to closing the construction loan, permanent financing must be obtained. Often, the permanent financing is in the form of another loan. These borrowed funds used for repayment of the construction loan are often referred to as permanent loans (or long-term financing) and are repaid over decades. Upon closing of the permanent loan (similar to a mortgage process on a residence), funds obtained from the permanent loan are used to pay off the construction loan.

A construction loan is borrowed only for the period of construction (usually just a few years or less); it is referred to as "temporary" or "short-term" financing. On the other hand, the loan repaid over a much longer period is regarded as "permanent" or "long-term" financing.

DELIVERY METHODS INVOLVING FINANCING OR OPERATIONS AND MAINTENANCE

Other Financing Options

Several other options are available to fund capital programs. These include cash, donations, letters of credit, and the sale of stock.

New Parties and Their Roles When Financing Is Included

A number of new parties can enter into the project team when financing becomes part of the project. These include the developer, the lender, the tenant and user, a financial consultant, and a construction inspector. A brief introduction to each of these parties and their roles follows:

- **Developer**—As discussed in Chapter 4: Program Management, the terms "developer" and "development manager" are distinguished by the developer's participation in the ownership of the project (in contrast to a development manager, which manages the development of a construction project but does not bring any financing to the project). Based on this distinction, the developer brings permanent financing to the project and assumes an ownership role. Thus, as the owner, the developer is also responsible for the maintenance and operation of the facility upon completion of construction. Some developers retain ownership as a long-term investment; others specialize in selling projects in the real estate investment market as an existing asset.

  The developer may be selected based on its qualifications and/or fees, a proposed lease rate, or a combination of factors. The developer might pick its own design and construction team ahead of time or might be selected on its own merit and work with the user of the facility to assemble the other members of the development team. The assignment of design and construction can then occur by way of the project delivery methods described in this book: Design-Bid-Build, CM at-Risk, Design-Build, or IPD.

- **Lender**—Loans, both the construction (short-term) and permanent (long-term), for private sector projects are typically provided by a bank.

- **Tenant and user**—This is the organization that takes the financial responsibility for paying for the use of the facility in the form of a lease. Payment is usually made in periodic installments, like rental payments for an apartment. The group occupying the facility is often referred to as the "user" of the facility.

- **Financial consultant**—Given the complexity of arranging for the financing of a construction project, it is common to seek the assistance of a financial consultant. A financial consultant will be familiar with the various sources of loans, loan structures, tax implications, and other valuable information to help determine the best financing alternatives.

- **Construction inspector**—The construction lender's inspector is employed by the lender to verify that the money being distributed in the periodic draws is appropriate.

NEW ROLES FOR THE ORIGINAL PARTIES

When financing becomes part of the project delivery process, the roles of the existing parties can change as well. The owner, the design firm, the constructor (or design-builder), and the owner's operations group are all affected in various ways:

- **Owner**—Often, the traditional "owner" of a project—a corporation, for example—changes from the role of owner to tenant or user of the facility when another entity provides the financing. This creates a delicate relationship in which the ultimate user of the facility is paying for the project, not by financing it, but rather through making lease payments to the financing entity. This is similar to a landlord-tenant relationship.

  One of the never-ending challenges in the industry is the ability to determine who the "owner" is in a practical sense during the construction of a project. Of course, there is always an entity that holds the title to the real estate, which may or may not be the same entity that is serving in the role of the "owner" contracting for the project delivery. In large institutions, is it the group paying for the facility? Or is it the group using the facility? The group maintaining the facility? When a third party brings financing to the project, identifying the owner grows even more complicated. Is it the developer? The tenant or user of the project? The lender or underwriter? The authority, the foundation, the bondholders, or trustee? There is no easy answer to this, and a successful argument can be made that any one of these entities is the owner.

- **Design firm**—The firm's primary role as the designer of the project is not unchanged by who is providing the financing. However, because of the confusion with identifying the owner, the challenge for the design firm is similar to its dilemma in Design-Build. The entity holding the contract for design services probably is not the same as the entity that will use the facility. Designing for the user, an approach in which design professionals have been trained, may be in conflict with designing for one or more of the "owners" on the project. Dealing with this dilemma is not impossible, but it does affect the role of the design firm when financing is included in the project delivery process.

- **Constructor**—The constructor's primary role as the builder of the project is unchanged by who is providing the financing. The exception is when the constructor's role is expanded to include financing of the project, in which case the constructor typically assumes the role of the design-builder (the same applies to the design firm if it provides the financing of the project).

- **Design-builder**—The design-builder's role as the designer and builder of the project is unchanged by who is providing the financing. As with the constructor or design firm, the exception is when the design-builder's role is expanded to include financing. The primary difference for the design side of the design-build team includes the same challenges as the design firm in working through the possible conflicts between the "owner" of the project and the needs of the design-builder.

PUBLIC/PRIVATE PARTNERSHIPS

Like so many other terms used in the industry, the term "Public/Private Partnership" describes a wide variety of situations. The National Council for Public-Private Partnerships offers this definition: "A Public-Private Partnership (PPP) is a contractual agreement between a public agency (federal, state, or local) and a private sector entity. Through this agreement, the skills and assets of each sector (public and private) are shared in delivering a service or facility for the use of the general public. In addition to the sharing of resources, each party shares in the risks and rewards potential in the delivery of the service and/or facility."[1]

Here are just a few of the common project scenarios involving both public and private parties:

1. A public owner has land and hires a private entity to finance, own, develop, and operate a new facility on the land that is leased to the private entity.
2. A public owner has land and hires a private entity to finance, own, and develop a new facility on the land that is leased to the private entity. The public owner operates the facility.
3. A public owner has land and hires a private entity to finance and own a new facility on land that is leased to the private entity. The public owner develops and operates the facility.
4. A public owner has land and finances, owns, and develops a new facility that is operated by a private entity.
5. A public owner has no land and leases a facility from a private entity that finances, owns, develops, and operates a facility on land owned by the private entity. The public owner pays rent to use the facility.
6. A public owner owns land and finances, owns, develops, and operates a new facility that is used for both public and private purposes. A private entity uses the facility or supports the facility.

Given the unique requirements of each of these scenarios, an entire book could be written on each one. Ways to handle the various types of projects are seemingly

---

[1] See: http://ncppp.org/howpart/index.shtml.

endless and are almost always modified to accommodate each project's unique conditions. Despite their differences, these all are examples of Public/Private Partnerships.

Elements of Public/Private Partnerships

Every facility has the same basic elements: the real estate (land), the building (or other improvements), and the operation and maintenance. The entity that will finance, own, and manage each element can be different on every project. These are just a few of the major issues that vary in every facility where public entities partner with private ones.

PROJECT RESPONSIBILITY MATRIX				
Issues/Elements	Financing?	Ownership?	Ownership Transfer?	Management?
Real Estate	?	?	?	?
Building	?	?	?	?
Operations & Maintenance	?	?	?	?

How each of these elements deals with each of these issues creates an infinite number of hybrids of Public/Private Partnerships. Consider financing alone: Will the private or the public entity finance the building? Will the entity solicit donations, collect taxes, sell bonds, or take out a loan? How will the debt be repaid and who will be responsible for it?

Another example involves the ownership of the project. Who will own the project during construction? Will the ownership transfer? If so, when will the transfer of ownership take place?

Every project is different and has its own unique combination of issues, including the political climate and the public's perception of the project. Because of the enormous number of variables that affect these projects and the fact that new creative solutions are being discovered every day, it is difficult to recommend helpful information. The best idea is probably to find a group of trusted advisers who are as familiar with as many of these options as possible.

Because these projects often involve a commitment of public resources (not necessarily dollars for development), it is very important that any Public/Private Partnership be conducted with full disclosure. Many issues can arise; for example, lenders cannot typically place a lien on a public facility, so security for the lender must be provided. Also, financing a public facility for private use usually has to be backed by some kind of guarantee.

The industry recognizes that this is a complicated field, and laws allowing Public/Private Partnerships are being passed throughout the country to address this issue. The field of Public/Private Partnerships is maturing, and as more public entities are facing tighter budgets, there is likely going to be an increase in the demand for funding from the private sector.

As Public/Private Partnerships have existed for centuries, so have the challenges that can come with them. For example, who is responsible for taking the appropriate measures to protect the public while using the facility? This is just one example of the kinds of issues that must be addressed.

It is important to note that implementation of one generic piece of Public/Private Partnership legislation will probably not be practical. Perhaps a future trend will be to evolve customized model legislation that takes these major elements and issues into consideration and addresses the unique challenges posed by the most popular hybrids. For now, existing procurement regulations may restrict the use of Public/Private Partnerships.

STRATEGIES FOR OFFERING FINANCING SERVICES

Construction firms seeking to expand their menu of services should understand how their surety would view their participation in any equity positions on their projects. Very few constructors invest in real estate projects for this reason. Instead, most bring financing to projects by creating relationships with a variety of lenders and other organizations that have the expertise to coordinate the financing options. An alternative for many constructors is to create a separate legal entity with financing capability that does not place their company's entire equity at risk.

AGREEMENTS INVOLVING FINANCING

Types of agreements used on projects with financing include:
- **Ground leases**—These are often used by owners of land who have a need for a capital project but do not have the resources to finance or develop the project on their own. Public owners can leverage their own land to develop a new capital improvement on it. The public owner does this by granting a long-term lease on the land and using private funds to develop the facility on the land. Examples include privatized military and university housing, prisons, and hotels.
- **Design-Build finance agreements**—These combine the responsibility for the design and construction of a Design-Build contract with the responsibility for financing of the construction. This is common for owners that want to keep from tying up their capital during the construction of the project.
- **Design-Build leasebacks**—These combine the responsibility for the design and construction of a Design-Build contract with a leaseback feature. A

property owner sells its property to an investor, which simultaneously leases it back, along with the improvement project to be built on the property. This is common when a property has significant value and the property owner wants to free that capital up for other uses.

OPERATIONS AND MAINTENANCE

The Lifecycle of a Facility

A lifecycle of a facility is the overall lifespan, from the original concept until the facility is either renovated or replaced. The overall lifecycle includes the need identification, the planning phase, funding and real estate acquisition, project delivery/development, occupancy, operation, and obsolescence. The lifecycle of a facility is measured in years, with the typical useful life being anywhere between 20–100 years.

The focus of this book thus far has been on the relatively short period of time representing the project delivery/development phase of this timeline—the planning, design, and construction phases. The project delivery/development portion is typically one to three years on a major building project and includes the design, construction, and occupancy phases. Thus, the project delivery/development phase is short when compared to the overall lifecycle of the facility.

The need identification, including the funding and real estate acquisition, is a process that could take months or years but is also relatively short relative to the overall life of the project. By far the longest period of time in the lifecycle of a facility is the operations phase in which the facility is used for its intended purpose. Owning and operating a facility is similar to owning and operating an automobile. The odds that the facility will last for the number of years intended is directly correlated to how it is maintained. Failure to operate and maintain a facility as recommended could significantly shorten its lifespan.

Once the facility is no longer useful, it is considered obsolete. Often the facility is renovated and used for a purpose different from its original one, or the facility may be demolished and replaced with a new structure.

The Impact of Operations on the Procurement Process

Procuring operations services in conjunction with design and/or construction services can be done simultaneously or in sequence. It is difficult, but not impossible, to add operations and maintenance services to Low Bid procurement. More commonly, the constructor or design-builder is expected to provide the expanded operations services as part of a Qualifications Based Selection process. This is accomplished by adding the additional scope to the Request for Proposals as part of the basic services or as an alternate for additional services. As a third alternative, the additional services may be handled as a separate negotiation with the successful constructor or design-builder. If the operations and maintenance are added to the Request for Proposals as either part of the basic services or as an alternate, the required services and expected basis for reimbursement must be specifically defined.

Performance-Based Contracting

When the contract includes operations and maintenance, it is possible to tie the performance of the facility to the contract with the service provider. The constructor or design-builder not only provides the services to operate the facility but also has its basis of reimbursement tied to the performance of the building. Sometimes the performance is tied to specific targets, such as expected energy savings. There are some providers that will guarantee these targeted savings. Facility owners evaluate the pros and cons of sharing in these risks, as well as the trade-offs in trying to achieve these savings when using performance-based contracts.

New Parties and Their Roles When Operations Is Included

A number of new parties can enter into the project team when operations and maintenance become part of the project. These include the various service providers and a developer. A brief introduction to these new parties and their roles follows:

- **Service provider(s)**—Service providers are entities that provide all or only some of the necessary services to operate and maintain the project after completion. This includes housekeeping, grounds/landscaping, toll collection, HVAC, electrical, building automation, etc.
- **Developer**—As discussed in Chapter 4: Program Management, the terms "developer" and "development manager" are distinguished by the developer's participation in the ownership of the project (in contrast to a development manager, which manages the development of a construction project but does not bring any financing to the project). As an owner, the developer is also typically responsible for the maintenance and operation of the facility. A developer acting as a development manager may also have operations management included as part of its services.

New Roles for the Original Parties When Operations Is Included

When operations and maintenance become part of the project delivery process, the roles of the existing parties can change as well. Here's a brief explanation of how the owner, the design firm, the constructor (or design-builder), and the owner's operations group are all affected in various ways:

- **Owner**—Often the traditional "owner" of a project—a corporation, for example—changes from the role of "owner" to tenant or user of the facility when another entity provides the operations.
- **Design firm**—The firm's primary role as the designer of the project is unchanged by who is providing the operations. However, as with financing, the challenge for the design firm is similar to its dilemma in Design-Build. The entity holding the contract for design services probably is not the same as the entity that will use the facility. Designing for the user may be in conflict with designing for one or more of the "owners" on the project. Dealing with this dilemma is not impossible, but it does affect the role of the design firm when operations are included in the project delivery process.
- **Constructor**—The constructor's primary role as the builder of the project is typically unchanged by who is providing the operations. The exception is when the constructor's role is expanded to include providing any or all of the operations of the project.
- **The design-builder**—The design-builder's role as the designer and the builder of the project is usually unchanged by who is providing the operations. As with the constructor or design firm, the exception is when the design-builder's role is expanded to include providing operations for the project. The primary difference for the design side of the design-build team includes the same challenges as the design firm in working through the possible conflicts between the owner of the project and the design-builder.

Strategies for Offering Operations and Maintenance Services

Construction firms looking to include operations and maintenance services should be aware of how labor intensive these services can be. Because they already have skilled labor forces, constructors (particularly specialty contractors such as HVAC and electrical contractors) are in a good position to make the leap into the expanded services of operations. For this reason, the constructor's expansion into operations is much more common than expansion into providing financial services.

Agreements Involving Operations and Maintenance

In addition to the agreements that include financing and operations outlined in the first part of this chapter, there are agreements that include operations but not design or financing. These are Operations or Service Agreements, Build-Operate Agreements (BO), and Build-Operate-Transfer Agreements (BOT).

- **Operations or Service Agreements**—Agreements between an owner of a facility and another entity to provide all or only some of the necessary services to operate and maintain the facility.

- **Build-Operate (BO) Agreements**—Agreements between the owner and constructor that combine the construction and operation of the facility. If design services are added, the agreement is with the design-builder and is referred to as a Design-Build Operate (DBO) agreement.
- **Build-Operate-Transfer (BOT) Agreements**—Similar to the Build-Operate Agreements, BOT agreements are distinguished by the builder (or design-builder) providing the financing and owning the facility up until a defined point in time, when the ownership is transferred from the builder to the ultimate owner of the facility.

It is important to note that, regardless of which agreement is used and who is responsible for the operation and maintenance of the facility, any project delivery method for design and construction might be utilized. An architect and constructor could be hired separately, and the project could be delivered using CM at-Risk or bid using Design-Bid-Build. Conversely, the design and construction responsibilities can be assigned to a single entity using Design-Build. Because Public/Private Partnerships are generally driven by a desire to consolidate services, Design-Build is typical with these partnerships.

In addition, in situations where the operations are part of the agreement, consideration is given to the impact that the design can have on the operations. For example, designing a more efficient prison that reduces the number of required guard stations dramatically reduces the labor cost of operating the prison.

Privatization—Combining Financing and Operations

The term "privatization" is often applied when the financing, development, and operations of a project are all combined. The same entity that is responsible for the financing, design, and construction also takes responsibility for the operation and maintenance of the facility. This is becoming increasingly common on projects that cannot be funded by public funds. Housing, parking decks, and prisons are examples of projects for which the demand has been met by private investors who have successfully developed models. Note that a well-structured Public/Private Partnership should retain the public entity's level of control. On the other hand, sometimes privatized projects may leave the public entity with little control.

SUMMARY

A New Definition of "Total Cost"

When the project delivery process includes more than just design and construction, keep in mind that the definition of the "total cost" must be broadened to include all project costs. The costs now required include more than just the planning, design, and construction costs.

DELIVERY METHODS INVOLVING FINANCING OR OPERATIONS AND MAINTENANCE

Be sure that all costs have been addressed without gaps or duplication. Delivering a brand new facility, only to later find out that there are shortfalls, could be disastrous. Facilities that sit empty while attempts are made to acquire the necessary funding to continue to operate it are very embarrassing. Duplication in costs could be equally disastrous if the project is cancelled due to a perceived lack of funds. Even if the project moves forward, a severely reduced program could significantly limit the use of the facility if it falls short of its original intent.

Few parties have the knowledge necessary to bring all pieces of a new project together. It is therefore critical to assemble a team of experts, each with experience with a part of the process. It also is essential to have a point person who is responsible for coordinating all these experts. Whether this expertise comes from within or is outsourced is not as important as working together and communicating, starting with the preparation of a complete and comprehensive budget that addresses all phases of the process.

Be sure that funding of each of the critical issues is addressed early in the process: Who is financing the cost of construction and the permanent financing (the mortgage)? Who is funding the real estate acquisition? Who is funding the operation and maintenance of the facility? The answers to each of these questions will inevitably result in a new definition of the "total project cost." They also will be more complicated than when the word "project" refers only to the planning, design, and construction.

Project Delivery Becomes More Complex

The ways financing and/or operations and maintenance are combined with the delivery of the facility vary tremendously. This chapter outlined some of the usual financing structures and operations and maintenance arrangements. It also addressed the impact they have on the procurement process and the involved parties and their roles.

When the delivery of financing and/or operations services is combined with the delivery of design and construction services, numerous questions arise. What services are required? How much should they cost? Who should I hire first? What type of contract should be used? Should one firm be used to provide all the services, or should they be separated? How should the services be procured? What criteria should be considered? How do I know what I am buying? How do I maintain control over the quality, cost, or schedule? Who will pay the cost of operating the utilities? Who will own the facility? Will the owner be more concerned about the "day one" cost or the total cost, including operating costs? Who will be responsible if the building does not work for its intended purpose? If something breaks, whose responsibility is it to fix it?

DELIVERY METHODS INVOLVING FINANCING OR OPERATIONS AND MAINTENANCE

When it becomes more complex to identify each party's responsibilities, it becomes more complex to select them. Contracts for design and construction are replaced with more complicated leases and operating agreements. The topic of alternative financing is an evolving one; there are many financial instruments available for funding new capital projects. Operations and maintenance is also a field that is changing rapidly, as new technologies and building systems continue to make the operation of a building more complicated.

As the topics continue to mature, more information on options for alternative financing and for operations and maintenance is created every day. This chapter has provided an introduction to these topics and touched on how the combination of financing and/or operations and maintenance can affect the project delivery process.

Every project has a real estate aspect, a financing piece, a development phase, and an operations and maintenance phase. The majority of this textbook has focused on the development phase, particularly the delivery of the design and construction services. For a variety of reasons, the responsibilities for the real estate, financing, or operations and maintenance of the project are often combined with the delivery of the design and construction.

When this occurs, the already challenging job of procuring and implementing the design and construction becomes even more daunting. Who to hire? When to hire? In what order to hire? These are just a few of the questions that arise when financing and/or operations and maintenance responsibilities are combined with the design and construction.

Every project's circumstances are unique. The factors that may lead an owner to one of the many strategies vary too much for any one set of rules to apply. The best advice is to always seek counsel from trusted advisers who have experience in dealing with the various strategies available. As long as there are challenges, there will always be someone looking for creative solutions. Thus, staying current with the latest evolutions in the industry is essential.

For additional information about construction financing, the AGC of America publication *Guide to Construction Financing – Second Edition* can be found at http://www.agc.org/building.

GLOSSARY

Agency Construction Management: A project management system based on an owner's agreement with a qualified construction management firm to provide coordination, administration, and management within a defined scope of services.

Allowances: Used for pricing materials or items not fully described in the specifications and which may be subject to later selection by the owner or designer. Examples include brick, cabinetry, and carpeting.

Alternate: A separately priced item on a bid form that the owner, in its discretion, may include in the contract.

Alternative Project Delivery Method: Any project delivery method other than Design-Bid-Build.

Arbitration: A more formal method of dispute resolution under which the parties' claims are presented to a single arbitrator or a panel of three arbitrators for a decision.

Architectural/Engineering Subcontract: With a constructor-led team or a joint venture design-builder, an architectural/engineering subcontract is the subcontract between the design-builder and the designer to provide the design to the design-builder. Note that the owner does not contract directly with the designer. Rather, the designer contracts directly with the design-builder.

Automobile Coverage by Constructors: This insurance covers against claims involving the use of vehicles by the constructor's employees. For example, it would cover the damages if a project superintendent had an automobile accident on his way from the project to a vendor's place of business.

Best Value: Fees: A procurement option defined as a competition where 1) price is part of the final selection criteria and 2) the price is the fees, but the fees are not the only criterion for final selection.

Best Value: Total Cost: A procurement option defined as a competition where 1) price is part of the final selection criteria and 2) the price is the total construction

GLOSSARY

cost (or design and construction costs if it is Design-Build), but the total construction costs are not the only criterion for final selection.

Bid Package: The group of documents issued by the owner to competing constructors so they can prepare bids.

Bonds: Securities issued by a private company or public governing body to secure funding. They are backed by a promise to pay a certain interest in installments during the term of the bond. Bonds are often used to secure financing for real estate projects.

Bridging: Used with the Design-Build delivery method, bridging is the process of creating documents containing partial design information that the owner uses as the basis of pricing when hiring a design-builder. Bridging documents can be preliminary (conceptual or schematic) or more complete (design development or partial construction documents). They can be prepared in-house if an owner has the design expertise available or by a consultant engaged by the owner.

Bridging Architect (or Bridging Designer): A consultant that assists the owner in developing the bridging documents used to communicate the owner's requirements to the design-builder. The bridging architect may also assist the owner by preparing specific design elements the owner wishes to describe within the project requirements. The bridging architect then monitors the actual construction of the project to ensure that it is consistent with the requirements of the program.

Builder's Risk Insurance: Property insurance that covers physical damage to the work while construction is in progress.

Building Information Model (BIM): An enhanced electronic representation of a facility for the purpose of design, analysis, construction, operations, and facility management. BIM consists of geometric representations of the building elements plus additional information that needs to be captured and transferred for the project delivery process and for facility operations. As the project moves through its lifecycle, different participants use BIM in different ways, each enhancing collaboration throughout.

Certificates of Participation: A Certificate of Participation (COP) is another form of lease-purchase financing often used to finance capital projects. A COP evidences ownership of a proportional interest in the right to receive payments provided for in a lease-purchase agreement. It is generally used for larger and more complex projects or when the public entity does not have a need for a public referendum.

Collaboration: A form of partnering. In a collaborative setting, the parties communicate regularly with one another in an effort to ensure that common goals are achieved. They attempt to come together as a team with the goal of completing the project. The parties foster this team approach to the project to resolve issues and problems in a cooperative (rather than finger-pointing) process.

GLOSSARY

Commissioning: Prior to occupancy, the project's systems and equipment are tested and adjusted so that they perform as designed and will satisfy the project's requirements.

Competitive Bidding: This process is at the heart of Design-Bid-Build. During competitive bidding, sealed bids are used (in public work, primarily) to demonstrate fairness and objectivity.

Conceptual Estimating: A requirement of companies offering preconstruction services. An estimator puts together a relatively detailed estimate of anticipated costs by considering a historical database of similar projects. The estimator may have very little design input, other than basic schematic drawings. Frequently, the estimator will create an "outline specification" to define how the estimate was completed and what it includes and excludes.

Conceptualization: In this phase of the IPD process, teams develop project goals concerning the desired outcomes of a successful project.

ConsensusDOCS: ConsensusDOCS are standard contracts developed by a diverse coalition of more than 30 leading construction industry associations with members from all stakeholders in the design and the construction industry.

Constructability Review: Conducted to evaluate whether there are major coordination, schedule, or technical obstacles posed by the design. The constructability review can identify project constraints at a time when adjustments can be made most economically.

Construction Documents Phase: The stage of the design during which the design details are finalized, and the full information required to perform the project is documented on both the plans and specifications.

Construction Management at-Risk: A project delivery method defined by the following characteristics: 1) design and construction are separate contracts and 2) the total construction cost is not a factor in the final selection. CM at-Risk can be procured with either Qualifications Based Selection or Best Value: Fees procurements. The constructor, referred to as the CM at-risk, holds the trade contracts and takes responsibility for the performance of the work. The CM at-risk typically provides essential preconstruction services and guarantees the construction costs and schedule. The CM at-risk serves as the general contractor assuming the risk of the performance, either by its own crews or by specialty contractors and suppliers.

Construction Phase and Project Contingencies: Used to adjust for minor changes in the work, changes in economic conditions, unanticipated problems, etc. The project contingency is generally held by the owner and is used to account for major problems and scope changes.

GLOSSARY

Construction Phase Service (or Construction Administration): The final phase of the design effort, which takes place during the actual construction activity.

Construction Subcontract: With a designer-led team or a joint venture design-builder, a construction subcontract is a subcontract between the design-builder and the constructor to provide construction services.

Constructor Controlled Insurance Programs (CCIP): The only critical distinction between a CCIP and an OCIP is that the constructor procures and holds the insurance policies. Both are comprehensive insurance programs, with coverage of most or all risks, for the benefit of all companies and persons on the project.

Cost-Plus: A basis of reimbursement in which actual costs associated with the project are marked up for overhead and profit by the contractor and then billed to the owner—the "plus" in Cost-Plus, referring to the contractor's fee.

Debt Financing: Short-term financing pays for the costs of planning, designing, and constructing a project. If short-term financing is borrowed in the form of a loan, it is often referred to as a construction loan. The lender will typically disburse the funds in increments (draws) tied to the completion of the work performed. To ensure that the lender does not lend more money than the value of the work performed, and to monitor how the borrowed funds are being used, the lender often hires a construction inspector to verify that the work is being completed as agreed upon and that the incremental draw on the loan is appropriate.

Defining Characteristics: Characteristics that uniquely distinguish one delivery system from the others.

Delivery System (or Delivery Method): The means by which design and construction work are provided. See also Project Delivery System.

Design Development: The stage of design at which relationships between various components of the design are finalized and the design team starts to flesh out more details, materials, standards, and the like.

Design Phase Contingency: The amount of money included in an estimate to represent the yet-to-be-detailed or yet-to-be-defined portions of the contract documents.

Design-Bid-Build: A project delivery method where the owner procures a design and bid package from an independent designer, uses a competitive procurement process to get bid prices for all work required to build the project as specified, and then selects a constructor to build the project on the basis of either Low Bid or Best Value: Total Cost procurements.

Design-Build: A project delivery method where one firm assumes responsibility for both the design and the construction of the project. By combining these two functions from the outset of the project, Design-Build can promote an interdisciplinary team approach throughout the duration of the project. The defining characteristic of Design-Build is that the design and construction contracts are combined.

Design-Build Prime Contract: The contract between the owner and the design-builder in which the design-builder agrees to design, construct, and deliver the project to the owner.

Design-Build Team: A group of design and construction professionals that deliver the project to the owner. They may all be part of one firm, called an integrated design-builder, or they may be members of different firms.

Direct Subcontracting: Applies when each trade contract and supplier is awarded individually and contracted directly to the owner. The number of direct contracts is typically greater than 10 and is often 50 or more.

Dispute Resolution Alternatives: The most common dispute resolution alternatives include mediation, case evaluation, dispute review boards, mini-trials, arbitration, and litigation.

Dispute Review Boards (DRB): Boards of project representatives who are appointed in advance of the project and who meet periodically during the project. At each meeting, the DRB is given an update on the project as a whole. In the event of any disputes that are not resolved directly by the parties, the DRB hears each side's position on the issue, and then renders a decision on that issue.

Fast-Track: Any project and process where there is overlap between two or more project phases.

General Liability Insurance: The most common form of insurance carried by constructors and others. It is sometimes called "comprehensive general liability" (CGL) insurance.

Guaranteed Maximum Price (GMP): A basis of reimbursement sometimes referred to as a "GMP" or "G-Max," this is a price mechanism sometimes used in construction contracts. The owner agrees to reimburse the cost of the work up to a prescribed ceiling amount—the Guaranteed Maximum Price.

Indefinite Delivery/Indefinite Quantity (IDIQ): An accelerated procurement approach that is generally used to describe open-ended contractual relationships that are not tied to specific scope. They are often used by owners who want to have contracts in place quickly to accommodate certain project types. Small projects or emergency projects, for example, benefit from having contracts that have already met the required procurement rules and can move quickly into the execution stage.

Indemnification/Hold Harmless Clauses: An indemnity is a risk-shifting mechanism between two or more parties. An indemnity occurs when one party

GLOSSARY

(the indemnitor) agrees to be responsible for any third-party claim or other hazard that might befall another party (the indemnitee).

Integrated Project Delivery: A project delivery method where the owner, designer, contractor, and other primary parties sign one agreement (referred to as a "multi-party" agreement). The term used to describe this type of contract is "relational" contracting as opposed to the "transactional" contracting, which is used in traditional contracting.

Invitation to Bid: The procurement process used on projects procured with the Low Bid procurement option (often referred to as the "traditional" process). Most owners, particularly public owners, have well established processes and procedures, many of which are regulated, for how they procure with Low Bid. Whether or not this process is specifically referred to as Invitation to Bid, it is probably very similar to the Low Bid process.

Job Order Contracting (JOC): A way to deliver projects more efficiently than going through a traditional advertisement/procurement/contracting process. Contractual terms flexible enough to work with many different projects, using typical rates and unit costs for common scope items, are negotiated one time. Terms to handle special or unique situations are also established in the contract. Once selected, JOC constructors are then under contract and available when needed.

Lean Construction: Construction aimed at minimizing costs and maximizing value to clients in all dimensions of the built environment: planning, design, construction, activation, operations, maintenance, salvaging, and recycling. The foundation of lean construction is a set of principles based on the holistic pursuit of minimizing waste to result in continuous improvement.

Letters of Credit: Negotiable instruments under which the issuer (usually a bank) agrees to pay the holder of the note, either upon a written demand for payment or upon the occurrence of some other well defined condition.

Lien Waiver: A relinquishment of lien rights to the extent of the amount that has been paid, and a record of the flow of funds down the chain of prime contractor, subcontractor, and supplier.

Litigation: Occurs when a lawsuit is filed in the court system, which will then proceed under the court's rules to a trial if no settlement is reached in advance.

Low Bid: A procurement option where the lowest bid is the sole criterion. Under Low Bid procurement, the owner takes the lowest responsible and responsive bidder qualified to perform the work.

Lump Sum Fixed Price: A basis of reimbursement where a fixed price for the scope of work is described in the contract documents. The general contractor assumes the risk of cost increases to complete the scope of work described in the original contract documents.

GLOSSARY

Management Method: The mechanics by which construction is administered and supervised.

Mediation: A voluntary, facilitated settlement negotiation. In mediation, each party to the dispute (and there may be more than two) meets with a mediator or facilitator.

Mini-Trials: Non-binding presentations of each side's case to a jury or panel of three persons.

Multi-Party Contract: A form of agreement where, at a minimum, the primary project participants comprised of the owner, the designer, and the contractor all sign one agreement.

Multiple Prime Contracting: A contracting approach that can be used with any of the delivery systems described in this book. As the name implies, instead of an owner contracting with a single general contractor, construction manager, or design-builder, the owner (or its representative) contracts directly with multiple trade contractors for the completion of the work and assumes the responsibility for the coordination of the work.

On-Call: An accelerated procurement approach that is generally used to describe open-ended contractual relationships that are not tied to specific scope. They are often used by owners who want to have contracts in place quickly to accommodate certain project types. Small projects or emergency projects, for example, benefit from having contracts that have already met the required procurement rules and can move quickly into the execution stage.

Open-Book Contracting: Refers to a contractual requirement to share openly information related to the project, particularly project cost information. This includes estimates, bids from subcontractors and suppliers, invoices, and any information directly related to the cost of executing the project.

Outline Specification: To define the pricing, the estimator must create a simple specification to define what the basis of the pricing is. At this stage in the design process, it is generally agreed that the construction estimates should be based on more of a systems analysis approach, as opposed to the form and format that will be used for the final project specifications.

Owner Controlled Insurance Programs (OCIP): The only critical distinction between an OCIP and a CCIP is that the owner procures and holds the insurance policies. Both are comprehensive insurance programs, with coverage of most or all risks, for the benefit of all companies and persons on a project.

Owner's Liability Insurance: Insurance that covers the same scope of damages as the constructor's liability insurance, except that it applies to claims arising from the actions of the owner.

GLOSSARY

Owner's Program: A statement of requirements for the project, provided to the design-builder as project requirements to be satisfied by the design-builder's design and construction services.

Partnering: Partnering is a collaborative process typically set up at the outset of a project. At a facilitated session attended by the major decision-makers of each principal participant, common goals and problems are discussed. The parties agree on a methodology by which to work out any issues that may arise. Partnering occurs throughout a construction project.

Payment Bond: A surety bond that secures a constructor's obligations to pay subcontractors, suppliers, and others lower in the hierarchical pecking order.

Performance Bond: Acts as security for performance, for the entity higher in the contracting chain than the bond principal.

Performance Specifications: These define the performance requirements of the completed system and leave the materials and methods of construction up to the constructor.

Performance-Based Contracting: When the performance of the facility is tied to the contract with the service provider. The constructor or design-builder not only provides the services to operate the facility, it also has its basis of reimbursement tied to the performance of the building.

Prequalification: The process by which prospective designers or constructors are examined before they are solicited to compete for a project. Persons and companies without the appropriate qualifications are not permitted to compete for the work.

Prescriptive Specifications: These specify details of the work the constructor is to perform and what materials it will use, perhaps listing the names and model numbers of products or manufacturers.

Privatization: This term is often applied when the financing, development, and operations of a project are all combined. The same entity that is responsible for the financing, design, and construction also takes responsibility for the operation and maintenance of the facility.

Procurement: The process of soliciting and engaging a designer or a constructor for a project.

Procurement Method (or Selection Method): The means of selecting the design and construction members. The method chosen can significantly affect the type of relationship created on the project and the project's ultimate outcome.

Professional Liability Insurance: Malpractice insurance against claims arising from the alleged malpractice of a designer.

Program Manager: The person(s) responsible for overseeing the construction of multiple structures on the same site or for overseeing coordinated building efforts involving construction work at multiple locations or under multiple contracts. Program managers can also oversee the construction of various structures for a single owner in multiple locations, such as retail centers, commercial office buildings, or certain types of public works projects.

Program Management: Oversight of the construction of multiple structures on the same site or responsibility of coordinated building efforts at multiple locations or under multiple contracts.

Programming (or Planning): The stage of design at which the designer assesses the owner's present usage of a facility and detailed requirements for the project and then develops lists of relationships and analyzes options and alternative courses of action.

Progress Payments: In most Design-Bid-Build contracts, the lump sum is a series of periodic (usually monthly) payments by the owner to the constructor. These are called "progress payments" because each is a percentage of the total lump sum price, based on the percentage of the total construction completed to date.

Project Delivery System/Project Delivery Method: The comprehensive process of assigning contractual responsibilities for designing and constructing a project. See also Delivery System.

Project Insurance: A multi-faceted policy that covers the interests of a number of the parties on the project.

Project Manager: A manager who provides construction oversight on a single-phase project or is responsible for overseeing the construction phase of a multi-building project. A project manager's scope of responsibility is more limited than that of a program manager.

Project Management: Oversight of a single-phase project or the construction phase of a multi-building project.

Public/Private Partnerships: A Public/Private Partnership (PPP) is a contractual agreement between a public agency (federal, state, or local) and a private sector entity. Through this agreement, the skills and assets of each sector (public and private) are shared in delivering a service or facility for the use of the general public. In addition to the sharing of resources, each party shares in the risks and rewards potential in the delivery of the service and/or facility.

Qualifications Based Selection: A procurement option based upon evaluation of the comparative qualifications of the competing companies without weighting price for determining the final selection.

Related Areas: Characteristics not unique to any one delivery method.

Request for Proposals (RFP): Occurs after the phase one Request for Qualifications (RFQ) process and involves more time, effort, and expense for all parties. Three to five competitors are usually invited to propose, and the proposals are reviewed and ranked following procedures specified in the solicitation. The firm determined best suited is selected, and the final negotiations for the award of the contract (if any) take place.

Request for Qualifications (RFQ): Used to identify which firms are interested in the project and to pinpoint their relative qualifications. The qualifications under consideration at this stage normally are limited to non-monetary issues. The owner should provide information about the project to the firms interested in applying for it. This material should provide some definition of the project under consideration.

Responsible Constructor: One that can perform and complete the work required by the contract documents, to the satisfaction of the owner. A responsible constructor must possess the necessary financial and technical capability to perform the work as well as the tenacity to do so, usually demonstrated by the constructor's past performance record.

Responsive Bid: An unequivocal offer to do everything required by the contract documents without exception.

Retainage: Money earned by the constructor but held by the owner pending completion of the project. Also refers to money earned by a specialty contractor but held by the general contractor pending completion of the project or a particular phase of the project.

Risk Shifting: Shifting of risk from the owner to its contractor. As a general rule, there is cost associated with the risk when it is shifted, and the more risk the owner shifts to the constructor, the greater that cost should be.

Savings: A result of the "risk sharing" between the client and constructor that is evolving as a part of the CM at-Risk delivery method. Often the client and CM at-risk enter into an agreement (as part of the contract) to share any savings generated by bringing the project in under the guaranteed price. The purpose for this is to create a common goal, encourage all parties to seek timely decisions, and give the CM at-risk an incentive to be as economical as possible in completing the project.

Schematic Design: The stage at which the design is developed on a conceptual basis.

Self-Insurance: Most insurance policies have a "self-insured retention," or deductible. The insured must contribute the amount of the deductible in advance of any obligation on the part of the insurance company to cover a loss.

Set-Based Design: Identified in lean construction theory as a tool to evaluate and prioritize multiple design options. With Set-Based Design (or concurrent engineering), when creating a product, the team develops multiple versions simultaneously, each version being a "set." Eventually, the designs will "compete" against one another and ultimately be consolidated to contain the best and most appropriate design elements from each set.

Shared Risk/Reward: The pooling of the team's contingencies along with sharing any of the unspent pooled contingency and linking at least a portion of the participants' profits to the project's overall target price. Used in the IPD project delivery method, shared risk/reward provides significant incentives for the team to work together.

Sole Source (or Direct Negotiation): A situation where the owner either elects to or has no choice but to negotiate directly with a single firm. In some cases, an owner may have reasons for believing that negotiating an award with a single contractor is in its best interest.

Spearin Doctrine: The result of a 1918 Supreme Court decision concerning a Federal Government construction contract, *United States v. Spearin*, 246 U.S. 132 (1918). Under this doctrine, the general contractor agrees to follow the contract documents without substantial variation; if that is done, the owner agrees to accept the work. This is also often called the owner's "warranty of the specifications."

Standard Forms of Agreements: Contract agreements that are in common use throughout the industry. Most owners, designers, and constructors either use standard forms or have custom forms that are modeled after the standard forms. These forms define the expectations and obligations of each party and, ideally, should mirror the parties' relationship.

Substitutions: Allow constructors to recommend different products from those specified. These tend to be regional and private in application.

Surety Bond: Surety bonds are specialized tri-party agreements. Each bond involves three parties, one of whom may be a class of companies rather than an individual company. These parties are 1) the bond principal, who is the one obtaining and directly paying for the bond, 2) the bond surety, who is providing security for the performance of the bond principal, and 3) the obligee, who is the beneficiary of the surety's commitment to provide this security. The surety under a surety bond agrees that if the bond principal does not fulfill its obligation to the claimant, the surety will step up to the plate and do so.

Sustainability (or Green Construction): The practice of designing and building facilities that are environmentally responsible. These facilities minimize the impact to the natural environment and resources consumed both during construction and throughout the building's lifecycle.

Target Price: A basis of reimbursement under which the project participants (at a minimum, those who are signers to the multi-party contract) collaboratively establish a target price for the project and then work together to maximize the

GLOSSARY

value that the owner receives for that amount—that is, to see to it that the value proposition proposed by the owner at the outset of the project is achieved for a cost no greater than the target price.

Teaming Agreement: An agreement between firms to jointly pursue an opportunity as an individual project.

Term Contracting: An accelerated procurement approach that is generally used to describe open-ended contractual relationships that are not tied to specific scope. Theses are often used by owners who want to have contracts in place quickly to accommodate certain project types. Small projects or emergency projects, for example, benefit from having contracts that have already met the required procurement rules and can move quickly into the execution stage.

Total Construction Cost (TCC): Construction cost of work plus the constructor's general conditions and constructor's fee.

Total Design and Construction Cost: Total construction cost (TCC) plus design fees.

Total Project Cost (TPC): Total design and construction costs plus the balance of all other project costs.

Typical Characteristics: Characteristics of a delivery method that are not required to define it.

Umbrella Liability Insurance: Provides excess coverage, over and above the limits of insurance carried by a constructor for any other type of insurance. If the general liability insurance provides coverage for personal injury claims up to the amount of $1 million dollars, then the umbrella insurance could provide coverage for damages incurred above that amount, up to the limits of the umbrella policy.

Unit Prices: A basis of reimbursement used to identify costs of materials or activities when actual quantities can only be estimated prior to construction. Paying for work by the unit may eliminate a need for contingencies to cover increased or decreased quantities.

Workers' Compensation: Every state has workers' compensation laws that require employers to obtain and maintain insurance against injury to their employees on the job. The statutory schemes provide that employees are barred from suing their employer in the event of an injury but must be content with workers' compensation proceeds.

Wrap-Up Insurance: One party obtains a variety of insurance coverages with a single carrier, or in a single policy.

SELF TEST ANSWERS

CHAPTER ONE—INTRODUCTION

1. a. Obtaining the funding for the project
2. e. None of the above
3. d. Both a and b
4. e. All of the above
5. b. Best Value: Total Cost
6. c. Best Value: Fees
7. d. All of the above
8. c. The number of contracts

CHAPTER TWO—PROCUREMENT OPTIONS

1. b. Invitation to Bid
2. a. Low Bid
3. e. all of the above
4. c. Request for Qualifications/Request for Proposal
5. False
6. c. Best Value: Fees

SELF TEST ANSWERS

CHAPTER THREE—BASIS OF REIMBURSEMENT

1. e. Lump Sum
2. a. Design-Bid-Build
   c. Design-Build Low Bid or Best Value: Total Construction Cost
3. e. All of the above
4. a. It (the design contingency) will be greater
5. b. Progressive GMP's
6. c. Referring to Target Price as "no GMP" is an accurate representation
7. c. A cost-plus contract

CHAPTER FOUR—PROGRAM MANAGEMENT

1. b. a project management system
2. c. by the expanded scope of work performed by the Program Manager
3. c. typically involved in all five phases of the construction process or providing services on most of them on a multiple structure or building site construction
4. c. whether or not responsibility of actual delivery of design and construction services is assumed
5. a. used with any delivery method
6. a. whether or not the developer holds an ownership or equity participation position

CHAPTER FIVE—AGENCY CONSTRUCTION MANAGEMENT

1. b. a project management system
2. d. the agent CM is not holding any of the trade contracts
3. b. the agent CM, is not at risk for the cost or schedule of building the job, i.e. the performance risk
4. d. all of the above
5. a. on the basis of qualifications and sometimes fee

SELF TEST ANSWERS

6. a. that it will not perform its services improperly
7. a. the salaries of the agent CM team
8. b. the CM at-Risk

CHAPTER SIX—PROJECT DELIVERY CONSIDERATIONS

1. False
2. True
3. False
4. True
5. False
6. True
7. True
8. True
9. True
10. True
11. True
12. False
13. True
14. True
15. False

CHAPTER SEVEN—DESIGN-BID-BUILD

1. a. a construction project delivery method
2. d. both a and b
3. c. an unequivocal offer to do everything required by the contract documents without exception
4. b. a separately-priced item on a bid form that the owner, in its discretion, may include in the contract
5. c. the owner assumes full responsibility for the performance of the designer
6. c. the constructor is typically not involved during the design phase

CHAPTER EIGHT—CONSTRUCTION MANAGEMENT AT-RISK

1. a. a construction project delivery method
2. c. a separate contract for design and construction, and final selection is based on factors other than just lowest construction cost
3. c. Guaranteed Maximum Price for the project
4. b. the constructor can begin construction before the completion of final construction documents
5. b. selection of the team members is based on criteria other than lowest cost

SELF TEST ANSWERS

6. a. the "schedule of values" basis

7. a. the "open-book" relationship with the owner

8. c. the owner's ability to provide input on the selection of trade or subcontractors

CHAPTER NINE—DESIGN-BUILD

1. a. a construction project delivery method

2. b. that one firm assumes responsibility for both the design and the construction of the project

3. b. is to first establish its project requirements, review and approve the design, approve project budgets and, if required, review and approve price proposals. The owner's requirements must be stated clearly and accurately for the project to be a success.

4. a. fewer design-related disputes during the construction phase than Design-Bid-Build

5. e. any of the above

6. a. selecting a Design-Builder with a low bid or best value bid procurement

7. d. all of the above

8. b. eliminated as a risk to the owner because the same entity is responsible for the construction cost and the design

CHAPTER TEN—INTEGRATED PROJECT DELIVERY

1. a. a project delivery method

2. c. Level 3

3. b. Pure IPD

4. d. None of the above

5. a. Qualifications Based Selection

6. False

7. a. Owner initiated changes

RELATED CONTRACTS

Below is a chart of standard construction contracts endorsed by AGC and the closest document equivalents for documents published by the American Institute of Architects (AIA), which AGC does not currently endorse. Updated and more detailed information can be found at www.consensusdocs.org.

DOCS#	ConsensusDOCS Name	2007 AIA #
\multicolumn{3}{c}{ConsensusDOCS 200 Series – General Contracting}		
200	Owner/Constructor Agreement & General Conditions (Lump Sum)	A101 (+A201)
200.1	Time and Price Impacted Materials	N/A
200.2	Electronic Communications Protocol Addendum	E201
202	Change Order	G701
203	Interim Directed Change	G714
204	Request for Information	G716 (2004)
205	Owner/Constructor Agreement, Short Form (Lump Sum)	A107
220	Constructor's Statement of Qualifications for Engineered Construction	A305
221	Constructor's Statement of Qualifications	A305
222	Design Professional's Statement of Qualifications	B305
235	Owner/Constructor Agreement & General Conditions, Short Form (Cost of Work)	A103
240	Owner/Design Professional Agreement	B101
245	Owner and Design Professional Agreement, Short Form	B105
260	Performance Bond	A312
261	Payment Bond	A312
262	Bid Bond	A310

RELATED CONTRACTS

263	Warranty Bond	N/A
270	Instructions to Bidders on Private Work	A701
280	Certificate of Substantial Completion	G704
281	Certificate of Final Completion	N/A
290	Guidelines for Obtaining Owner Financial Information	N/A
290.1	Owner Financial Questionnaire	N/A
291	Application for Payment (GMP)	G702
292	Application for Payment (Lump Sum)	G702
293	Schedule of Values	G703

ConsensusDOCS 300 Series – Collaborative Agreements		
DOCS#	ConsensusDOCS Name	2007 AIA #
300	Tri-Party Integrated Project Delivery (IPD) Agreement	C191
301	Building Information Modeling (BIM) Addendum	E202
310	Green Building Addendum	D503

ConsensusDOCS 400 Series – Design Build		
DOCS#	ConsensusDOCS Name	2007 AIA #
400	Preliminary Owner/Design-Builder Agreement	N/A
410	Owner/Design-Builder Agreement & General Conditions (Cost Plus w/ GMP)	A141
415	Owner/Design-Builder Agreement & General Conditions (Lump Sum)	A141
420	Design-Builder & Design Professional Agreement	B143
421	Design-Builder's Statement of Qualifications for a Specific Project	N/A
450	Design-Builder/Subcontractor Agreement	A441
460	Design-Builder/Subcontractor Agreement (Sub GMP)	A441
471	Performance Bond (Surety Not Liable for Design Costs)	A312
472	D-B Payment Bond (Surety Liable for Design Cost)	A312
473	D-B Payment Bond (Surety Not Liable for Design Cost)	A312
481	Certificate of Substantial Completion	G704 (2004)
482	Certificate of Final Completion	N/A
491	Application for Payment (Cost Plus, w/GMP)	G702
492	Application for Payment (Lump Sum Contract)	G702
495	Change Order (Cost Plus with GMP)	G701
496	Design-Build Change Order (Lump Sum)	G701

RELATED CONTRACTS

ConsensusDOCS 500 Series – Construction Management		
DOCS#	ConsensusDOCS Name	2007 AIA #
500	Owner/Construction Manager Agreement & General Conditions (At-Risk)	A133 (+A201)
510	Agreement and General Conditions between Owner and Construction Manager (Cost of Work, Preconstruction Option)	A134 (+A201)
525	Change Order/Construction Manager Fee Adjustment	G701 CMa

ConsensusDOCS 700 Series – Subcontracting		
DOCS#	ConsensusDOCS Name	2007 AIA #
703	Purchase Agreement for Noncommodity Goods	
705	Invitation to Bid/Subbid	N/A
706	Performance Bond	A312
707	Payment Bond	A312
710	Application for Payment	G702
721	Subcontractor's Statement of Qualifications	
725	Subcontractor/ Subsubcontractor Agreement	N/A
725 Exhibit E	Insurance Requirements to 725	N/A
750	Contractor/Subcontractor Agreement	A401
750.1	Rider b/t Contractor & Subcontractor for Storage of Materials at Site	
751	Contractor/Subcontractor Agreement, Short Form	A401
752	Subcontract for Federal Construction, and FAR Exhibit	N/A
760	Bid Bond	A310
781	Certificate of Substantial Completion	G704
782	Certificate of Final Completion	N/A
790	Request for Information	G716
795	Change Order	G701
796	Interim Directed Change	G714

RELATED CONTRACTS

ConsensusDOCS 800 Series – Program Management		
DOCS #	ConsensusDOCS Name	2007 AIA #
800	Owner/Program Manager Agreement and General Conditions	N/A
801	Owner/CM Agreement (CM is Owner's Agent)	A132
802	Owner-Trade Contractor Agreement (CM is Owner's Agent)	A133
803	Owner-A/E Agreement (CM is Owner's Agent)	A133
810	Agreement b/t Owner and Owner's Representative	A132
812	Trade Contract Interim Directed Change	G714
813	Trade Contract Change Order	G701
814	Certificate of Substantial Completion	G704
815	Certificate of Final Completion	N/A
907	Equipment Lease	N/A

INDEX

A

Alternative Project Delivery Method, 275

Arbitration, 106, 145, 180, 275

Architectural/Engineering Subcontract, 193, 199, 275

Automobile Coverage by Constructors, 99, 101, 111, 275

B

Best Value, xi, 8, 9, 15, 19–21, 23, 25–28, 33, 37, 41, 43–45, 48, 49, 52, 63, 64, 97, 98, 102, 122, 123, 125, 127, 133, 137–139, 157, 159, 160, 162, 171, 177, 185, 193, 198, 199, 202, 204, 209, 210, 216, 217, 219, 220, 222, 223, 233, 236, 238, 250, 258, 275, 277, 278, 287, 288

Best Value: Fees, 8, 15, 19– 21, 23, 26–28, 33, 37, 41, 43, 45, 48, 52, 63, 64, 102, 123, 157, 159, 160, 162, 171, 177, 185, 193, 202, 204, 209, 216, 223, 233, 238, 250, 275, 277, 287

Best Value: Total Cost, xi, 8, 9, 15, 19–21, 23, 25, 27, 33, 37, 41, 44, 45, 48, 52, 63, 64, 102, 123, 125, 127, 133, 137–139, 159, 162, 193, 198, 199, 202, 204, 209, 210, 216, 217, 219, 222, 236, 238, 250, 275, 278, 287

Bid Day, 21, 32

Bid Package, 125, 129, 276

Bids, 32, 154

Bonding of Subcontractors and Trade Contractors, 100, 102, 120

Bonds, 100, 102, 119, 120, 126, 149, 158, 184, 194, 215, 224, 246, 251, 259, 276

Bridging, 193, 194, 199, 207, 276

Bridging Architect (or Bridging Designer), 276

Builder's Risk Insurance, 99, 101, 110, 276

Building Information Model, 102, 104, 250, 276

C

Certificates of Participation, 251, 260, 261, 276

Change order, 36

Claims, 98, 99, 101, 105, 126, 144, 158, 179, 194, 210, 224, 242

INDEX

Collaboration, 99, 101, 105, 126, 145, 158, 179, 194, 210, 223, 225, 226, 230, 276

Commissioning, 79, 89, 125, 135, 157, 168, 193, 201, 277

Competitive Bidding, 125, 130, 137, 277

Conceptual Estimating, 157, 160, 277

Conceptualization, 223, 235, 277

ConsensusDOCS, 18, 117, 118, 144, 149, 178, 184, 188, 209, 215, 241, 245, 277, 291– 294

Constructability, 36, 79, 86, 277

Constructability Review, 277

Construction Administration, 278

Construction Documents, 157, 167, 277

Construction Documents Phase, 277

Construction Management, x, 4, 7, 12, 13, 19, 21, 41, 47, 52, 63, 68, 70, 71, 79, 81, 109, 117, 123, 129, 146, 152, 157, 159, 171, 188, 190, 221, 222, 275, 277, 288, 289, 293

Construction Management at-Risk, x, 19, 21, 41, 47, 52, 63, 68, 70, 71, 109, 123, 129, 146, 152, 157, 159, 171, 188, 190, 221, 222, 277, 289

Construction Phase and Project, 157, 161, 193, 198, 277

Construction Phase and Project Contingencies, 157, 161, 193, 198, 277

Construction Phase Service (or Construction Administration), 278

Construction Subcontract, 193, 200, 278

Constructor Controlled Insurance Programs, 102, 113, 278

Contingency, 157, 160, 193, 197, 278

Contract Documents, 18, 117, 149

Contractor, 34, 47, 54, 104, 122, 126, 142, 151, 154, 186, 217, 247, 293, 294

Cost-Plus, 43, 47–53, 57–60, 62, 64, 65, 109, 157, 172, 175, 177, 194, 205, 206, 278

D

Debt Financing, 251, 262, 278

Defining Characteristics, iv, v, 125, 135, 157, 169, 193, 202, 223, 237, 278

Delivery Method, iii– v, 1–3, 10, 12, 13, 19, 47, 62, 67, 70, 122, 125, 132, 150, 157, 163, 185, 193, 200, 217, 223, 226, 233, 275, 278, 283

Delivery System (or Delivery Method), iv, v, 125, 128, 157, 160, 193, 197, 223, 227, 278, 283

Design, x, xi, 3, 4, 6, 9, 12–14, 16, 19, 21, 23, 25–29, 36, 37, 39, 41, 43, 44, 47, 50, 52, 53, 60, 63, 64, 68–71, 79, 81, 84, 93, 95, 97–99, 101, 103, 104, 107–111, 114, 117, 121–123, 125–131, 133–154, 156–160, 162–166, 168–171, 173, 177, 178, 180–185, 187, 190, 193, 194–227, 230, 232, 233, 235– 237, 239, 241–243, 245, 246, 248, 249, 256, 263–265, 267, 270, 271, 275–279, 283, 284, 286, 288–292

Design-Bid-Build, x, xi, 3, 6, 9, 12–14, 19, 21, 25, 27, 37, 41, 43, 47, 50, 52, 63, 64, 70, 71, 81, 93, 95, 97, 101, 109, 110, 122, 123, 125, 127–131,

133–154, 156, 159, 164, 168–171, 178, 180–185, 190, 196, 201–203, 205, 208–212, 214–217, 219–221, 245, 263, 271, 275, 277, 278, 283, 288– 290

Design-Build, x, 4, 6, 12, 13, 16, 19, 21, 23, 25–27, 37, 39, 41, 43, 47, 50, 52, 53, 60, 63, 64, 68, 70, 71, 81, 84, 97, 98, 101, 109, 111, 117, 122, 123, 129, 135, 141, 146–150, 152, 159, 162, 164, 168, 169, 173, 177, 181, 185, 187, 190, 193, 195, 196–222, 225– 227, 230, 232, 233, 237, 239, 241, 242, 246, 248, 249, 256, 263, 264, 267, 270, 271, 276, 278, 279, 288, 290, 292

Design-Build Prime Contract, 193, 199, 279

Design-Build Team, 193, 198, 279

Design Development, 278

Designer, 126, 142, 158, 176, 219, 223, 239, 276

Design Phase Contingency, 157, 160, 193, 197, 278

Design Phases, 99, 101, 107, 126, 146, 158, 180, 194, 211, 224, 242

Developer, iv, 67, 74, 263, 269

Direct Subcontracting, 1, 17, 20, 279

Dispute Avoidance/Management, 99, 101, 106, 126, 145, 158, 180, 194, 211

Dispute Resolution, 99, 101, 105, 126, 145, 158, 180, 194, 210, 279

Dispute Resolution Alternatives, 99, 101, 105, 126, 145, 158, 180, 194, 210, 279

Dispute Review Boards (DRB), 279

E

Estimating, 157, 160, 277

F

Fast-track, 109

Fee, iv, 25, 28, 47, 49, 54, 74, 79, 80, 91, 92, 94, 157, 161, 162, 175, 194, 206, 215, 293

Financing, vi, 69, 25–254, 256–258, 260–263, 266, 267, 271, 273, 278

G

General Conditions, 47, 54, 79, 89, 118, 149, 184, 215, 291–294, 296

General Contractor, 126, 142, 154

General Liability Insurance, 99, 101, 110, 279

Guaranteed Maximum Price (GMP), xi, 6, 19, 47– 49, 52, 54, 55, 57, 60, 64, 65, 109, 127, 157, 161, 166, 169, 173, 188, 194, 205, 206, 221, 279, 289

H

Hard Bid, 26, 51

I

Indefinite Delivery/Indefinite Quantity, 279

Indemnification, 99, 101, 110, 126, 146, 158, 182, 194, 212, 224, 242, 279

Indemnification/Hold Harmless Clauses, 99, 101, 110, 126, 146, 158, 182, 194, 212, 224, 242, 279

Insurance, 80, 94, 99, 101, 102, 110–113, 126, 147, 158, 182, 194, 212, 224, 243, 276, 278, 279, 281–284, 286, 293, 297–300

Integrated Project Delivery, vii, x, xi, 4, 6, 13, 21, 23, 41, 47, 49, 52, 57, 58, 60, 63, 64, 186, 218, 223, 225–229, 242, 245, 246, 250, 280, 290

Invitation to Bid, 21, 24, 30, 31, 32, 38, 42, 45, 62, 137, 280, 287, 293

J

Job Order Contracting (JOC), 14–16, 62, 280

L

Lean Construction, 99, 102, 113, 126, 147, 158, 182, 194, 213, 224, 244, 280

Letters of Credit, 100, 102, 121, 280

Liability, ii, 99, 101, 110–112, 132, 229, 279, 281, 282, 286

Licensing; Licenses, 93, 100, 102, 114, 115, 126, 147, 158, 182, 183, 194, 195, 213, 224, 244

Lien Waiver, 280

Litigation, 106, 280

Low Bid, 8, 9, 14, 15, 19–21, 23, 25, 26, 31, 38, 41, 43, 45, 48, 52, 63, 64, 102, 116, 122, 123, 125, 127, 133, 134, 136, 137, 151, 159, 164, 177, 193, 198, 199, 202, 205, 209, 210, 212, 214, 216, 217, 219, 220, 222, 236, 238, 250, 258, 268, 278, 280, 287, 288

Lump Sum, 3, 14, 30, 33, 38, 47–53, 55, 60–65, 92, 118, 125, 127, 129–131, 136, 139, 144, 149–152, 157, 164, 167, 168, 171, 172, 175, 184, 193, 198, 205, 230, 280, 288, 291, 292

Lump Sum Fixed Price, 125, 129, 175, 280

M

Management Method, 67, 70, 281

Mediation, 105, 145, 281

Mini-Trials, 281

Multi-Party Contract, 223, 228, 281

Multiple Prime Contracting, 1, 17, 20, 281

O

Occupancy, 69, 79, 90, 125, 135, 157, 169, 193, 202

On-Call, 1, 14, 15, 62, 281

Open-Book Contracting, 47, 50, 281

OSHA, 117, 132

Outline Specification, 157, 160, 281

Owner, 12, 14, 34, 64, 99, 101, 102, 112, 118, 125, 126, 128, 140, 149, 158, 176, 184, 193, 194, 200, 207, 215, 223, 239, 243, 250, 264, 270, 281, 282, 290–294

Owner Controlled Insurance Programs (OCIP), 102, 112, 281

INDEX

Owner's Liability Insurance, 99, 101, 112, 281

Owner's Program, 193, 200, 282

P

Partnering, 99, 101, 105, 123, 126, 145, 151, 152, 158, 179, 194, 210, 282

Payment Bond, 282, 291–293

Performance-Based Contracting, 251, 269, 282

Performance Bond, 282, 291–293

Performance Specifications, 282

Preconstruction Services, 79, 87

Prequalification, 12, 21, 25, 26, 100, 102, 116, 123, 126, 147, 148, 151, 158, 183, 194, 214, 224, 245, 282

Prescriptive Specifications, 282

Prime Contract, 193, 199, 279

Privatization, 252, 271, 282

Procurement, iii, iv, v, 1, 7, 8, 12–14, 21, 22, 25, 26, 29, 40, 41, 43, 102, 125, 137, 157, 171, 193, 203, 223, 237, 250, 251, 257, 268, 282, 287

Procurement Method (or Selection Method), 1, 7, 282

Professional Liability Insurance, 99, 101, 111, 282

Program Management, iii, 12, 13, 67, 68, 71, 72, 79, 81, 263, 269, 283, 288, 294

Program Manager, iv, 67, 73, 74, 283, 288, 294

Programming (or Planning), 79, 84, 85, 125, 133, 157, 164, 193, 200, 223, 234, 283

Programs, 79, 88, 102, 112, 113, 278, 281

Progress Payments, 125, 130, 283

Project Delivery Method, iii, 1, 2, 3, 19, 47, 62, 275, 283

Project Delivery System, iv, v, 125, 128, 157, 160, 193, 197, 223, 227, 278, 283

Project Insurance, 99, 102, 112, 283

Project Manager, 67, 73, 283

Public/Private Partnerships, vi, 251, 266, 267, 271, 283

Q

Qualifications Based Selection, 8, 15, 19–21, 23, 25, 26, 28, 29, 33, 37, 40–43, 45, 49, 52, 63, 92, 97, 98, 102, 122, 123, 157, 159, 160, 162, 164, 168, 170, 171, 173, 177, 179, 184, 185, 193, 198, 203, 209, 216, 217, 221–223, 225, 230, 237, 241, 250, 258, 268, 277, 283, 290

R

Related Areas, iv, 1, 11, 13, 99, 101, 283

Request for Proposals (RFP), 21, 23, 24, 28, 33–37, 43–45, 139, 162, 171, 204, 256, 268, 269, 284

Request for Qualifications, 23, 24, 33, 171, 284

299

INDEX

Request for Qualifications (RFQ), 23, 24, 33, 171, 284

Responsible Constructor, 125, 130, 284

Responsive Bid, 125, 130, 284

Retainage, 100, 102, 116, 123, 126, 148, 158, 183, 194, 214, 224, 245, 284

Risk Shifting, 47, 50, 284

S

Safety, 35, 79, 88, 100, 102, 117, 123, 126, 132, 149, 158, 183, 194, 214, 224, 245

Savings, 157, 161, 193, 200, 284

Schematic Design, 284

Selection Method, 282

Self-Insurance, 99, 102, 112, 284

Set-Based Design, 114, 223, 233, 284

Shared Risk/Reward, 223, 233, 285

Sole Source (or Direct Negotiation), 22, 41, 42, 285

Sole Source, 285

Spearin Doctrine, 53, 125, 128, 153, 156, 173, 179, 206, 210, 220, 240, 285

Specifications, 125, 128, 160, 174, 282

Standard Forms of Agreements, 100, 102, 117, 126, 149, 158, 194, 224, 285

Subcontractor, 22, 43, 120, 121, 194, 208, 292, 293

Substantial Completion, 292, 293, 294

Substitutions, 125, 139, 285

Surety, 100, 102, 119, 124, 126, 149, 150, 158, 184, 194, 215, 224, 246, 285, 292

Surety Bond, 285

Sustainability (or Green Construction), 100, 102, 121, 126, 150, 158, 185, 194, 216, 224, 247, 285

T

Target Price, xi, 30, 43, 47–49, 51, 57–65, 177, 223, 228, 230–233, 238, 241, 250, 285, 288

Teaming Agreement, 193, 199, 286

Term Contracting, 1, 14, 286

Total Construction Cost (TCC), 286, 288

Total Design and Construction Cost, 286

Total Project Cost (TPC), 286

Turnkey, 256

Typical Characteristics, iv, v, 125, 135, 157, 169, 193, 202, 223, 237, 286

U

Umbrella Liability Insurance, 99, 101, 111, 286

Unit Prices, 125, 139, 286

W

Warranty, ii, 125, 128, 292

Workers' Compensation, 99, 101, 111, 286

Wrap-Up Insurance, 99, 102, 112, 286